D0811888

# Atlas of Southeast Asia

# Atlas of Southeast Asia

RICHARD ULACK • GYULA PAUER

*with the assistance of*
*Jane Johnshoy Domier & Julsun D. Pacheco*

MACMILLAN PUBLISHING COMPANY
NEW YORK

Collier Macmillan Publishers
LONDON

Macmillan Publishing Company
866 Third Avenue, New York, N.Y. 10022

Collier Macmillan Canada, Inc.

Library of Congress Catalog Card Number: 88-17543

Printed in the United States of America

printing number

2 3 4 5 6 7 8 9 10

**Library of Congress Cataloging in Publication Data**

Ulack, Richard.
Atlas of Southeast Asia.

1. Asia, Southeastern—Maps. 2. Asia, Southeastern—Economic conditions—Maps. 3. Asia, Southeastern—Social conditions—Maps. I. Pauer, Gyula. II. Title.
G2360.U4 1988 912′.59 88-17543
ISBN 0-02-933200-1

*Dedicated to*
*Frederick L. Wernstedt and Robert S. Chauvin*

# MAP SYMBOLS

## NATIONAL MAPS

|  |  |
|---|---|
| | River, Canal |
| | Lake, Reservoir |
| 32,995 △ | Ocean Depth |
| Mt. Halcon 8,218 ▲ | Mountain Peak |
| Mu Gia Pass | Mountain Pass |
| *Boroboudour* ▲ | Point of Interest |
| *Angkor Wat* | Ruin |
| | Highway |
| | Railroad |
| | International Boundary |
| | CITIES AND TOWNS |
| **BANGKOK** | National Capital |
| **MANILA** | 5 million and over |
| **Haiphong** | 1,000,000 to 5,000,000 |
| Chittagong | 500,000 to 1,000,000 |
| Bien Hoa | 100,000 to 500,000 |
| *Sabang* | less than 100,000 |

## METROPOLITAN MAPS

|  |  |
|---|---|
| | Super Highway |
| | Major Road, Street |
| | Minor Road, Street |
| | Mass Rapid Transit (Singapore) |
| | Light Rail Transit (Manila) |
| | Railroad |
| *ATENEO DE MANILA* ■ | Point of Interest |
| *POST OFFICE* ■ | Major Structure |
| | Park |

# Contents

*Preface* ix
*Acknowledgments* xii

Part One. *Regional Overview*

Introduction 1
1. The Physical Environment and Resources 3
2. Historical and Political Background 15
3. Cultural Characteristics 26
4. Regional Population and Urban Characteristics 32

Part Two. *The Nation-States*

Introduction 45
5. Republic of Indonesia 47
6. Republic of the Philippines 62
7. Malaysia 74
8. Republic of Singapore 85
9. Negara Brunei Darussalam 93
10. Kingdom of Thailand 99
11. Socialist Republic of the Union of Burma 111
12. Socialist Republic of Vietnam 123
13. People's Republic of Kampuchea 136
14. Lao People's Democratic Republic 144

*Selected Bibliography* 153

*Index* 159

# *Preface*

Long-term interests in the Southeast Asian region on the part of Dr. Ulack and in cartography on the part of Dr. Pauer have come together to produce this work, the first comprehensive reference atlas of the entire Southeast Asian region since Hall's *Atlas of South-East Asia,* published in 1964. The atlas is a reference work designed for libraries and for individuals with an interest in the region, including scholars, students, government workers and businessmen assigned in the region, and tourists. Whereas the atlas may appear directed to an American audience, we would stress that the atlas should be of importance to any English-speaking audience with an interest in the region. Certainly the text and illustrations have been produced with this in mind. However, because the volume is being published in the United States, and because it presumably will be used primarily by Americans, we have included the locations of American embassies on the major metropolitan area maps and we have opted to use the non-metric system of measures, although we usually provide metric equivalents.

The primary aim of the atlas is to provide detailed and current maps and information (as of the mid-1980s, when possible) on the Southeast Asian region and on each of the ten nations that comprise the region. Although this is a reference work, the four regional chapters are meant to convey to the reader a general overview of the region's characteristics and problems. The reader should come away from these early chapters with a good sense of the importance of the region to the United States and the rest of the world, and of what its major characteristics and problems are. The four thematic chapters and the ten national chapters provide detailed information about landforms, climate, history, culture, population and urban structure, political characteristics, and economic conditions. The text, statistical information at the beginning of each chapter, 70 maps, 66 diagrams, and 50 color photographs have all been carefully selected and integrated to provide the reader with a regional understanding.

It is impossible to list here (or in the bibliography) all the sources from which information for the many maps and other illustrations was taken. Among the important sources for maps and other information were various United States government agencies including the Central Intelligence Agency, the Departments of Defense and the Army, and the Defense Mapping Agency. Maps from these agencies were often used as base maps for the regional, national, and urban maps included herein. The national maps are Lambert Conformal Conic Projections;

the two-page regional map, taken from a Department of Defense base, is an Azimuthal Equidistant Projection. The various national reference maps are of course at different scales given the widely varying sizes of each nation. The region's largest metropolitan areas (Jakarta, Manila, and Bangkok) are mapped at the same scale (1:75,000) for ease of comparison. Similarly, most of the smaller metropolitan areas are also presented at the same scale (1:37,500).

National and thematic maps have been updated with more recent information taken from a wide variety of sources (e.g., the *Area Handbook* series, regional and national atlases, maps received from agencies in the Southeast Asian nations). Metropolitan area maps have been updated through the use of recent maps received from foreign government agencies and tourist bureaus, urban maps found in atlases and texts, and from tourist maps. In this regard, early in the project letters were written to every organization that could be identified in each of the ten nations (as well as their embassies in the United States) requesting maps and information of the nations and cities. Such requests often resulted in current information that allowed us to update our maps. Vietnam Tourism, for example, forwarded post-1980 tourist maps of Hanoi and Ho Chi Minh City. Additionally, tourist maps published in recent travel guides such as the wonderfully illustrated and written *Insight Guide* series or those published by Lonely Planet Publications often yielded valuable information. The Southeast Asian regional map published by Bartholemew, the Hildebrand Travel Maps, and the Apa Maps by Nelles Verlag were also very useful and provided another means to check and update earlier sources. The regional climate maps by Robert Huke, published by the International Rice Research Institute, were also very helpful, as were maps published by the National Geographic Society. Morgan and Valencia's excellent and detailed *Atlas for Marine Policy in Southeast Asian Seas* also deserves special mention. In short, scores of maps were compiled to produce the maps used in this work.

One of the major goals of this work has been an attempt to be as consistent as possible in the presentation of maps, statistics, and other information. Anyone who has worked with data and maps from a Third World nation is aware of the difficulties encountered. Our problems here have been multiplied since ten separate nations are included. Information for several of the nations, most notably Singapore and Malaysia, is quite good, but this is the exception and means, of course, that consistency has not been possible. Indeed, recent information for several of the nations, especially Kampuchea and Laos, is particularly unreliable. We have attempted to present maps and statistics that reflect information as of the early or mid-1980s, but in the case of Kampuchea and Laos the information often reflects the situation prior to 1975. Thus, the reader who has recently lived in Vientiane, for example, may find fault with our map of that city because it omits (or includes) some feature that it should (or shouldn't) include. We offer apologies for such instances, but our information is based on the best and most recent information that we could find. Certainly our map of Phnom Penh reflects the city in the early-1970s, and the economic activities maps of the two countries (and of Vietnam) reflect activities prior to 1980. It is our suspicion that in some instances (though perhaps not in Kampuchea and Phnom Penh) the situation has remained pretty much the same as it was in the 1970s, at least at the scale presented.

The statistics presented at the beginning of each national chapter, in the text, and in the graphs, come from several principal sources. These include the most recent editions of the *Europa Yearbook*, the *Encyclopedia Britannica Book of the Year*, and a variety of United Nations sources, including annual and other publications of the UN Conference on Trade and Development (UNCTAD), the UN Department of International Economic Affairs, the Food and Agriculture Organization (FAO), and the UN Economic and Social Commission for Asia and the Pacific (ESCAP). Specific citations can be found in the bibliography. National populations and demographic data found at the beginning of each chapter are from ESCAP. Population data for individual urban areas and other subnational administrative areas were taken from a variety of sources including those already cited and individual national censuses or statistical yearbooks. The *Europa Yearbook* was especially useful in this regard. Except where noted otherwise, urban populations are for entire metropolitan areas. Since the definition of terms like "urban" and "metropolitan" may be quite different from that understood by Westerners (and may be quite different among the nations in the region), comparisons should be made with care. Data for the climate diagrams were taken from Wernstedt's *World Climatic Data*. In general, we have included references for those maps and diagrams where there were only one or two major sources; it was not possible to do so in all cases since numerous sources would have to be cited. Hopefully, the information given here and in the bibliography will indicate to those who are interested all the major and many of the minor sources from which we gathered data and information. Readers are encouraged to contact Professor Ulack if further information is desired or if errors are found.

In terms of the spelling of place names we have usually followed the spellings given on the most recent U.S. agency maps. In some instances we have kept with a more commonly used spelling, or at least we have indicated the more common spelling in parentheses. For example, the most recent CIA map of Kampuchea shows the cities of Batdambang and Kracheh. On most maps (even recent maps) these places are spelled Battambang and Kratie and thus we have included these more common spellings as well. On the other hand, for example, we have kept with Kuala Trengganu (Malaysia), rather than Kuala Terengganu as it is found on US agency maps. Street spellings on some of the urban maps also often caused considerable consternation, especially in the case of Bangkok. Given a half dozen or more maps of the city, there were sometimes as many as three different spellings for the same street. In such cases, we often had to make our own judgement, even after a native Thai had been consulted! Finally, the term Indochina when used herein refers to that portion of mainland Southeast Asia that was formerly a French colony, that is, Vietnam, Kampuchea, and Laos.

Whereas the expert or resident will undoubtedly find errors and omissions, we hope that the maps, illustrations, and text reflect with reasonable accuracy a sense of the Southeast Asian region.

# ACKNOWLEDGMENTS

Dr. Ulack's interest in Southeast Asia began as a graduate student in geography at Penn State University where he studied under the guidance of Professor Frederick L. Wernstedt, noted for his work on the Philippines. Wernstedt, and Charles Fisher's excellent *South-East Asia: A Social, Economic, and Political Geography,* were instrumental in the development of Ulack's early interest in the region. A debt of gratitude is indeed due these two scholars.

An undertaking such as this atlas could not be accomplished without the help of numerous individuals, and we want to acknowledge here those individuals and institutions without whose aid and contributions this atlas could not have been completed. During the stage of gathering maps, statistics, and other information one week was spent in Washington, D.C. The Woodrow Wilson Center publication *Scholar's Guide to Washington, D.C. for Southeast Asian Studies* was particularly helpful in locating sources of information. Among the institutions visited in Washington, several yielded especially significant materials including the Library of Congress and the World Bank. At the former, special thanks are due to the staff of the Geography and Map Division and especially to Thomas DeClaire, reference librarian, who was a great help in locating obscure materials. Mr. A. Kohar Rony provided valuable assistance in the Library's Asian Division. At the University of Kentucky a large debt of gratitude is due Gwen Curtis, the Map Collection librarian, who spent much time locating materials. Thanks also to the Government Publications section at the university, and especially to Barbara Hale, and to the staff at the Agriculture Library at the University of Kentucky. Materials from numerous other international, American, and foreign agencies and organizations were utilized and we would especially like to acknowledge the maps and publications of various United Nations agencies, the U.S. State Department, the U.S. Departments of Defense and the Army, the Central Intelligence Agency, and a large number of agencies and embassies in Southeast Asia. Examples of organizations located in Southeast Asia that provided recent city and national maps and other publications include Vietnam Tourism, Tourist Development Corporation Malaysia, the Embassy of Brunei Darussalam, the U.N. Economic and Social Commission for Asia and the Pacific (ESCAP), the Singapore Ministry of Communications and Information, and the Philippine Convention Bureau. Special thanks are due to Professor I Made Sandy of the Indonesian Department of Home Affairs, Directorate of Land Use, for providing Indonesian atlases and city maps, and to Pamela Slutz of the U.S. Embassy in Jakarta who coordinated the effort. While it would be impossible to include in this brief volume all who directly and indirectly contributed to this atlas, more detailed information on sources both domestic and foreign can be found in the bibliography.

The many fine color photographs found throughout the atlas were copied from slides contributed by colleagues who have spent many years living, traveling, and studying in various parts of the region. Many thanks are due to the following geographers: Bob Huke at Dartmouth; Jim Hafner at the University of Massachusetts; Tom Leinbach at the University of Kentucky; Aulis Lind at the University of Vermont; Bob Reed at the University of California-Berkeley; Bill Thomas, Professor Emeritus at California State University-Hayward; Bill Wood at the U.S. State Department; and Matrini Nathalang, a doctoral student at the University of Kentucky. Thanks also to historian Bill Duiker at Penn State, to anthropologist Joel Halpern at the University of Massachusetts, and to Jeff Baker of the Patterson School of Diplomacy at the University of Kentucky. These colleagues also often provided advice or contributed other maps or materials, as did Bill Withington at the University of Kentucky. Such a project could not have been undertaken without the encouragement and support of Stan Brunn, chairman of the Department of Geography at Kentucky. Without the many hours of work by Jane Domier and Julsun Pacheco, research assistants in the Department's Cartographic Laboratory, the project could not have been completed. Thanks are also due the reviewers of the text and maps; their comments certainly helped to improve the product. A special note of gratitude is due Lloyd Chilton, Executive Editor of the Professional Books Division at Macmillan. Without his encouragement, support, flexibility, and unflappable nature it is doubtful that the project would have been undertaken. The valuable assistance during the editing process given by Elyse Dubin, Managing Editor at Macmillan, is also gratefully acknowledged. Finally, our families must be acknowledged for their encouragement and support. We do so here, and say thanks, especially to our wives Karen and Magda. A sincere debt of gratitude is offered to all.

# Atlas of Southeast Asia

INDIA
CHINA
BANGLADESH
BURMA
Mandalay
SHAN PLATEAU
Akyab
Ramree
Pegu
Rangoon
Bassein
Moulmein
Gulf of Martaban
VIETNAM
Thai Nguyen
Hanoi
Haiphong
Nam Dinh
Thanh Hoa
Vinh
Gulf of Tonkin
HAINAN
CANTON
HONG KONG (BR.)
LAOS
Luang Prabang
Vientiane
Chiang Mai
THAILAND
Savannakhet
Khon Kaen
KHORAT PLATEAU
Ubon Ratchathani
Pakxe
Nakhon Ratchasima
DANGREK RANGE
ANNAMITE CHAIN
Hue
Da Nang
Qui Nhon
BANGKOK
Chon Buri
KAMPUCHEA
Tonle Sap
Phnom Penh
VIETNAM
Ho Chi Minh City
Long Xuyen
Andaman Islands (India)
Mergui Archipelago
Mergui
Tenasserim
ANDAMAN SEA
Gulf of Thailand
Isthmus of Kra
Nicobar Islands (India)
Phuket
Nakhon Si Thammarat
Songkhla
Hat Yai
Kota Baharu
George Town (Penang)
Malay Peninsula
Kuala Trengganu
Ipoh
MALAYSIA
Kuantan
Kuala Lumpur
Melaka (Malacca)
Strait of Malacca
SINGAPORE
Singapore
Banda Aceh
Medan
Pemantangsiantar
Simeulue
Lake Toba
Nias
SUMATRA
Pakanbaru
Padang
Siberut
Mentawi Islands
Jambi
BARISAN RANGE
Palembang
Lingga Islands
Natuna Islands
Anambas Islands
Bangka
Belitung
Karimata Strait
SOUTH CHINA SEA
Kota Kinabalu
Bandar Seri Begawan
BRUNEI
SARAWAK
MALAYSIA
Kuching
KALIMANTAN (BORNEO)
Pontianak
SCHWANER MOUNTAINS
Balikpapan
Banjarmasin
JAVA SEA
INDO
INDIAN OCEAN
Sunda Strait
JAKARTA
Bogor
Bandung
Cirebon
Semarang
Magelang
Surakarta
Yogyakarta
Surabaya
Madura
Kediri
Malang
Bali
Lombok
JAVA
Denpasar
Java Trench
Christmas Island (Australia)
SCALE 1:17,600,000
0 100 200 300 400 Miles
0 100 200 300 400 500 600 Kilometers

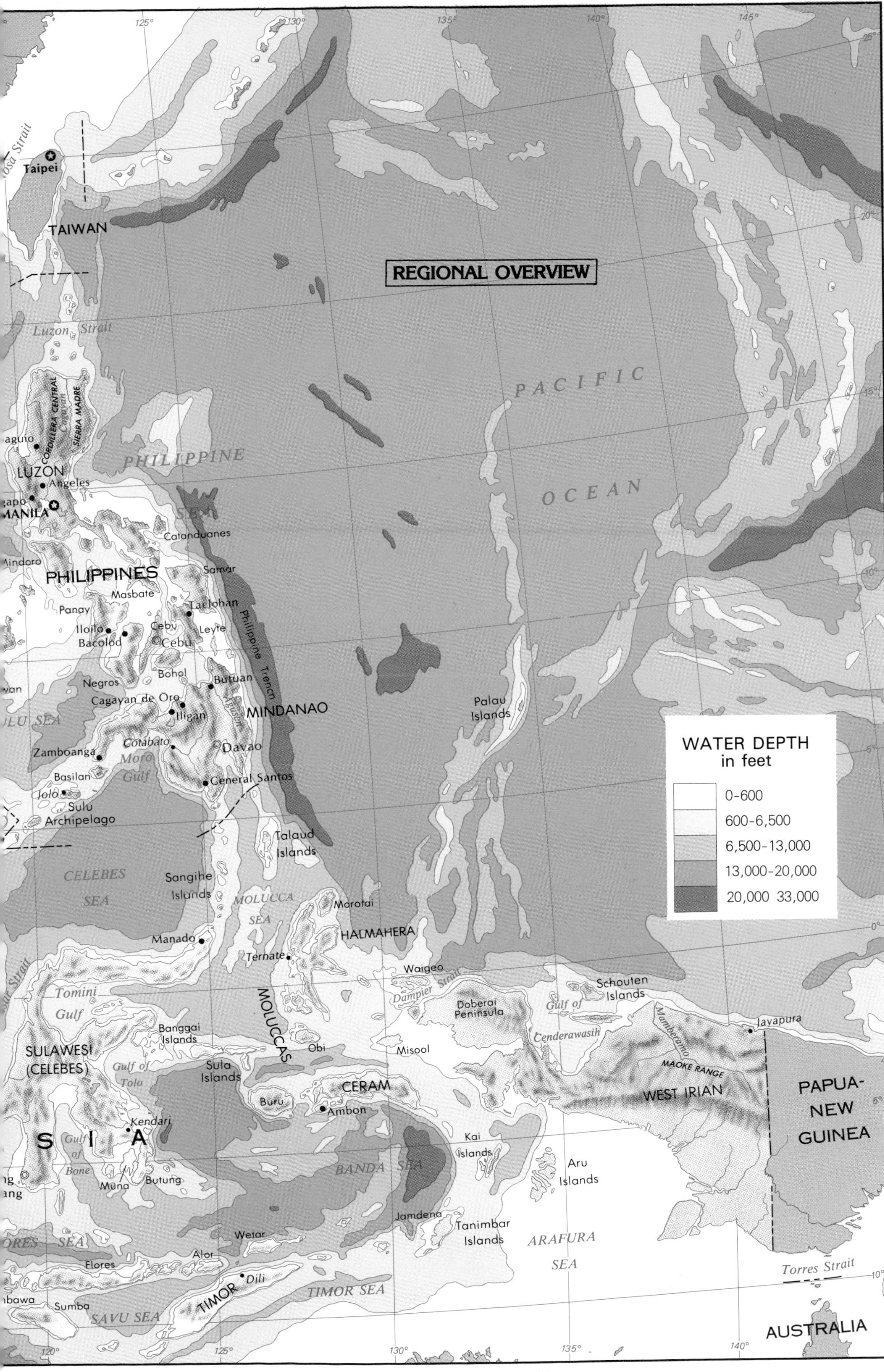
REGIONAL OVERVIEW
PACIFIC
OCEAN
PHILIPPINE
SEA
Philippine Trench
WATER DEPTH
in feet
0-600
600-6,500
6,500-13,000
13,000-20,000
20,000 33,000
Taipei
TAIWAN
Luzon Strait
LUZON
Angeles
MANILA
Catanduanes
PHILIPPINES
Samar
Masbate
Panay
Tacloban
Leyte
Iloilo
Bacolod
Cebu
Bohol
Negros
Butuan
Cagayan de Oro
Iligan
MINDANAO
Zamboanga
Cotabato
Moro Gulf
Davao
Basilan
Jolo
General Santos
Sulu Archipelago
CELEBES SEA
Sangihe Islands
Talaud Islands
MOLUCCA SEA
Morotai
HALMAHERA
Manado
Ternate
Palau Islands
Tomini Gulf
MOLUCCAS
Waigeo
Dampier Strait
Doberai Peninsula
Schouten Islands
Gulf of Cenderawasih
Jayapura
Mamberamo
MAOKE RANGE
WEST IRIAN
PAPUA-NEW GUINEA
Banggai Islands
SULAWESI (CELEBES)
Obi
Misool
Gulf of Tolo
Sula Islands
CERAM
Buru
Ambon
Kendari
Gulf of Bone
Muna
Butung
BANDA SEA
Kai Islands
Aru Islands
Jamdena
Tanimbar Islands
ARAFURA SEA
Wetar
Alor
Flores
Dili
TIMOR
TIMOR SEA
Sumba
SAVU SEA
Torres Strait
AUSTRALIA
125°
130°
135°
140°
145°
120°
25°
20°
15°
10°
5°
0°

# PART ONE

# *Regional Overview*

It is the purpose of this reference atlas to provide the reader with an overview of the region known as Southeast Asia and its ten independent nations. We begin with four chapters on the physical, historical, political, cultural, and population characteristics of the region; these are followed by ten chapters, one for each of the nations.

In attempting to understand the contemporary human characteristics of this very complex region of more than 400 million people, one must keep in mind several pivotal facts. First, the region had a relatively high indigenous civilization; that is, many of its groups were quite sophisticated when influences from India, China, and elsewhere began to diffuse into the region. Thus, for example, there were irrigated ricefields, metals were being used, the importance of women and of maternal descent had been established, ancestor worship was practiced, and, in Java, batik was being made. Second, the island and peninsular portion of the region has historically been very accessible by sea whereas the mainland areas have been accessible through a series of generally north-south trending river valleys. And third, the region is sandwiched between the two great cultural realms of India to the west and China to the north. The diffusion of peoples and ideas from the Indian subcontinent and from China are a major explanation for the cultural characteristics of the region's population. More recent arrivals, including Arabs, Europeans, and Americans, have brought about further mixing and added to Southeast Asia's human diversity.

For centuries Southeast Asia has been a region of great turmoil and conflict. When external participants have been involved, the reason has been in large part to maintain the region's accessibility or to control its strategic location and natural resources. On the other hand, numerous internal conflicts have resulted from the human diversity that exists. This volume's theme is to portray the physical and human diversity of the region. As we shall see, the phrase "shatter belt" (meaning a region caught between colliding external cultural and political forces and, as a result, fragmented) continues to be quite appropriate in the context of Southeast Asia. To be sure, the region also has unifying elements. Examples of such unifying elements include the fact that with the exception of much of Vietnam, most of the region was influenced culturally by elements derived from India. Thus, the majority of the mainland population today adheres to Theravada Buddhism which arrived from India. And certainly the fact that the vast majority of the region is influenced heavily by a tropical monsoon climate has brought about similarities, for example, in agricultural practices. And finally, with few exceptions (most Singaporeans and the handful of local elites in other nations), the regional population is unified in that it is basically impoverished.

# 1

# *The Physical Environment and Resources*

*Land Area:* 1,735,700 square miles (4,495,465 sq km); almost one-half the size of the United States.
*Highest Elevation:* Hkakabo Razi, Burma; 19,285 ft (5,878 m)
*Typical Annual Rainfall:* 60 (150 cm) to 120 inches (300 cm); unevenly distributed throughout year
*Annual Average Temperature:* 80°F (27°C) at sea level
*Principal Mineral Resources:* Petroleum, natural gas, tin, copper
*Principal Agricultural Crops:* Rice, maize, cassava, bananas, rubber, coconut, sugar cane, oil palm, opium poppy
*Other Commercial Products:* Hardwoods including teak, sandalwood, and rosewood; bamboo and rattan; fish and fish products

In terms of physical geography, Southeast Asia can best be described as fragmented. Also called a "shatter belt," much of the region is divided into literally thousands of islands and islets. The mainland, a peninsula, is also fragmented in the sense that the region is rugged and the generally north–south trending series of mountain and hill ranges have sometimes hindered east–west human interaction. The land is divided into numerous smaller pockets of lowland mountain basins and river valleys. Some of these, especially the valleys associated with the region's major rivers, are heavily populated and are major core areas for agriculture.

Climatically the region can be described as humid equatorial and humid tropical. Temperatures near sea level average around 80°F (27°C) throughout the year and annual average rainfall is typically between 60 inches (150 cm) and 120 inches (300 cm). Rainfall is unevenly distributed throughout the year in the humid tropical areas because of the monsoonal conditions that prevail in much of the region. Upland areas have cooler temperatures and often higher rainfall; because of this more temperate climate, upland "hill stations" emerged during the colonial period which continue as resort towns to be popular tourist attractions.

Although forests have been cut down or burned throughout the region there are still extensive areas of forest, especially in Indonesia, Laos, Thailand, and Burma. Such forests produce teak and other hardwoods and bamboo, to name but a few commercial products. The region today accounts for one-tenth of the world's roundwood production. Minerals of major commercial importance include tin and copper and, more recently, petroleum and natural gas. Major subsistence crops are rice (in Thailand it is the major export), maize, and several root crops, including cassava. Rubber, coconuts, and sugar cane are the most important commercial crops.

## LANDFORMS AND DRAINAGE

Three different tectonic plates collide in the Southeast Asian region. Near these collision, or subduction, zones there has been considerable volcanic and earthquake activity. Many volcanoes have erupted in recent times, among the best known of which occurred on the tiny island of Krakatoa, located in the Sunda Strait be-

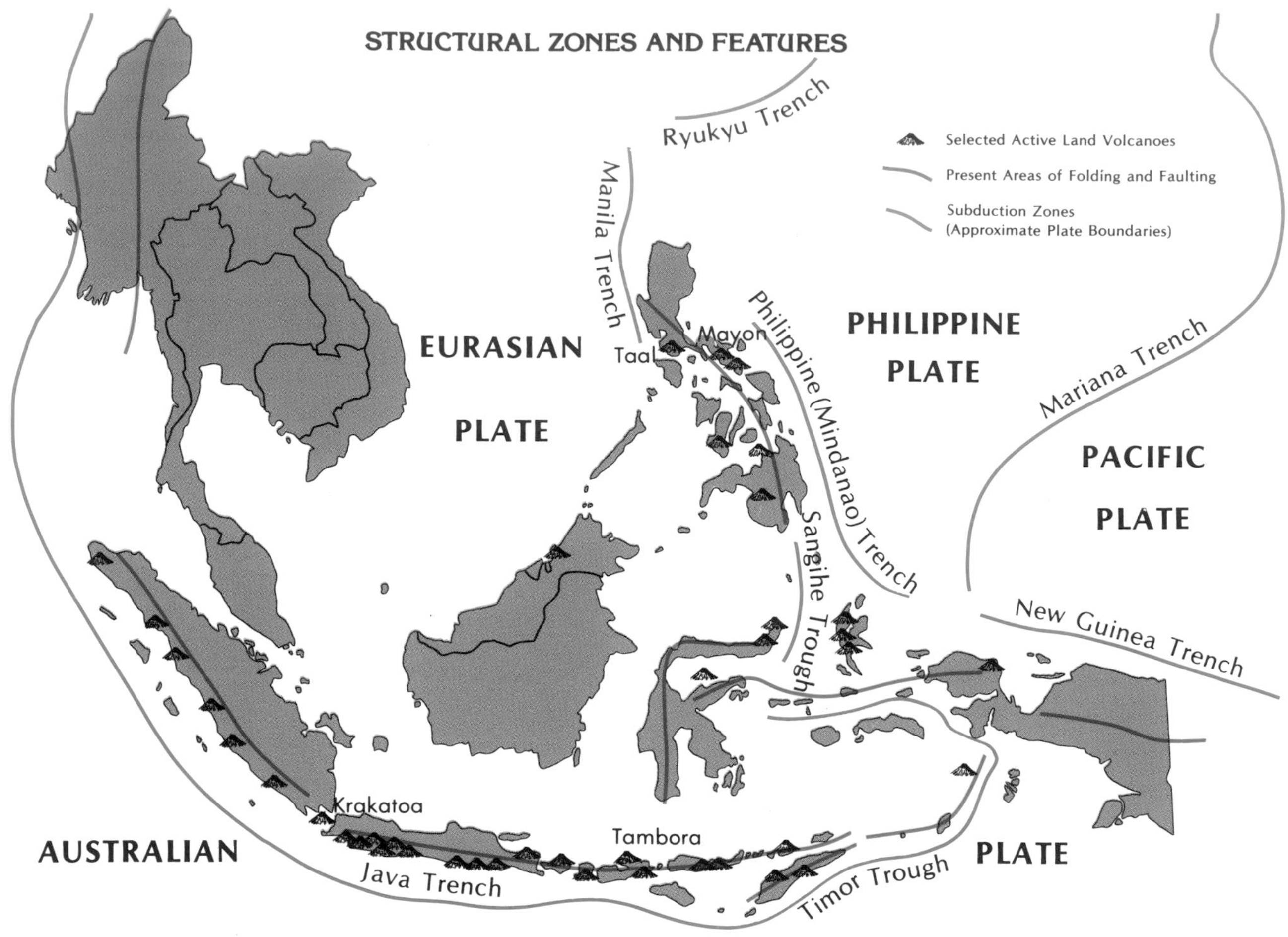


tween Java and Sumatra, in 1883. Java alone has more than 50 volcanoes that are periodically active. One-sixth (223) of the world's major earthquakes that have occurred in this century have been in the Southeast Asian region, accounting for over 35,000 deaths. Mainland Southeast Asia today is geologically stable but it, too, is rugged as a result of past mountain-building activity. The subsequent erosion and deposition that has taken place on the mainland has created a landscape of great complexity.

An understanding of the topographic and drainage characteristics of the region is important to an understanding of human migration, settlement patterns, and population distribution. It is in the great river valleys and deltas, and on the lowland areas of fertile volcanic soils, where the densest clusters of population and settlement are located. Mainland Southeast Asia contains four major rivers where dense rural populations can be found. The region's principal river, and the sixth longest in the world at 2,600 miles (4,200 km), is the Mekong. This river begins in the high mountain areas of Tibet and reaches its delta in southern Vietnam where each year it discharges a huge amount of water and sediment, ranking it fifth among the world's rivers in this category. Until the Vietnam War rice production totals and surpluses in the lower Mekong area were among the highest in Southeast Asia.

The other major regional rivers are Burma's Irrawaddy which, together with its tributaries, provides 5,000 miles (8,000 km) of navigable waterways in the wet season and 3,600 miles (5,900 km) during the dry season; the Chao Phraya in Thailand, only 200 miles (320 km) long but especially significant because it supports one of the world's great rice-growing and exporting regions; the 500-mile-long (800 km) Red River (Song Hai) of northern Vietnam where rural population densities are among the world's highest; and Burma's Salween (1,700 miles; 2,800 km), one of the world's least useful rivers, since it passes through areas of narrow, deeply incised gorges and generally poor soils, major reasons for the low population densities here.

There are no major rivers in Southeast Asia's Malay Peninsula or its island areas. Because this part of the region is also wet and rugged there are of course numerous rapidly-flowing, short rivers which quickly drop off to the sea from the mountainous interior. Where this occurs, falls and rapids are found and the potential exists for the development of hydroelectric power. One example of such a river is the Agus and its Maria Cristina Falls, located near Iligan City on the northern coast of the Philippines' second largest island, Mindanao. This short 22-mile (35 km) river falls from about 2,300 feet (700 m) to the sea creating a series of falls and rapids. About 40% of the total hydroelectric potential in the entire Philippines is found here, only a portion of which has been developed. Another example, in northern Sumatra, Indonesia, is the Asahan River, which drains the scenic upland Lake Toba region. The hydroelectric power from the falls along this river spurred the development of the Asahan industrial project.

Maria Cristina Falls on the Agus River, Iligan City, the Philippines (R. Ulack)

## CLIMATE, SOILS, FLORA, AND FAUNA

With the exception of a few highland areas and the extreme northern portion of mainland Southeast Asia, the entire region can be classified within the equatorial and tropical wet categories of climates. Total annual precipitation amounts are generally high, well over 100 inches (250 cm) in many places as attested to by the climate graphs found throughout this volume. Average temperatures throughout the year are also generally high, about 80°F (27°C) with monthly averages near sea level rarely varying two or three degrees Fahrenheit from the annual average.

The winds that carry the moisture-laden air are controlled by the seasonal migration of the equatorial low (or Intertropical Convergence Zone) and subtropical highs, which are located to the north and south of the equatorial low. These belts of high and low pressure migrate north in the winter of the northern hemisphere, and south in the summer. Thus the region is most affected by these winds, called monsoons, which carry the moisture-laden air in opposite directions during the two seasons (wet and dry) of the year. Those areas on or near the equator, such as Singapore, receive a relatively even annual distribution of rainfall. Areas affected by the monsoon, on the other hand, receive the majority of their rainfall in a few short months. Rangoon, Burma, for example, receives nearly 90% of its annual rainfall in the five-month period from May to September when the summer (or southwest) monsoon blows out of the southwest (see climate graph for Rangoon in Chapter 11). Such an uneven distribution of rainfall is of course important from the standpoint of agriculture. Areas such as those near Rangoon that are dry for more than half of the year must be irrigated to produce crops during the dry season.

Regions that are warm and moist the year round typically have soils that have undergone a process called laterization. Such soils are de-

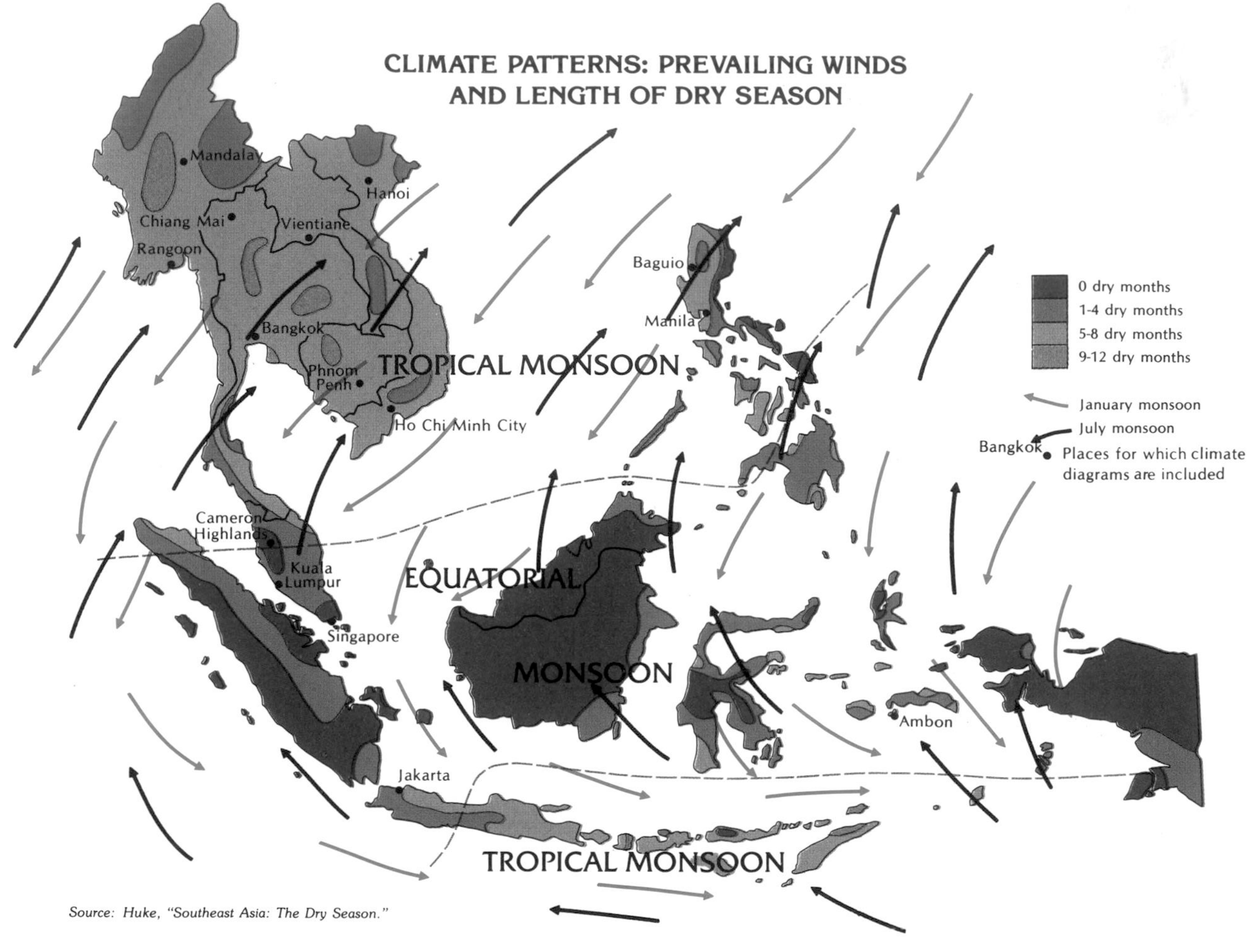


Source: Huke, "Southeast Asia: The Dry Season."

nuded of their nutrients because of bacteria that thrive all year in such warm, moist conditions and because the heavy rainfall dissolves basic elements out of the soil as it seeps down through the upper soil layer. Typically, soils of the tropics are not fertile insofar as most agricultural crops are concerned. This may seem surprising, as indeed it was to the first Europeans who ventured into the tropics, since the natural vegetation looked so lush. But the tropical forest species have adapted their root systems to the shallow soil where they are nurtured by the rapidly-decaying plant matter and microorganisms. Once the forest cover is burned or cut down, as has happened in so many tropical areas through commercial exploitation, expansion of permanent settlement, shifting cultivation, and natural causes, the soil erodes and is leached of its nutrients much more rapidly than under natural conditions, since it is now exposed directly to the sun's rays, and to heavy rains.

There are two major exceptions to the generally infertile soils of Southeast Asia. First, soils derived from volcanic materials which, when they are composed of basic materals (as opposed to acidic), can be extremely fertile. Among the classic areas for such rich soils are the central and eastern parts of Java, an Indonesian island that comprises less than 7% of the country's land area, yet contains nearly two-thirds of its 170 million people. Fertile soils are certainly one reason for such high population densities. The second major exception are the alluvial (water-deposited) soils found in the floodplains and deltas of the region's rivers. The sediments carried by the rivers constantly renew the fertility in the densely-populated rice-producing areas associated with the region's core area of settlement. All of Southeast

Asia's most densely-populated agricultural areas are located on soils of either alluvial or recent volcanic origin. In addition to Java, these include the Philippines' Central Plain, and the valleys of the mainland's major rivers, already discussed.

The region's tropical forests exhibit an abundance and diversity of flora and fauna which are without parallel anywhere in the world. As the noted geographer Charles Fisher stated, "Nor is this surprising when it is recalled that, besides possessing both a climate and a degree of topographical fragmentation which are conducive to such profusion and variety, the region is focally situated between the main Asian and Australian centers of plant dispersal" (Fisher, 1964, p. 43). The latter part of Fisher's comment refers to the fact that in the eastern part of Indonesia, immediately to the west of Sulawesi and Lombok, is the dividing line between two great floral and faunal realms, the Oriental to the west of the line and the Australian to the east. The boundary was originally defined by A. R. Wallace over a century ago and became known as "Wallace's Line"; since then the boundary has been modified (by Weber, for example; see map of natural vegetation regions) because it has become increasingly evident that Oriental species have been much more widely disseminated to the east than Wallace proposed, and Australian varieties are found farther west than the original line. Wherever the exact boundary, it is clear that during the geological time period known as the Pleistocene epoch (the ice age), which began about two million years ago and ended only ten thousand years ago, most of what is today insular Southeast Asia was attached to the Asian land mass since sea levels were much lower

Stream erosion, Cebu Island, the Philippines (R. Ulack)

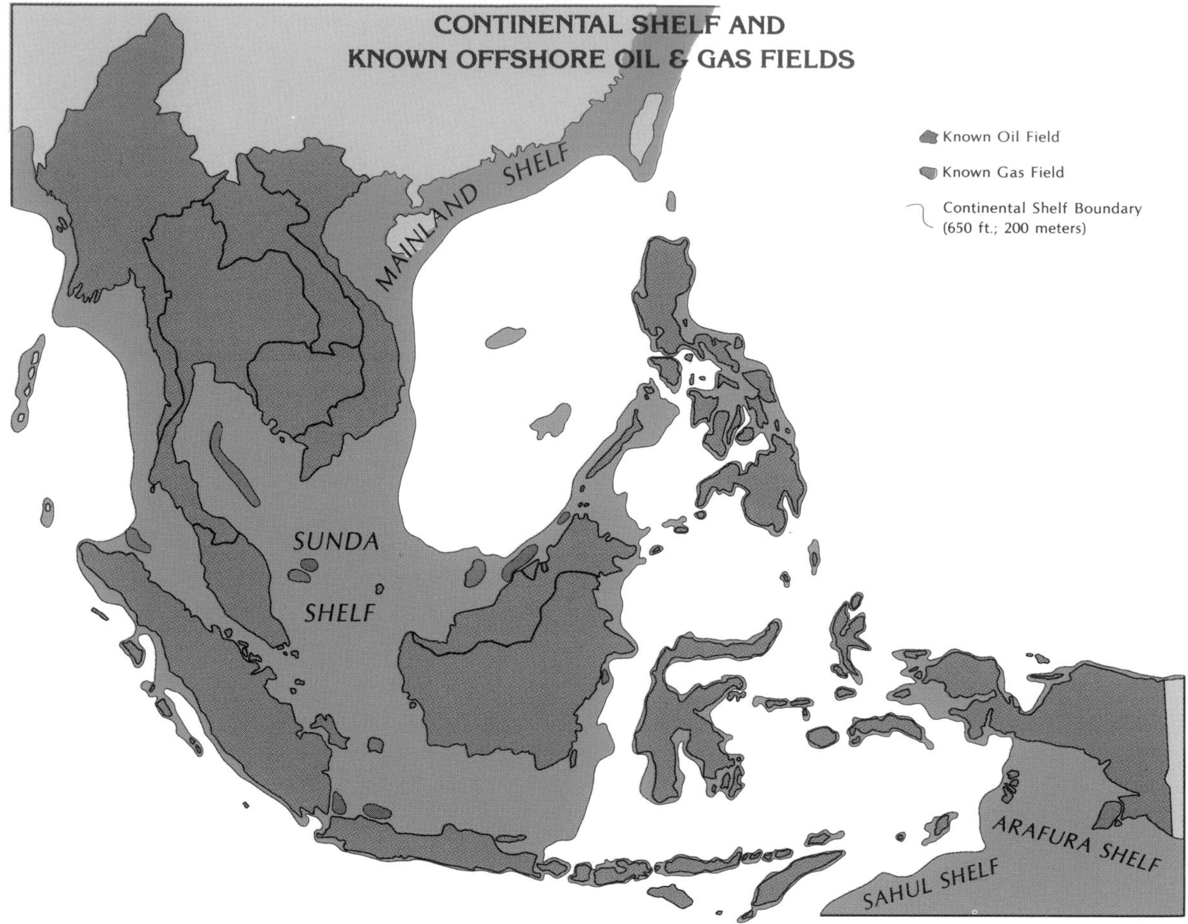


than they are today. Land areas then exposed included the continental shelf (called the Sunda Shelf, or Sundaland, in Southeast Asia), maritime areas that are today less than about 650 feet (200 m) deep. In the area around Wallace's Line, however, greater oceanic depths kept the areas physically separated by at least 40 miles (65 km). The water barrier acted as an effective deterrent to the migration of some life forms, especially land-based flora and fauna, including mammals, reptiles, and insects. This was also a barrier, of course, to human movement and it is estimated that man did not reach those areas to the east of the line until perhaps 40,000 or 50,000 years ago.

Only a few of the better-known examples of plant and animal life can be mentioned in this brief volume and several of these are given as examples in the individual national chapters. Commercially, the forests of Southeast Asia, and especially Burma and Thailand, yield the greatest share of the world's production of teak. Other hardwoods such as rosewood, sandalwood, and ebony, and such products as bamboo and rattan are also of commercial importance. Unfortunately, deforestation is bringing about the destruction of the rich and varied life forms of tropical forest regions. Indigenous animals to Southeast Asia, the better-known of which include the orangutan, Javan and Sumatran rhinoceros, tiger, leopard, and monkey-eating eagle, are already extinct in most areas, or are near extinction. Many of the perhaps millions of species of plants (most not yet discovered) in tropical areas may be valuable to man for medicinal, industrial, or other purposes. Numerous species are endemic (locally found) and therefore deforestation of a small area can mean the disappearance forever of a species. One study estimated that one forested mountain in

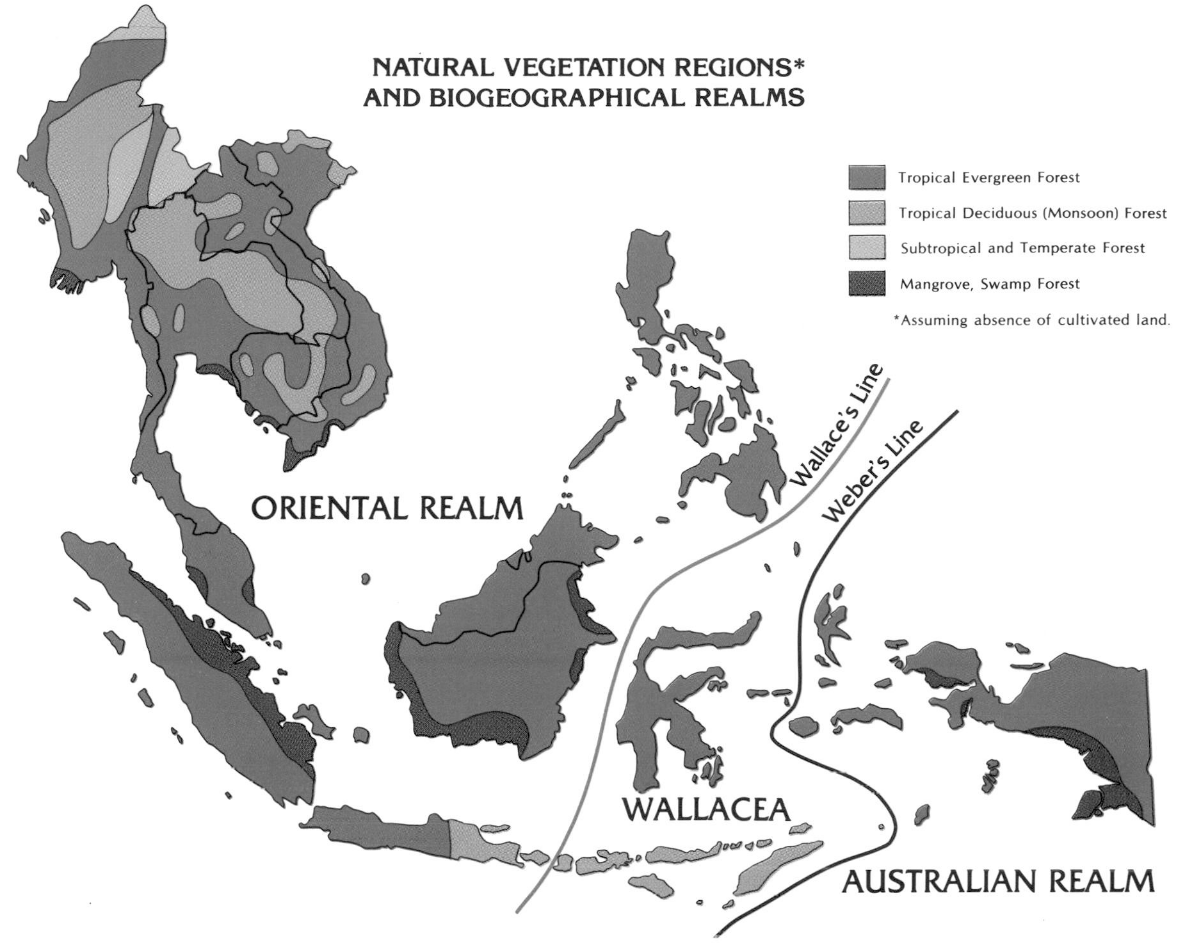

Hauling teak logs, Burma (courtesy R. Huke)

the Philippines contained more woody plant species, many of them endemic, than the entire United States.

## MINERAL RESOURCES

Whereas the economies of nearly all the nations of the region are dependent primarily on agriculture, there are some mineral resources of importance. Relative to total world production, by far the most significant of these is tin ore. Malaysia is the world's leading producer and accounts for nearly one-fifth of total production; Indonesia and Thailand are also important producers and together these three nations account for over two-fifths of total world production. Other mineral resources of commercial importance include chromite in the Philippines (which ranked eighth in world production in 1983); copper in the Philippines (ranked tenth); and nickel in Indonesia (fifth) and the Philippines (ninth). Iron ore, bauxite, phosphate, lead, zinc, and gemstones are produced in limited amounts. In short, except for tin and some copper, nickel, and chromite, the region is relatively poor in mineral resource production.

Two fossil fuels, petroleum and natural gas, have become increasingly important to the economies of several nations in the region, especially during the past two decades. The first commercial petroleum production in the region was by the British in Burma beginning in 1886. By the 1970s the major regional producers were Indonesia, Malaysia, and tiny Brunei, but offshore exploration and production had also begun in the Philippines, Vietnam, and Thailand. Taken together, the Southeast Asian nations produce less than 5% of the world's petroleum and natural gas. The largest producer is Indonesia, an OPEC member that produced over 450 million barrels of oil in 1983 and ranked ninth among world producers (with 2.5% of world production). Indonesia derives over three-quarters of its export earnings from petroleum and natural gas and Brunei derives nearly all its earnings from these fossil fuels. Such a dependence upon one or a few primary commodities can severely strain the economy of a nation when the world price for that commodity declines. Petroleum is a good example of a commodity whose price has fluctuated enormously since the early 1970s. The other major fossil fuel, coal, is commercially important only in northern Vietnam.

Tin mining, peninsular Malaysia (courtesy T. Leinbach)

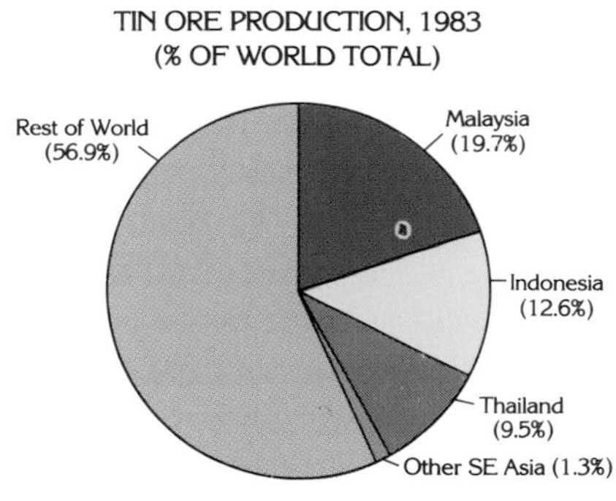


*Source: UNCTAD, 1985. Yearbook of International Trade Statistics 1985. (N.Y.: UN, 1985).*

## AGRICULTURE SYSTEMS AND RESOURCES

The economies of all Southeast Asian nations, except Singapore, have historically been based on agriculture. Today agriculture remains the dominant sector in most nations and comprises over 50% of the labor force.

Long before the arrival of outsiders, agriculture flourished throughout much of the region. Indeed, the geographer Carl Sauer (1952) proposed that sedentary cultivation was first practiced in mainland Southeast Asia, rather than in the Near East. More recent archeological discoveries in northern and northeastern Thailand have demonstrated that plants, including rice and beans, and animals were domesticated very early (Solheim, 1972). When the Europeans finally did begin to arrive in the region two kinds of agricultural systems were evident: shifting cultivation and intensive subsistence cultivation. Shifting cultivation, also known as "slash-and-burn" agriculture, is very widespread throughout most humid tropical regions of the world and is found where intensive cultivation is not possible, especially in upland areas. Once thought by Westerners to be a type of agriculture harmful to the environment, it has since become clear that this practice is not harmful so long as population densities never reach a point where land is used too intensively. In Southeast Asia the practice involves cutting away and burning a small patch of forest and then planting in it a wide variety of food crops, including upland (or rain-fed) rice, for several years. The land is eventually abandoned and the forest is allowed to replenish itself. If the same land is used for too long a period of time, or too frequently, then the soil and forest are destroyed and may be replaced by a savanna-like vegetative cover. Such a cover means grass, often of the type called *lalang* in Malaysia and *cogon* in the Philippines, a grass too coarse and sharp-edged to be used even for grazing animals.

Intensive subsistence, or sedentary, agriculture, although not geographically as widespread as shifting cultivation, involves far greater numbers of people. Rice was, and remains, the principal subsistence crop in the region. Production is most intensive in those areas where physical conditions are best suited to lowland (or wet) rice production: broad river valleys and deltas with fertile alluvial soils. In 1983 nearly one-half of the region's cultivated land was in rice, a greater share than in any other major world region, and the Southeast Asian nations together produced over one-fifth of the world's rice. Rice as cultivated in the region is very labor-intensive and involves first the preparation of the wet-field (*sawah* in Indonesia), or the rice padi. This often means leveling the land and constructing a dike around the padi so the field can be flooded. Practices vary but the next step usually involves planting seeds close together in nursery beds followed several weeks later by transplanting the seedlings to the main fields. By then the main fields have been flooded and the soil worked into a soft mud through repeated plowing and harrowing, most often with the aid of the water buffalo, the work animal of monsoon Asia. Following transplanting, water

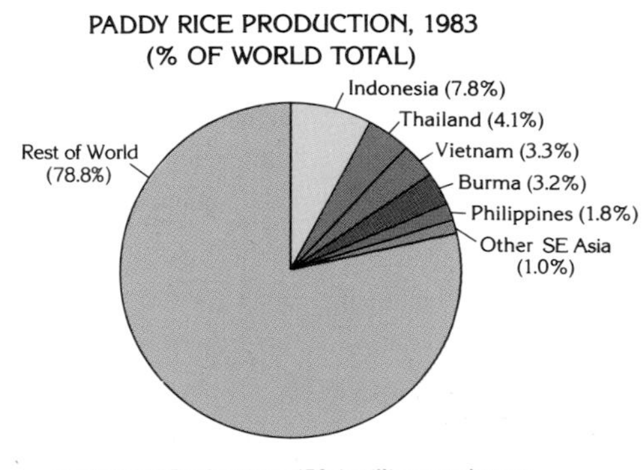


*Source: UN, FAO, 1985.*

Transplanting rice seedlings, Kedah, Malaysia (courtesy T. Leinbach)

in the padi has to be carefully regulated so that the upper portion of the plant is not submerged. As the rice reaches maturity, the padi is drained and the rice harvested, usually by hand. In some upland and even mountainous areas lowland rice can be produced in terraces that have been painstakingly built into the hillsides. The most dramatic example of this is found in the mountain areas of northern Luzon, in the Philippines, where such practices began centuries ago (see photo in Chapter 6). The construction of the padi in both lowland and terraced upland areas provides protection against excessive soil erosion. Also, new flood waters in the padi each growing season mean that mineral matter is replaced. Such areas have produced rice for centuries without serious loss of soil fertility.

Beginning in the 1960s, the "Green Revolution" brought with it new, high-yielding varieties of rice and other grains, and today some of the nations of Southeast Asia are self-sufficient, or nearly so, in rice production. Thailand remains the world's principal rice-exporting nation and Burma, Kampuchea, and southern Vietnam could regain their historic positions as exporters if the political and economic turmoil in those countries is brought under control.

The Europeans introduced a new agricultural

Woman tapping rubber tree, peninsular Malaysia (courtesy T. Leinbach)

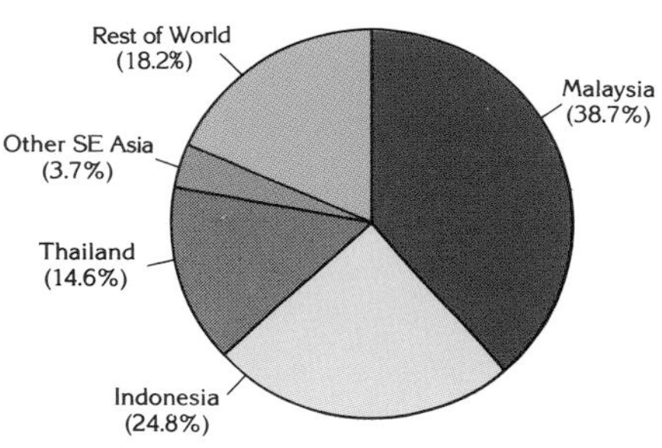

Source: UN, FAO, 1985.

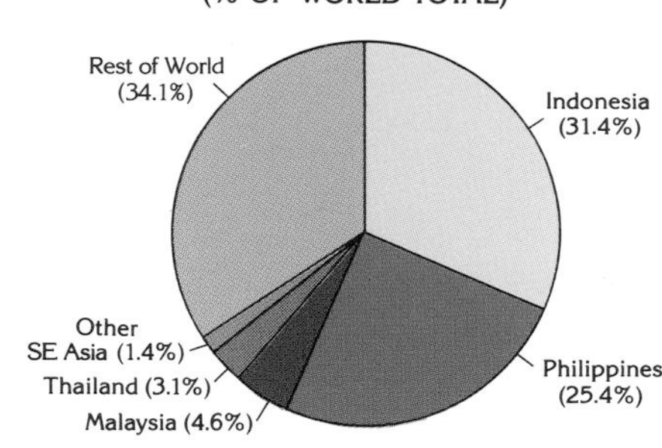

Source: UN, FAO, 1985.

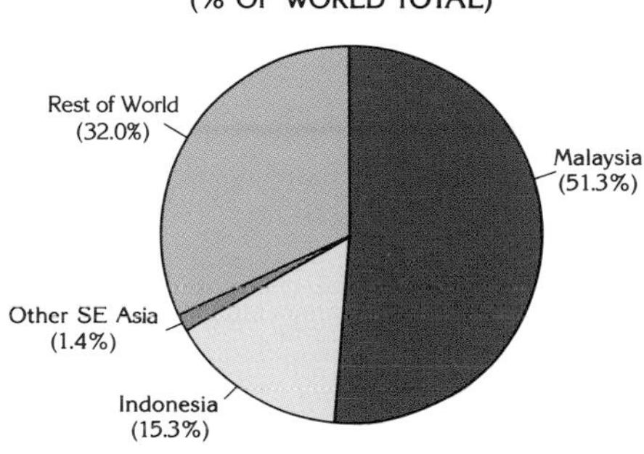

Source: UN, FAO, 1985.

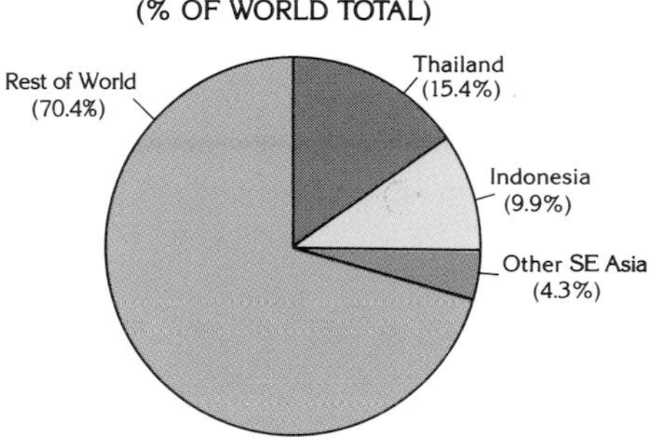

Source: UN, FAO, 1985.

system to the region, plantation agriculture. In so doing the colonizers, in particular the British and the Dutch, introduced a wide range of new commercial plants from other tropical lands. Indeed, except for rice, sugar, coconuts, and some spices, all of the major commercial crops produced in Southeast Asia today were introduced during the colonial period. By transfer from other parts of the world, Europeans introduced maize, coffee, tea, cinchona (quinine is obtained from the bark of the tree), tobacco, oil palm, and rubber. In 1983 the region produced a major share of the world's natural rubber (82% of total world production in 1983), coconuts (66%), copra (74%), palm oil (68%), sugar cane (9%), and jute and like fibers (9%). Other crops of importance included cassava (30% of the world's manioc was produced in the region) and maize (4% of the world total). Finally, in parts of Burma, Thailand, and Laos the illegal opium poppy is yet another crop of local commercial importance. These areas comprise most of what has been

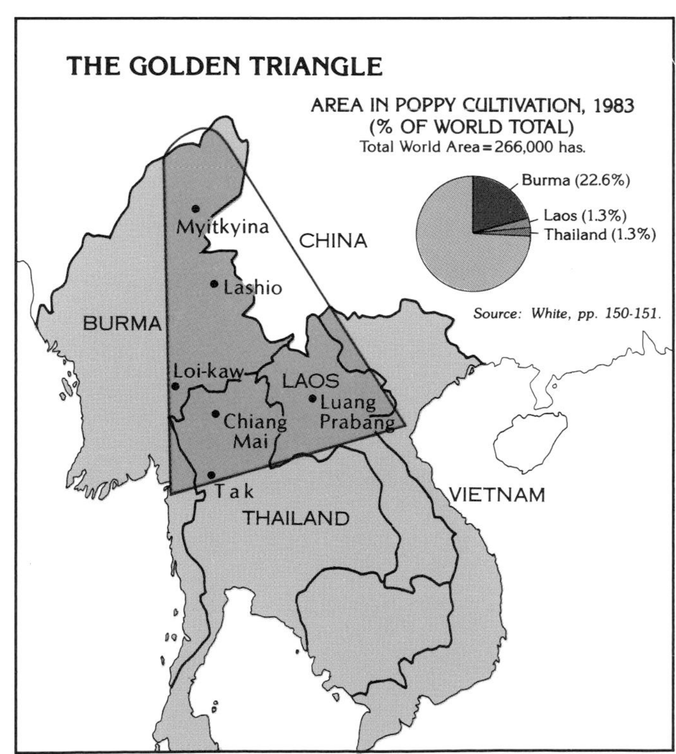

termed the "Golden Triangle," one of the world's most important source regions for opium and its addictive derivative, heroin.

Given the region's archipelagic nature, fisheries are of course another important resource. In the 1980s over one-tenth of the world's fish catch came from Southeast Asia and fish processing and canning has become commercially important in some areas. By far the region's primary producers were Indonesia, Thailand, and the Philippines, which together accounted for three-quarters of the regional catch. Given the rich, warm marine waters of the region, fisheries offer great potential as a resource; on the other hand fisheries, as well as offshore oil and gas, also offer potential for conflict as the nations of Southeast Asia vie over who controls the seas.

# 2

# *Historical and Political Background*

In addition to a basic knowledge of the physical environment, an understanding of the cultural, political, and economic characteristics of contemporary Southeast Asia is not possible without some background in the history of the region. Over the past several thousand years a wide variety and diversity of peoples have migrated into, and through, the region, both by land and by sea. In the ensuing national chapters we will examine the specific historical backgrounds of the individual nations; it is our purpose here to give a general overview of those historical forces that give the region the diverse character it has today.

## PRE-EUROPEAN INFLUENCES

While the evidence is fragmentary and open to alternative interpretations, it is possible that Southeast Asia was settled very early, perhaps as long as 500,000 years ago, during the Pleistocene epoch. As we saw in the previous chapter, during that time most of the Indonesian archipelago was a part of the mainland since sea levels were much lower than they are today, thus exposing much of the continental shelf. Archeologists have found early evidence of humans on Java who migrated there from the north across the land bridge. Since that time many different racial and ethnic groups have migrated into this very accessible region. The earliest groups included Australoids, Negritos, and Melanesoids (possibly a mixture of the former two groups), all today considered minor racial groups in that their total numbers are quite small. Most of these earliest groups are thought to have come from the Indian subcontinent. Today only a few relatively pure groups of Negritos and Australoids remain in Southeast Asia and these are found only in remote mountainous areas.

A more recent and much more numerous migration to the region has been that of peoples of the Mongoloid racial group, who began arriving in large numbers from southern China several thousand years ago. Over time this movement increased due in large part to the population pressures in southern China and the subsequent competition for new land on which to settle. Some earlier writers have argued that these more recent, more numerous, and more advanced settlers pushed the earlier inhabitants to less desirable locations, namely, to the more remote interior upland areas. This is the basis for the historic animosity that exists even today between the lowland majority and upland minorities as described by the anthropologist Robbins Burling, among others. Today, of course, the racial identity of the vast majority of Southeast Asians, both upland and lowland, is Mongoloid. In more recent centuries there has been a continuation of migration from China but peoples from the Indian subcontinent and later from the Middle East and Europe have contributed to an even greater diversity and mixing of the population.

The Indianization of Southeast Asia began more than two thousand years ago when traders, often accompanied by Hindu and Buddhist priests, ventured by sea to the nearby ports of Southeast Asia. Their numbers were never very large but these traders and priests brought with them influences that have permanently left their mark on the region: For example, new religious ideas from India, sacred languages such as Sanskrit in written form, a new concept of royalty (the "god-king"), codes of law, art, architecture, literary forms, and agricultural techniques. The first great indigenous empires have been called Indianized kingdoms because they followed closely these influences. With these kingdoms also came the first true cities in the region. During this period the most astute local leaders rose to prominence by blending advice from the Indian priests with indigenous concepts and belief systems. As early as the first century A.D. kingdoms and cities had begun to emerge.

In mainland Southeast Asia the best known and most powerful kingdoms were the mainland empires of Funan, Champa, Ayutthaya, Dvaravati, Pagan, and the Khmer or Angkorian state, which all flourished at various times between the fifth and fifteenth centuries A.D. Although not the earliest, perhaps the best known of all was the Khmer empire, founded in the ninth century. One of its most elaborate capitals, the temple complex of Angkor Thom was one of the largest cities in the world at its zenith in the twelfth century. It is estimated that the city, and the surrounding rural villages serving it, had a population that approached one million. The structure of this sacred city was in strict accordance with Indian Hindu-Buddhist cosmology. A large brick or stone temple complex or monument was at the city center, and nearby were other religious buildings as well as the buildings of royalty, the aristocracy, and administration. These were surrounded by a walled or moated area. Angkor Thom was an excellent example of what the geographer T. G. McGee has described as the precolonial "inland sacred city."

Indianized empires were also established in insular and peninsular Southeast Asia and the most powerful of these were Srivijaya, Majapahit, and the trading empire centered on Malacca (now Melaka). Srivijaya lasted from about 700 to 1200 and included most of Sumatra, western Java, the west coast of Borneo, and

Angkor Wat, Kampuchea (courtesy W. Duiker)

the Malay Peninsula. Its capital, also Srivijaya, was located near present-day Palembang, in southern Sumatra. Srivijaya represented a second type of city in precolonial Southeast Asia: the "coastal market city." Majapahit, a Javanese-centered empire, emerged about 1300 and for the next century and a half held suzerainty over much of the Indonesian archipelago. The Malacca sultanate was founded about 1400 and until it fell to the Portuguese in 1511, was the major trading center of the region. Other important early empires in the Indonesian archipelago included Mataram and Kediri, both centered on Java, and that of the Sailendra dynasty in central Java. The ornate eighth-century Buddhist temple complex built at Borobudur during the time of the Sailendra dynasty is one of very few places in the region that rivaled Angkor in terms of the size and splendor of its monumental architecture. The late ninth century Hindu temples at Prambanan built by Mataram rulers in central Java are examples of other great architectural achievements.

Arab traders arrived in the region well before the Europeans, and by about the eleventh century Islam had begun to make its appearance in the region. A number of Islamic sultanates emerged and soon much of the indigenous population of insular Southeast Asia had embraced the religion.

## WESTERN COLONIZATION

It was left to the European and American colonizers, however, to divide the region amongst themselves and thus establish the current boundaries and bases for the ten independent nation-states in the region. There was often little cultural or historical rationale for the land boundaries that were established and today this remains a very real problem throughout the re-

Prambanan temple, east central Java (courtesy W. L. Thomas)

gion. In short, today's nation-state in Southeast Asia, as in other parts of the world, is a product of the colonial period and not a natural development.

The first European ships to arrive in the region came from eastward and belonged to the Portuguese. They arrived in 1509 and two years later the Portuguese had established the first European garrison in Malacca after defeating the Malacca sultanate. Shortly thereafter Spanish ships under Ferdinand Magellan crossed the Pacific and reached the Philippines in 1521. Magellan was slain near the central Philippine island of Cebu but his ships successfully completed the first European circumnavigation of the globe. There followed a period of intense competition between Portugal and Spain over the spice trade, especially in that part of the Moluccas centered on Tidore and Ternate, the area known to the Europeans as the "Spice Islands." The Dutch, British, and French came to the region next and by the latter half of the nineteenth century nearly all of Southeast Asia was colonized by one of these five European powers. Only Thailand was never colonized, although it was heavily influenced by the West and its national boundaries were also drawn by the Europeans. American victory in the Spanish-American War at the end of the nineteenth century brought the final Western actor into the region, and from 1898 until the Japanese occupation in 1941, the Philippines was an American colony.

It is of utmost importance that the broad impacts of the Western colonial experience in Southeast Asia be understood, since without this information it is not possible to comprehend the present-day economic and political characteristics of the region. Furthermore, each of the colonizers had a somewhat different style and impact but all eventually had one overriding reason for control: raw materials and profit. The colonial period left many legacies that are too numerous to cite here but some of the more important can be mentioned. First was the development of mineral and forest resources and of the plantation system and associated crops. Second, a transportation system and related infrastructure was constructed for the purpose of getting the primary commodities to port so that they could be shipped on to the mother country. Third, and related to the former legacy, was the rapid development of one major, or "primate," city that served as principal port, capital, cultural and educational center, and financial and manufacturing center of the colony. Today these former colonial port cities are the very largest in each nation and the vast majority of wealth and power is concentrated within these cities. They are what has been called the "core" area of the nation, serving the vast hinterland or "periphery". Today such nations are characterized by huge spatial income inequalities between the core and periphery. Fourth was the introduction of alien political systems and institutions and boundaries. Fifth was the introduction of Western languages through educational systems. And sixth was the introduction of Christianity. These impacts often varied greatly from colony to colony. A good example of this is the

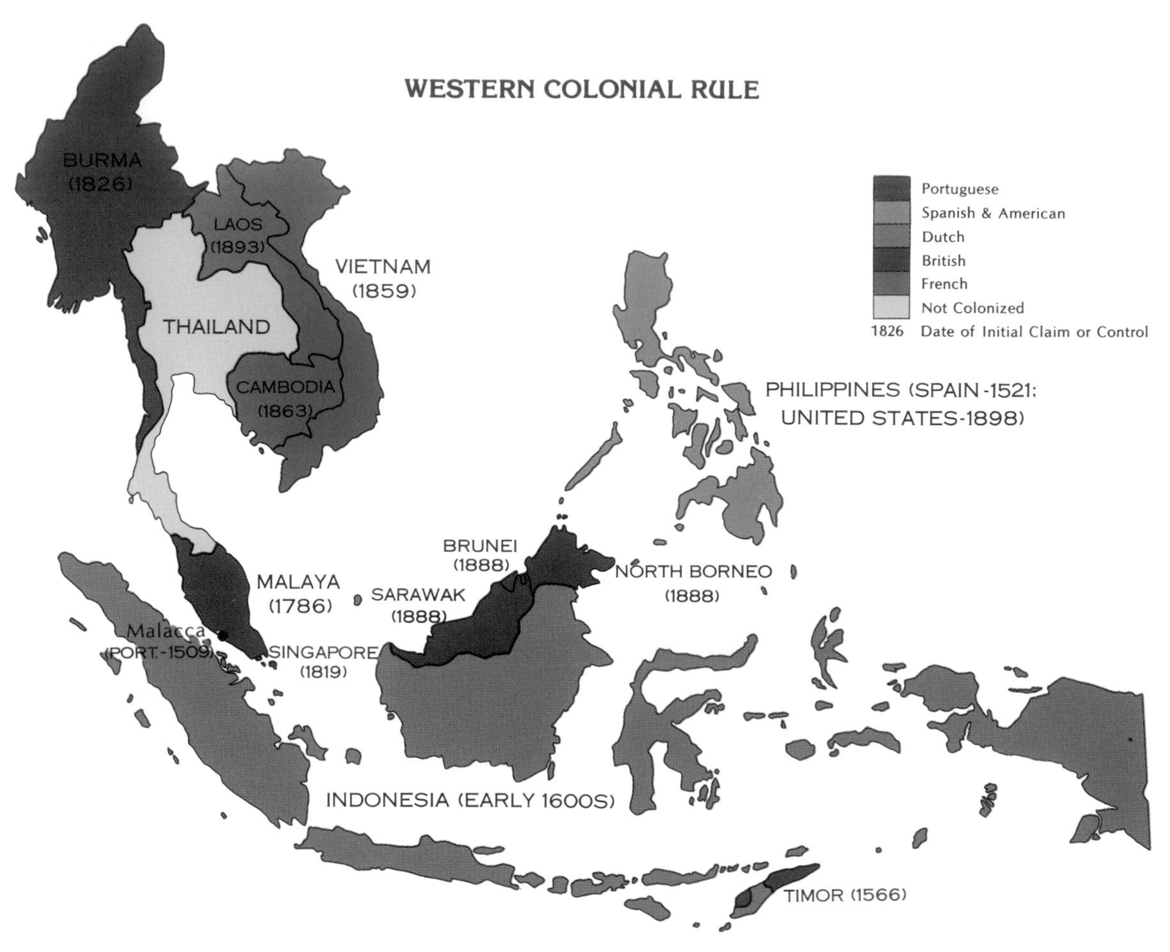

Manila Cathedral in Intramuros, Manila (courtesy W. L. Thomas)

Government building, Singapore (R. Ulack)

introduction of an educational system and European language. The British and American colonizers brought both of these into their colonies and as a result English is today quite widely spoken in the Philippines and Malaysia; on the other hand, Dutch and English are rarely spoken in Indonesia and Burma, respectively, because the Dutch and British did not put great emphasis on the development of education and language in these colonies except where they provided education for the local bureaucratic elite who staffed the colonial government.

## CONTEMPORARY POLITICAL REALITIES

Southeast Asia today is composed of ten independent nation-states which can be subdivided into two groups of nations based on their political-economic philosophies. The member states of the Association of Southeast Asian Nations (ASEAN), an economic "common market" which began in 1967, is comprised of the six free-market nations of Indonesia, the Philippines, Thailand, Malaysia, Singapore, and Brunei. All were charter members except tiny Brunei, which joined in 1984 shortly after it became independent. Most of these nations describe themselves as nonaligned but their economies, trade, and alliances are clearly oriented toward Western Europe, North America, and Japan. On the other hand, the four remaining nations, Burma, Vietnam, Kampuchea, and Laos are socialist states. The latter three have been oriented toward the Soviet or Chinese style of Communism since 1975, following the end of the Vietnam War and the conclusion of twenty years of American military involvement in the Indochina area. Burma has been organized as a neutral, one-party state since 1974 and if there is such a thing as a nonaligned nation in the region, Burma comes the closest to being one. All of the nations are members of the United Nations but Kampuchea is represented at the United Nations by a government-in-exile as of 1988, rather than by that which is actually in power.

## DEPENDENCE AND INTERDEPENDENCE

In varying degrees the nations of Southeast Asia are dependent economically and militarily upon extraregional developed nations. The degree of

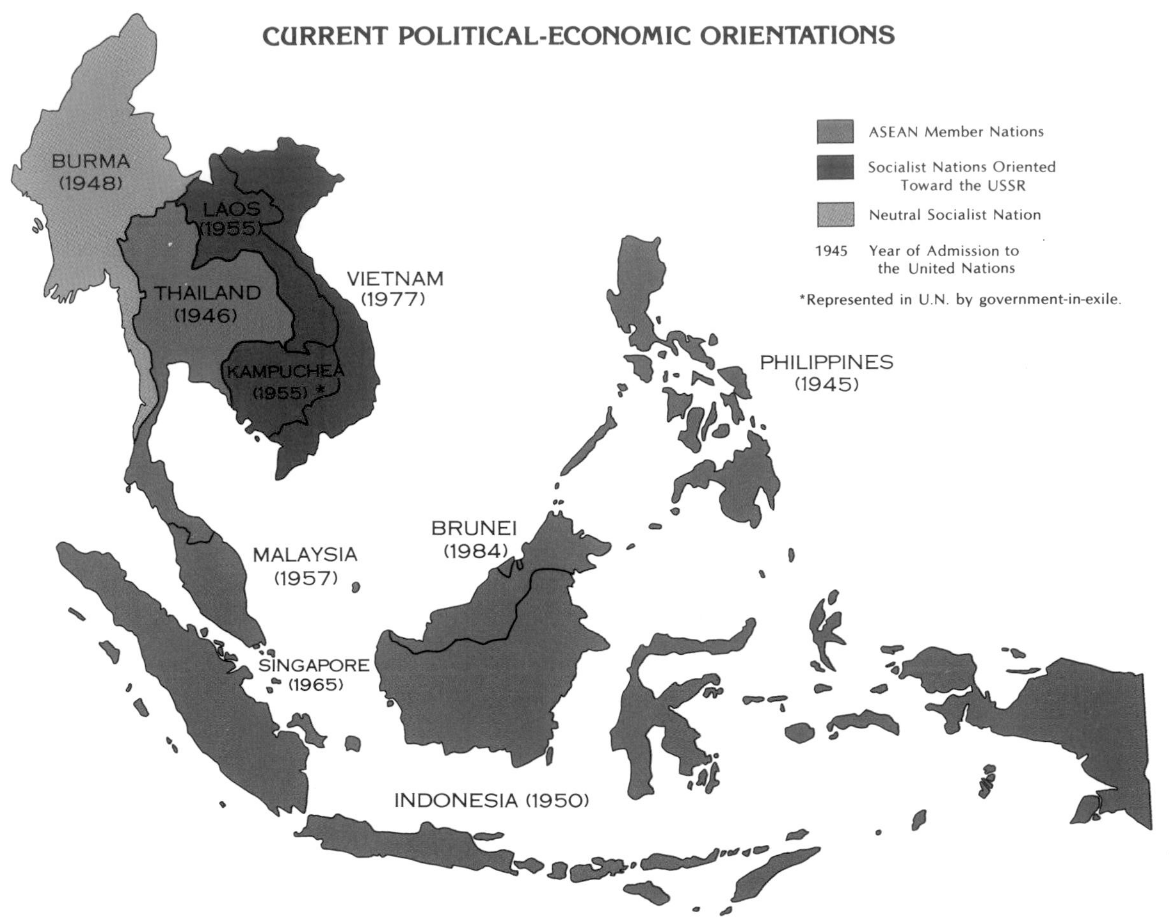


dependence can be measured by such things as foreign investment, military alliances and assistance, economic aid, the direction and share of foreign trade, and tourist flows. The individual national chapters that follow give evidence for both extra- and intra-regional linkages among and between nations. Such examination supports clearly the existence of the two distinct political-economic groupings of nations already noted.

The six ASEAN nations, for example, have adopted in varying degrees a rather liberal policy toward foreign economic involvement and have in fact actively promoted such foreign investment through a variety of fiscal and other incentives. For example, a reason that the inflow of such capital has occurred more rapidly in ASEAN than other regions is because corporate taxes are much lower (15–20%) than elsewhere, as for example in South Asia (55–65%). Thus, multinational corporations are increasingly being welcomed as a means to increase output, capital, technological levels, exports, and employment. Such corporations have often been subjected to severe criticism related to excessive repatriation of profits. The cry of neocolonialism has derived in part from the power of such Western and Japanese-owned corporations. Oftentimes the benefits derived by the host country are minimal, in part because of the very high import content involved in such activity. Nevertheless, foreign direct investment has grown rapidly, by more than four times during the 1970s. And recently Japan has become the major source of such investment.

Today, formal military alliances among groups of nations are rare in the region, but this has not always been the case. Thailand and the Philippines, along with Pakistan, the United States, Great Britain, New Zealand, Australia, and originally France, were members of the now defunct Southeast Asia Treaty Organization (SEATO). SEATO was a defensive and anti-Communist alliance which was created as a response to what was perceived as Communist expansionism in the region. This fear, expressed as the "domino theory," grew out of the creation of a Communist state in North Vietnam in 1954 and the likelihood of a united North and South Vietnam. It was feared that such a united Communist Vietnam would ultimately lead to Communist domination of the entire region. Each nation would fall, like dominoes, under Communist control. SEATO ceased to exist in 1975 but the geopolitical philosophy among ASEAN members and the United States is still guided by this principle.

Since 1975 there have been some changes in bilateral military alliances. One basic change has been related to the Soviet-Chinese split. Vietnam and the Soviet Union have emerged as allies against China. Since 1979 Vietnam has even provided the Soviet Union with at least two military bases at the sites of the former American bases at Cam Ranh Bay and Da Nang. China and Vietnam have clashed along their common boundary several times since 1979, due to Hanoi's tilt toward Moscow and because of the 1978 Vietnamese invasion and subsequent occupation of Kampuchea. The situation is very complex and has affected all of the region's nations. For example, neighboring Thailand is very much concerned about the Vietnamese occupation of Kampuchea and has attempted, with little success, to negotiate a Vietnamese withdrawal. On the other hand, strongly anti-Chinese Indonesia tends to favor a Soviet-backed Vietnam as a barrier to Chinese influence in the region. In short, current policies in the region's non-Communist nations are still a response to Communist expansion, but now such policies take into account two opposing players, China and the Soviet Union.

International labor migration and remittances and tourism are other reflections of the economic and political ties between nations. Not surprisingly, the geographical origins of tourists traveling to the region reflects in part the colonial past with the United States, Great Britain, and France among the major origins of international travelers. In recent years, however, the Japanese have become the largest single group of extraregional visitors. This is not surprising given the high income levels of the average Japanese, Japanese economic investments in the region, and Japan's close proximity to Southeast Asia. Labor migration and subsequent remittances (money sent home by workers) such as those resulting from, for example, Thai and Filipino workers in Middle Eastern oilfields, yield very significant revenues.

## FUTURE POLITICAL PROBLEMS AND PROSPECTS

The Southeast Asian region has a long history of conflict and there have been several different reasons for such conflict. First, issues of national identity have been a major source of conflict, both currently and historically. Such issues have derived, for example, from long-standing ethnic differences, from religious antagonisms, from differences between alien minorities (most notably the Chinese) and the indigenous population, and most recently, from revolutionary social challenge (Leifer, 1981). In terms of the former, one of the major characteristics of the region is its tremendous ethnic diversity. Nations in the region often include within their colonial-imposed boundaries ethnic minorities unwilling to reconcile themselves to political dominance by other cultural groups. Burma is perhaps the best-known example of a nation with insurgent groups made up of ethnic minorities, but examples of such conflict could be given for nearly all the other nations as well. Attempts by such minority groups to secure separate political status have not generally been successful and major regional conflicts have not emerged as a result. But such separatist movements are endemic within the region and will continue to have a negative impact upon national unity.

A source of conflict that has had a much greater impact on the region since independence has been brought about by revolutionary social change. Stark poverty and gross class and spatial disparities of wealth have facilitated such revolutionary movements. The most common feature of this type of conflict has been the organized armed guerrilla movements against the local elites who replaced the former colonial rulers. It has nearly always been an insurgent Communist Party that has proffered such change. In only one area, North Vietnam, did the Communist Party succeed to power immediately after colonial withdrawal and it has only been since 1975 that the Communists have controlled all of Indochina. In every other nation of the region (except Brunei), the Communist Party has played an active political role at different times. In the Philippines, for example, it was formed originally in the 1940s in response to the Japanese occupation. This Hukbalahap (or "Huk") movement, as it was called, is the origin of the Communist Party of the Philippines and its armed wing, the New People's Army, which today includes perhaps 20,000 active guerrillas operating throughout most of the nation. Communists are probably least active today in Indonesia, where the Party has been strictly outlawed since it was implicated with an abortive coup in 1965.

Another source of regional conflict derives from the colonial period. The political boundaries that failed to take into account ethnic realities were originally drawn by the colonial powers. As a result virtually every international boundary in the region has been in dispute at one time or another since independence. Some boundary disputes are still not resolved, and occasionally military action results. Recent boundary disputes have occurred between Brunei and Malaysia, Malaysia and the Philippines, Malaysia and Thailand, Indonesia and Papua-New Guinea, Burma and China, and Vietnam and China. Boundary disputes have also been the source of conflict between Thailand and Kampuchea.

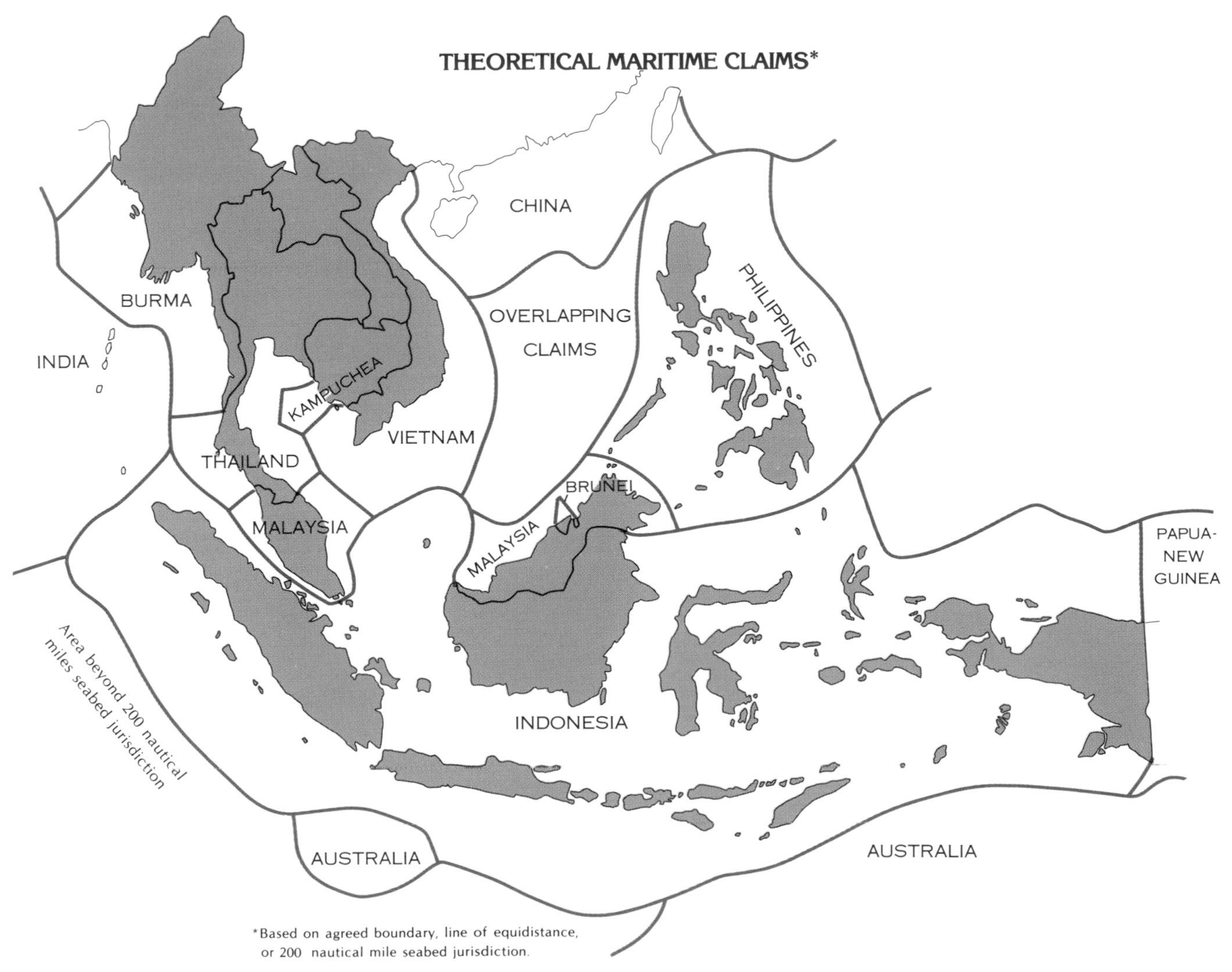

In the future, boundary disputes also will involve those over who controls the oceans. An important point for consideration in the development of oceanic resources—especially in archipelagic areas like Southeast Asia, where rich fisheries and offshore oil and natural gas are found—relates to territorial oceanic claims. The United Nations has sponsored "Law of the Sea" conventions in which participating nations have worked with little success to resolve such claims. The United Nations recognizes a 200-mile claim for nations even though initially many nations claimed only three miles of the bordering seas. Other nations, like the United States, do not recognize such an extensive claim and this question will undoubtedly remain a major problem.

Perhaps the major regional problem today is that surrounding the question of Kampuchea. Until this issue is resolved there can be little hope for any kind of agreement between the Communist and ASEAN states or between the major external powers of regional influence. The issues involved in this conflict go beyond those that are simply political; bitter differences between Khmers and Vietnamese existed long before the French colonized the area. In the 1830s, for example, the Vietnamese attempted to eradicate the traditional culture of the area and replace it with its own. The Khmers, and for that matter the Thais as well, have historically feared the expansionist Vietnamese. Thailand views the new Vietnam-dominated status of both Kampuchea and Laos, traditionally considered buffer states to Vietnam, as a major threat to its own security. It is thus not surprising that Thailand, as well as other ASEAN states that harbor similar fears, have encouraged (and even supplied arms to) anti-Vietnamese groups in Kampuchea to oppose these newest colonizers.

# 3

# Cultural Characteristics

The region's accessibility by sea and land, its fragmented physical character, and the historic migrations into the region and subsequent intermixing of diverse peoples all combine to explain the great cultural diversity that characterizes the region today. The region can also be described culturally, as it was physically, as a shatter belt. Literally hundreds of different ethnic groups are found throughout the region.

## LANGUAGE

Languages stemming from four major, and one minor, indigenous language families are spoken in the region. Malayo-Polynesian, or Austronesian, languages and dialects predominate in the island areas and in the Malay Peninsula; Sino-Tibetan languages predominate in Burma; Tai languages are used principally in Thailand, Burma, and Laos; and Austro-Asiatic languages are spoken widely in Kampuchea and Vietnam. Various dialects of Chinese are widely distributed, but dominate in Singapore. Papuan languages, which include much smaller numbers of speakers, occur in West Irian on New Guinea and in a few other areas of eastern Indonesia.

Such a brief and simple summary of such a complex topic does not reveal the variations in the geographical distribution of these families; the reader should refer to the individual maps of ethnolinguistic groups in each of the national chapters in order to understand better the great diversity that exists. It should also be noted that there is often disagreement as to language classification. For example, whereas we have chosen here to include the Vietnamese language with the Austro-Asiatic family, Vietnamese has also been classified as a Tai and Sino-Tibetan language. According to one author, "The fact that it is tonal and can seem monosyllabic accounts in part for the confusion. The further fact that Vietnamese is heavily (laden) with loan words from Chinese adds to the uncertainty. . . . Possibly the linguists will someday conclude that it is in a family of its own" (Williams, pp. 18–19). Finally, it might be noted that there is also often disagreement as to whether a language should be classified as a separate langauge or a dialect (a variant of a language). The point is that the way in which languages are classified and mapped here will not satisfy everyone.

Each of the language families found in the region includes hundreds of separate languages and dialects. For example, there are over 600 Papuan languages spoken in Indonesia, Papua-New Guinea, and the nearby islands of the western Pacific. Many of these are spoken by only a few thousand people. And although the languages of individual nations are predominantly of the same family, there are many mutually unintelligible languages spoken. In the Philippines, for example, about 70 different major languages and dialects are spoken and in Indonesia the number is around 250. Often a dialect is so unlike the language with which it is classified that it is in reality a separate language. Clearly, we can include only the relatively few widely spoken languages in our discussion here and in the succeeding national chapters.

Of the Southeast Asian nations, certainly Burma has had at least as many problems in national development and unity caused by ethnolinguistic differences as any other nation in the region. Whereas the ethnic Burmans comprise about two-thirds of the total population, various upland groups who speak dif-

ferent languages are the most numerous in their own regions. Upon independence from England in 1948, the federal constitution of the Union of Burma established six more or less autonomous units based on ethnolinguistic considerations in an attempt to satisfy the aspirations of the larger minority groups. Separate states were established for those who spoke Shan (a Tai language), Karen, Kachin, Chin, and Burmese (all Sino-Tibetan languages). Occasionally, such groups have even held military control over their states. In addition to these major ethnic groups there are scores of smaller groups throughout Burma, most often in upland areas. These comprise the numerous small hill tribes found all over Southeast Asia. In Burma these include the Palaung-Wa and Nagas, among many others.

Besides indigenous languages there are also those that have been introduced more recently. For example, a number of mutually unintelligible Chinese dialects are spoken by the millions of ethnic Chinese who are found throughout Southeast Asia, principally in the cities. Mandarin Chinese is taught in many private Chinese schools that exist in the region's cities. Singapore is culturally a Chinese nation in that about three-quarters of the total population is of Chinese ancestry. Malaysia's population is about one-third ethnic Chinese. While no other nation in the region has as large a proportion of Chinese as Singapore or Malaysia, all have significant shares.

Indians of recent origin also brought with them their languages such as Tamil (of the Dravidian family) or Hindi (Indo-European family) and other cultural attributes. For example, many contemporary ethnic Indians in Malaysia can trace their ancestry to immigrants who came in the late nineteenth century from the Tamil-speaking area along the coast of southeastern India to work on Malaysia's rubber plantations or in its tin mines. Today, like the Chinese, Indians often own shops and businesses in

Meo tribal girl, near Thailand-Burma border (courtesy J. Baker)

the "Indiantowns" found throughout the cities of Southeast Asia.

Finally, the European and American colonizers brought with them their educational systems and schools, and thus another overlay of languages. One of these languages, English, is today widely spoken as a second language in much of urban Southeast Asia. England brought the language to its colonies and today it is one of four official languages in Singapore (and is the medium of instruction in schools). The United States introduced English into the Philippines through its educational system and today English is spoken as a second language by about two-fifths of all Filipinos. It is also the medium of instruction, in part because of the great diversity of native languages spoken within the Philippines. With a few exceptions, the English-speaking visitor to the region will have little difficulty in making himself understood, especially in the largest cities.

Surprisingly, although the Spanish colonial period lasted for nearly 350 years in the Philippines and most Filipinos have Spanish names, Spanish is a language spoken today by only a very few Filipinos, most notably by a few of the old, landed aristocracy. Portuguese, Dutch, and French are also relatively unimportant languages among the indigenous population. None of these former colonizers were noted for extensive educational advances in their colonies.

Continued external influences, notably by the Russians in Vietnam, Laos, and Kampuchea, and by the Japanese all over the region, will further add to the degree of cultural complexity in the Southeast Asian region.

## RELIGION

There are three major world religions found throughout Southeast Asia: Buddhism, Islam, and Christianity. The very first religions introduced into the region from the outside were "brahmanism" (or Vedism), a precursor of Hinduism, and Buddhism. These religions were brought from India by Brahmin and Buddhist priests beginning about 2,000 years ago. Hinduism is today adhered to by only 1% of the total regional population but its historic influences are much greater than current numbers suggest. As we have already noted, its early influences could be witnessed over most of the region in the great early kingdoms that were established. Today, Hinduism is practiced among most ethnic Indians, the descendents of earlier immigrants to the region. This group is most concentrated in the urban areas of Malaysia, Burma, and Singapore. Also, Hinduism is the religion of the majority of Balinese on the island of Bali, immediately east of Java. The several million Hindu Balinese represent the only major non-Indian population anywhere in the world that adheres to Hinduism.

Buddhism, on the other hand, is a major religion in the region and accounts for about one-third of the total population. The people of Burma, Thailand, Laos, Kampuchea, and Vietnam are predominantly Buddhist. North-

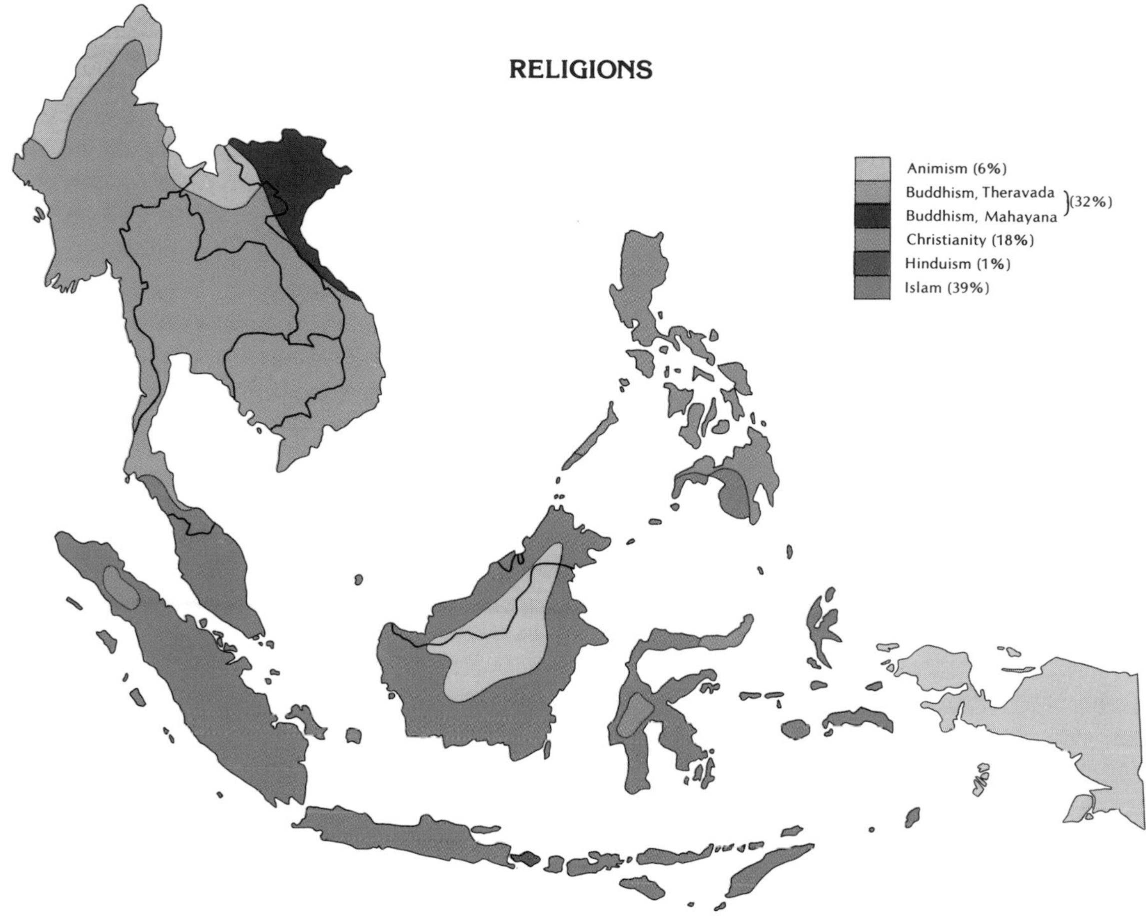


ern Vietnam has historically been influenced by nearby China whereas until about the fifteenth century southern Vietnam had been more influenced by India. In religion, too, this is evident as the followers of the religion are Mahayana Buddhists in the north, and Theravada Buddhists in the south. The former is perhaps less orthodox, entering northern Vietnam by way of China whereas that in the south diffused into Burma, Thailand, Kampuchea, and southern Vietnam by way of Ceylon (Sri Lanka). Certainly this strict delineation in Vietnam, as well as the proportion of adherents to Buddhism (and other religions), has been altered since 1975 as the secular Communist government has deemphasized religion and as large numbers of northern Vietnamese have been encouraged to migrate to the New Economic Zones of the south. But strong traditions and belief systems that have lasted for centuries are difficult to alter and it is certainly so that the majority of Vietnamese maintain their loyalty to such beliefs.

Islam was the next great world religion to enter the region and today nearly two-fifths of the population are Muslims, making it the region's largest religion. Although Muslim merchants have frequented the trading ports of Southeast Asia since the seventh century A.D., it was not until about the twelfth or thirteenth century that, beginning in northern Sumatra, it became an official religion. Today it is the predominant religion in Indonesia, Malaysia, and Brunei, and there are important minorities in the extreme southern portions of the Philippines, Thailand, and Burma. Perhaps even moreso than the other great religions of the region, Islam has greatly affected the cultural, economic, and political institutions and processes in those nations where it is predominant.

Christianity was of course introduced into the region by the Europeans. Catholicism was first brought by the Spanish and Portuguese in the sixteenth century to the island and peninsular areas, and later by the French to their In-

Buddha statue, Bangkok (R. Ulack)

Magellan's cross, Cebu City, the Philippines (R. Ulack)

dochinese colony. Catholicism is today still important in southern Vietnam, and before 1975 many of the nation's local elites were Catholic. Catholicism is of course the major religion in the Philippines, adhered to by 85% of the population. Protestantism has more recently made some inroads into the region, principally among some of the interior hill tribes. Today, two major ethnic groups in Sumatra, the Minangkabau and Bataks, are predominantly Protestant. Another example are the Karen Baptists in Buddhist-dominated Burma.

These "external" religions replaced, and to some extent have been modified by, the indigenous tribal religions that are still widely distributed throughout Southeast Asia. Animism remains a dominant belief system for many of the upland minority tribal groups, especially in the most remote areas of Burma, Laos, the Philippines, eastern Indonesia, and Borneo. Animism today accounts for 5–10% of the total regional population.

## CULTURAL CHANGE

Political strife, economic change, more elaborate transportation systems, new communication technologies, and the media have brought about alterations in cultural patterns through migration and the exposure to new and often alien ideas and values. For example, the continuing conflict in the Indochinese area means that refugees are still leaving in the hope of gaining a new and better life elsewhere. In Indonesia, the government is pursuing its Transmigration policy whereby persons on densely populated Java are encouraged to migrate to distant and sparsely populated places such as Kalimantan and Irian Jaya (western New Guinea).

And as already noted, the Vietnamese government has brought about massive internal mobility through the development of New Economic Zones in the south.

By far the most significant movement, however, has been the massive relocations from rural areas throughout the region to the largest cities in each nation. This rural-to-urban migration has brought to the cities people from every background and geographical origin possible. While often residing in the cities among people of similar background and ethnic origin, such migrants clearly are affected by new ideas and lifestyles. Upon return to their rural origins, be it temporary or permanent, the migrant carries with him or her new ideas and material goods from the city. This diffusion process has gradually altered traditional lifestyles.

Today throughout nearly all of the large cities in the region (especially those in the ASEAN nations), the evidence of alien culture is evident. For example, bluejeans are ubiquitous, Western rock-and-roll music dominates the air waves, fast-food chains such as McDonald's reflect new tastes (at least for the few who can afford it), and the elderly, who traditionally have been cared for by younger family members, are beginning to become more isolated. Exposure to Western movies, television, visitors, technology, and consumption patterns in these cities suggests that such places act as the filter through which external cultural influences, by way of migrants, diffuse to the small towns and rural areas of the periphery. Additionally, such places act as meeting places for people of all backgrounds from within each nation. In short, cultural convergence of a type seems to be occurring throughout the region. Such convergence, of course, means gradual change in ideas but, unfortunately, it does not also necessarily mean a concomitant improvement in economic or social condition.

# 4

# Regional Population and Urban Characteristics

*Population (1986):* 408,444,000

*Population Density:* 235 persons per sq mi (91 persons per sq km)

*Urban Population:* 24%

*Annual Average Rate of Natural Population Increase:* 2.0%

*Crude Birth Rate:* 30.9 per 1,000 population

*Crude Death Rate:* 10.5 per 1,000 population

*Infant Mortality Rate:* 73 infant deaths per 1,000 live births

*Life Expectancy:* Male—56.6 years; Female—60.2 years

*Percentage Aged 0-14:* 38.5%

*Percentage Aged 65+:* 3.7%

*Per Capita GNP (1986):* $710

Southeast Asia has a population in excess of 400 million, or over 8% of the world total. Within the region Indonesia is by far the most populous nation, accounting for over two-fifths of the region's total. Spread over more than 12,000 islands and islets, Indonesia's total land area also accounts for about two-fifths of the regional total. Vietnam, the Philippines, Thailand, and Burma follow Indonesia in population; the next four most populous nations are notably smaller and form a third grouping. Tiny Brunei, with a population of only one-quarter of a million, is the region's least populous nation.

## POPULATION DISTRIBUTION AND DENSITY

Within the region, population distribution is quite uneven. The heaviest population concentrations are found in the fertile river valley and delta regions and near the sea. At least seven primary "cores" of high population density can be identified. These are: Java and the nearby smaller islands of Madura and Bali; the Philippines from the Central Plain north of Manila south to the central Visayan Islands; the western coast of peninsular Malaysia; the lower Mekong Valley of southern Vietnam and Kampuchea; Thailand's Chao Phraya drainage area; the lower Irrawaddy; and the Red River valley and coastal areas of northern Vietnam. These core areas include all of the region's largest metropolitan areas and its most densely-populated rural areas.

Whereas overall population densities for the entire region are not as high as those of Southeast Asia's much larger neighbors (235 persons per square mile compared to 606 for India and 290 for China), land for agriculture is more limited because of the rugged topography. Thus, population densities in the limited lowland areas that are available for farming are very high. At the extreme is fertile Java, where densities in rural areas attain levels of over 2,000 persons per square mile (775 persons per sq km). There is limited land remaining for new agricultural settlement and therefore many seek opportunities in cities or in other nations.

Aside from the special case of the city-state Singapore, the nations with the highest overall population densities are the Philippines and Vietnam, with densities of 487 persons per square mile (188 persons per sq km) and 480 persons per square mile (185 persons per sq km), respectively. A cursory examination of the regional population density map reveals that there are very limited sparsely populated areas

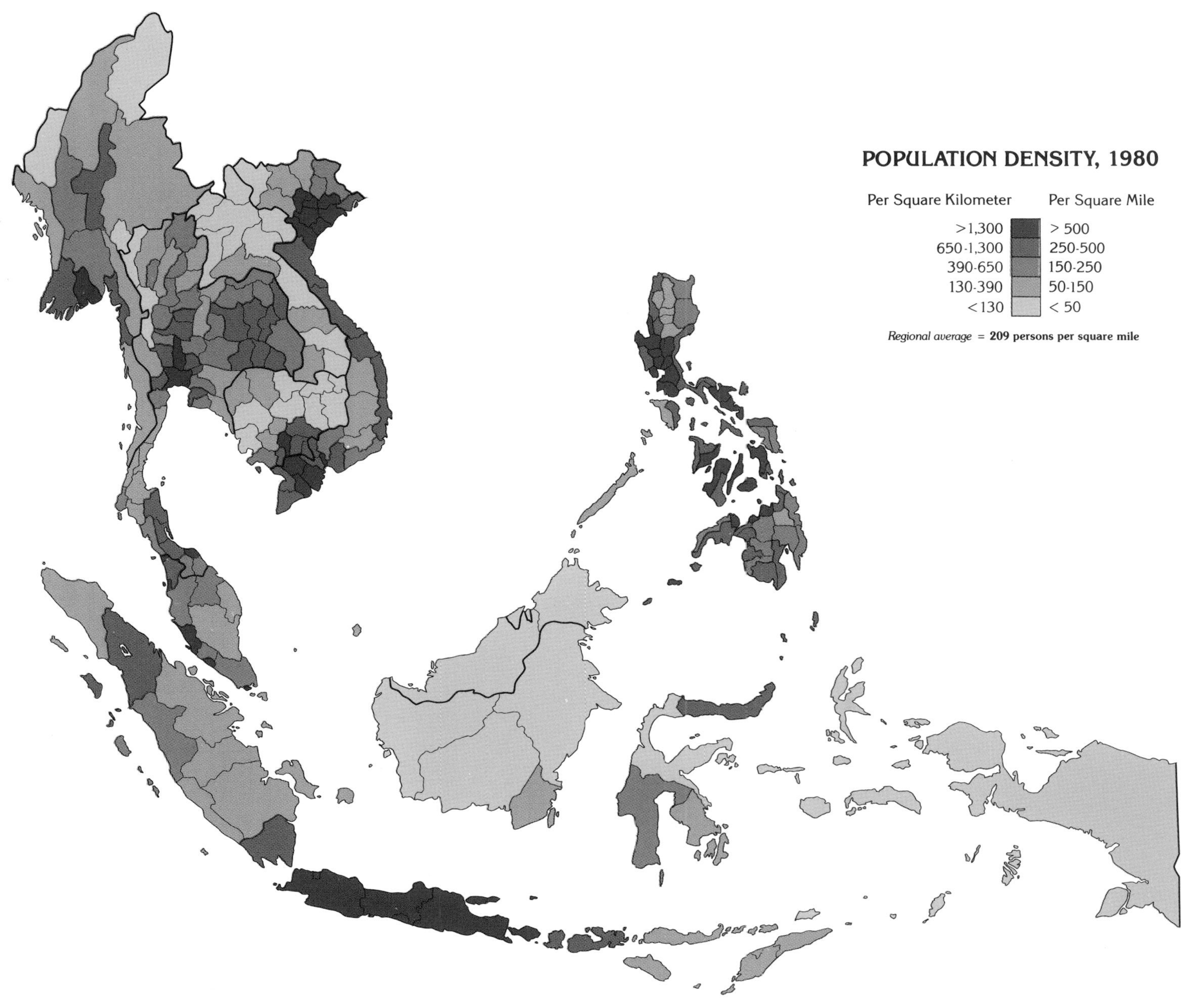
POPULATION DENSITY, 1980
Per Square Kilometer
Per Square Mile
>1,300
> 500
650-1,300
250-500
390-650
150-250
130-390
50-150
<130
< 50
Regional average = 209 persons per square mile

Upland tribal village, northern Thailand (courtesy J. Hafner)

in these two countries. In Vietnam only the interior and upland provinces of northern and central Vietnam are sparsely populated and in the Philippines only the northern interior uplands and portions of central Mindanao have low densities. This, of course, confirms that movement on a large scale to new agricultural lands within these nations is not possible. On the other hand, Indonesia's Outer Islands, eastern peninsular Malaysia and Sabah and Sarawak on northern Borneo, and much of Laos and Kampuchea are still sparsely populated.

## POPULATION CHANGE

Population change varies throughout the region because of differences in fertility, mortality, and migration characteristics. As is so of the Third World generally, rates of natural population increase in most of Southeast Asia are high because birth rates in the region have generally been high. Overall, the annual rate of natural population increase is slightly over 2%, which means that the regional population will double in about 35 years, assuming that the growth rate remains at about the same level. While fertility levels have recently declined in a few nations, rapid population growth remains a problem for nearly all the nations of the region. Singapore is an exception and is unique in the region, as it can be classified as a "developed" nation. As such most of its demographic and socioeconomic indicators reflect a higher level of development (for example, a rate of natural increase of just over 1% annually). In Thailand and Indonesia population growth rates, while still high relative to developed nations, have declined significantly through strong government support of family planning programs. On the other hand, the Malaysian government has advocated increased population growth. Given the rapidly growing urban populations and high densities in farming areas it would seem to be to the social and economic advantage of the region's nations to further lower rates of population increase.

One implication of high birth rates and rapid population increase is that a large proportion of the population is in the young and dependent age group. Thus, in the region as a whole nearly two-fifths of the population is under 15 years of age (compared with just over one-fifth in the United States or Europe). The population age structure of nations with such high

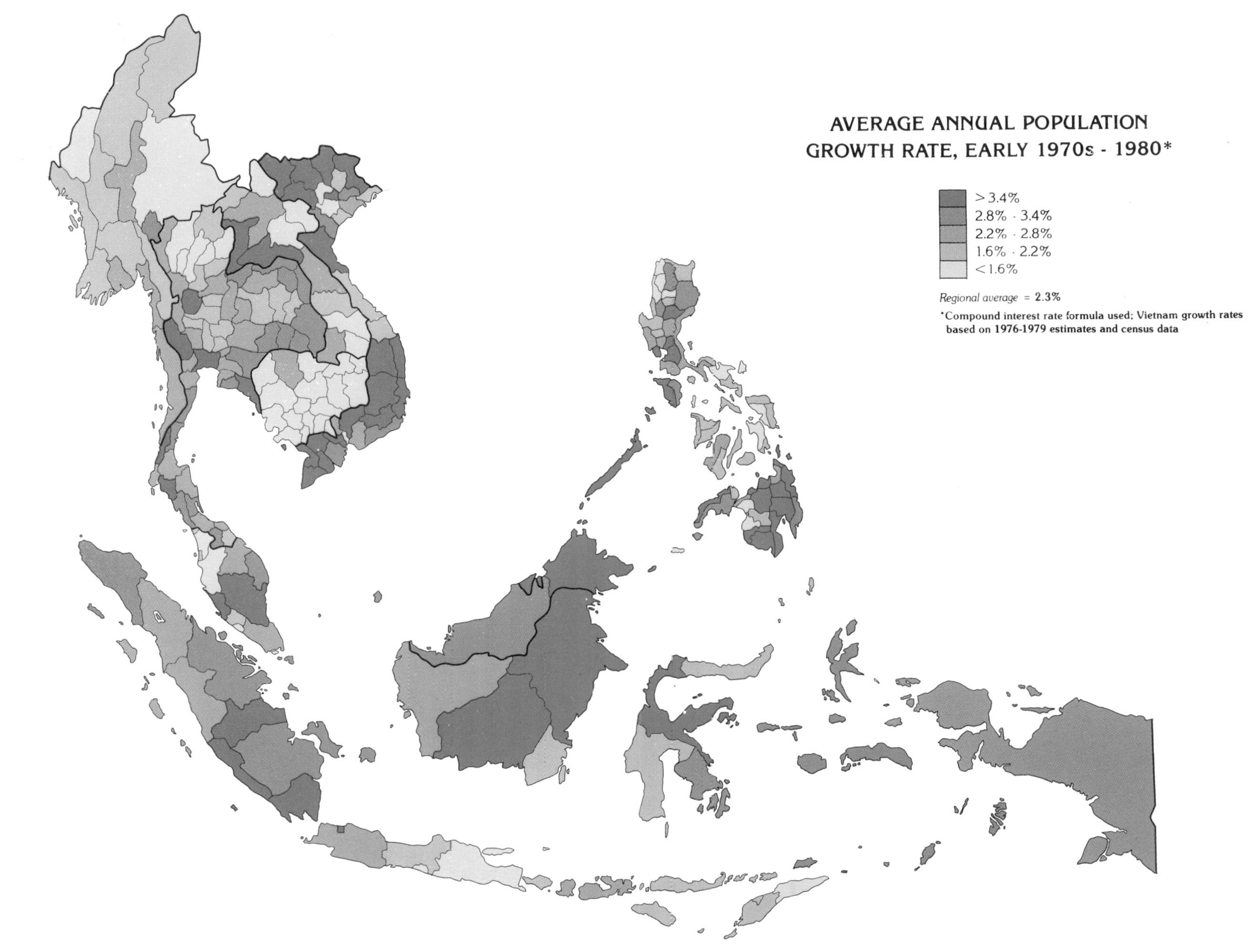
AVERAGE ANNUAL POPULATION
GROWTH RATE, EARLY 1970s - 1980*
>3.4%
2.8% - 3.4%
2.2% - 2.8%
1.6% - 2.2%
<1.6%
Regional average = 2.3%
*Compound interest rate formula used; Vietnam growth rates
based on 1976-1979 estimates and census data

Explaining family planning in Java (courtesy World Bank)

young dependency rates typically has a very broad base which rapidly narrows in the older categories (see page 37). Thus it is not surprising that only 3.7% of the region's total population is over 65 years of age (compared with 13% in Europe). Population pyramids for three nations with different age and sex characteristics can be used to show the three regional types of age structure that exist today. The population pyramid for the Philippines is most typical of the region and has the broad base of nations with high fertility. Singapore has a narrower base and a higher percentage in the later age groups, more typical of the lower fertility and higher life expectancy associated with higher levels of economic development. Vietnam has the broad base but relatively fewer in the middle age categories, especially among males, as a result of the high mortality associated with the Vietnam War years. Mortality measures including crude death rates and infant mortality rates are particularly high in Kampuchea (crude death rates were estimated by the UN to be 17.6 per thousand in 1986), Laos (17.9), and Burma (13.4) because of continuing military conflict in some areas of each nation combined with generally low levels of development (few doctors, limited health care, low educational and income levels, and so forth).

Thus, population growth has been uneven throughout the region partly because of differences in levels of fertility and mortality. However, the major reason for variations in population change is due to in-, or out-, migration. Within Southeast Asia there has been considerable migration between nations in the form of refugee movements, but the vast majority of human migration has been of a more voluntary nature within nations. Since World War II population redistribution within individual nations has been massive as large numbers have migrated to cities, especially the very largest, or primate, cities of each nation, and to frontier agricultural regions. During the 1970s the region's largest

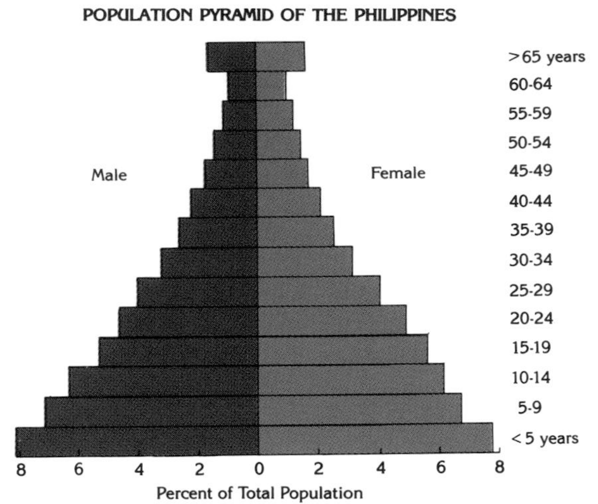


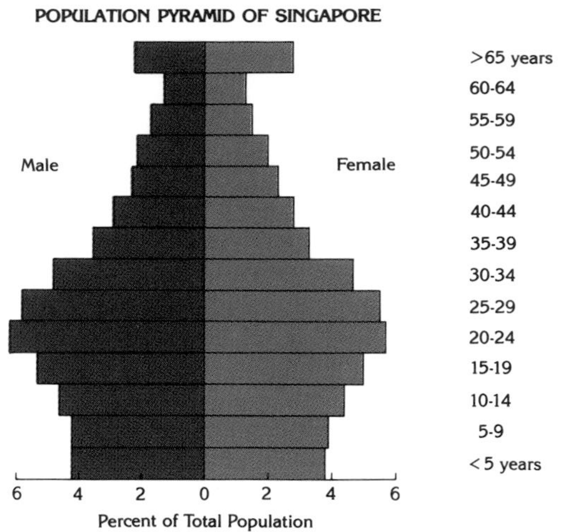


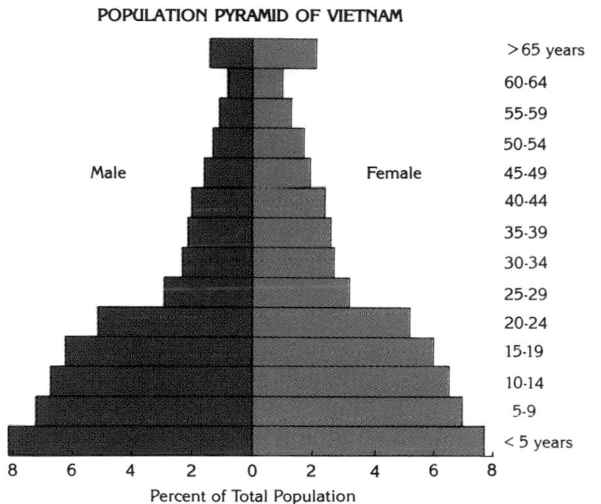


cities, and some of the smaller cities as well, have continued to grow the most rapidly in population. Rates of growth have generally been much higher in the cities than the regional average, which of course implies heavy migration, especially from the densely-populated rural areas. Thus, for example, Jakarta has experienced especially heavy migration from the great concentrations in Java's rural areas.

There are a few "pioneer" areas that still remain in parts of Southeast Asia and it has been to such areas that rural migrants have moved, either spontaneously or through government incentives. An example of the former has been the heavy migration of Filipinos to rural Mindanao Island beginning in the early twentieth century. Such movement has continued but rural Mindanao has fast filled up and there are few areas that can still be called pioneer settlement areas. An example of government-encouraged migration to sparsely populated rural areas is Indonesia's Transmigration program. Begun in 1905 during the Dutch colonial period and having continued since independence, the purpose of the program is to alleviate population pressures on overcrowded Java through the migration of people to the "Outer" Islands, especially Sumatra and Kalimantan (Borneo). The program, according to some critics, has been unsuccessful since the provision of suitable sites has been costly and it has directly affected only a tiny fraction of Java's population. Nonetheless, comparison of the maps of population density and population change do show evidence that some areas of low density (Sumatra, Mindanao, Kalimantan) have recently experienced especially rapid population growth.

The patterns of population change within Vietnam, Kampuchea, and Laos, especially since 1975 after the withdrawal of American forces, has differed somewhat from other parts of the region. At least one primate city, Phnom Penh, has lost population. Government-forced migration in Vietnam has sent North Vietnamese to settle in the New Economic Zones of the South. And of course the end of the war and subsequent turmoil caused thousands to flee to other, nearby nations, both over land any by water. Because of the continuing flight of refugees and civil war, in Kampuchea there has in fact been an absolute population decline in the majority of that nation's political subdivisions, which is unprecedented in contemporary Southeast Asia. During the 1970s it was estimated that Kampuchea's population declined from 7.1 million to 5.2 million, or by over 26%. This can be attributed mostly to the atrocities that occurred during the Khmer Rouge period under Pol Pot's leadership and to the subsequent emigration.

Other areas of the region that sometimes experienced growth well below the regional average (about 2.3% annually in the 1970–1980 period) during the 1970s have been border states and provinces and other areas distant from the national core regions, where many of the disenchanted minority and insurgent groups have been waging war against government forces. This has sometimes meant an exodus of refugees, either to other parts of the nation or to other nations.

## URBAN GROWTH AND URBAN CHARACTERISTICS

With the exception of the microstates of Singapore and Brunei, Southeast Asia remains predominantly rural. In 1980 the United Nations estimated that less than one-quarter (24%) of the region's total population lived in urban areas. That the region is undergoing urbanization is indicated by the fact that in 1950 only 15% of the population resided in cities, whereas it is estimated by the United Nations that 36% will be urban by the year 2000.

The metropolitan areas that have grown the most rapidly are the very largest. Today, there are ten metropolitan areas in the region with populations in excess of one million (as compared to four such areas in 1950) and three of these are over five million. By the year 2000 it is estimated by the UN that three of the region's cities, Jakarta, Manila, and Bangkok, will rank among the world's 30 largest urban areas with populations of 17, 13, and 11 million, respectively. Nations having one large city that completely overshadows all other cities in size, such as Thailand, Burma, and the Philippines, are said to have a high index of primacy. Such an index is derived by dividing the population of the very largest city by that of the next largest urban area. In the region's two most populous nations, Indonesia and Vietnam, this index is low because there is more than one very large city. In the case of Indonesia, this is partially because of the large population and areal extent of the nation. Such size has meant that economically Indonesia is able to support several "million" cities. In addition to Jakarta these are: Surabaya, Bandung, and Semarang in Java and Medan in Sumatra. Vietnam also has more than one such city. Ho Chi Minh City (formerly Saigon) is the largest, but Hanoi in the north is close behind and by the year 2000 may surpass Ho Chi Minh City. Vietnam has had a long history whereby the nation has been divided into two parts at various periods. Between 1954, the year in which French colonial forces were forced to withdraw from the country, and 1975, which marked the withdrawal of American forces, there were in fact two nations. Hanoi was the capital of the Communist North and Saigon was the capital of the American-supported South.

As was also so during the colonial period, the

Traffic jam near Quiapo market, Manila (R. Ulack)

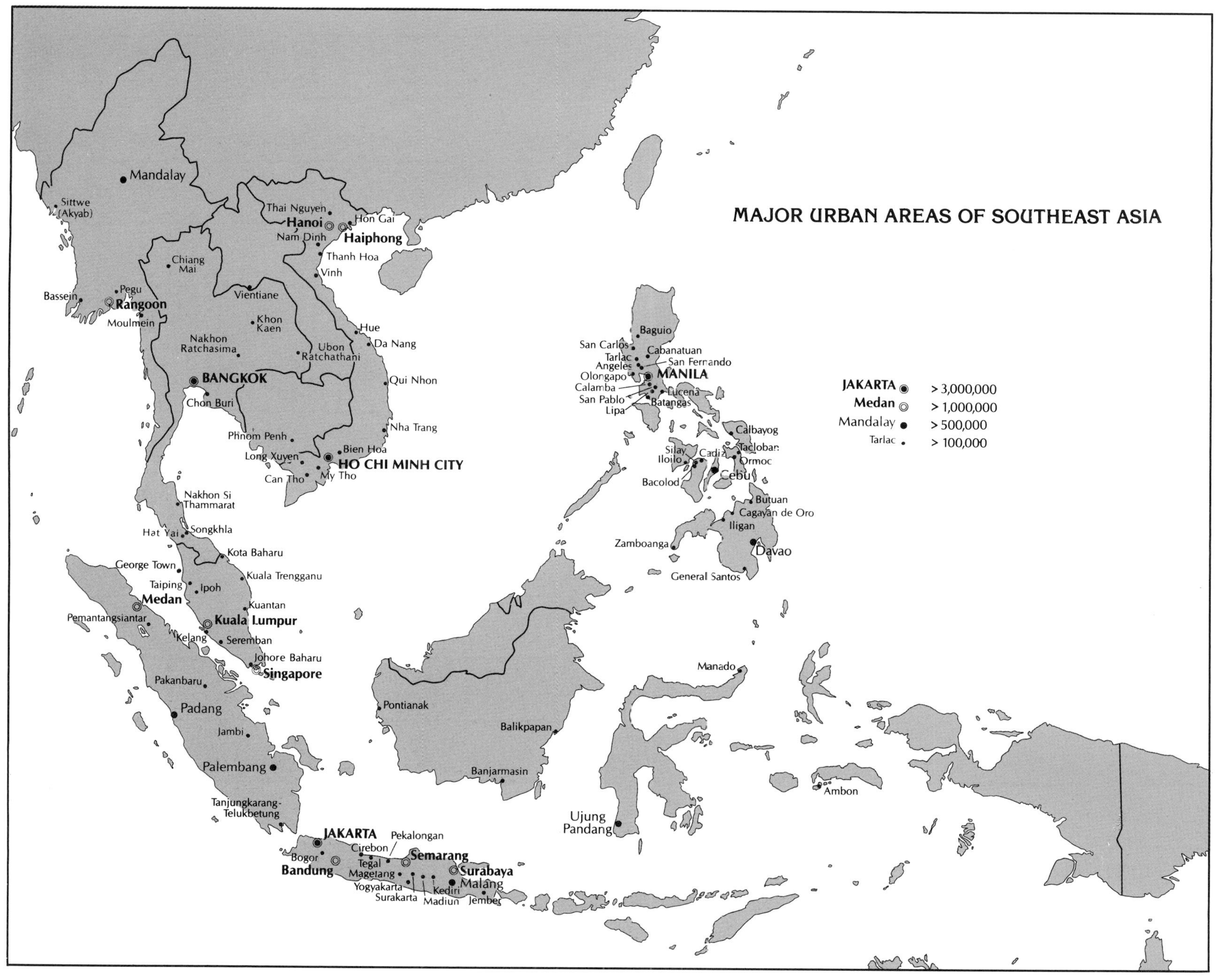
MAJOR URBAN AREAS OF SOUTHEAST ASIA
JAKARTA > 3,000,000
Medan > 1,000,000
Mandalay > 500,000
Tarlac > 100,000
Mandalay
Sittwe (Akyab)
Bassein
Pegu
Rangoon
Moulmein
Chiang Mai
Thai Nguyen
Hanoi
Hon Gai
Haiphong
Nam Dinh
Thanh Hoa
Vinh
Vientiane
Khon Kaen
Nakhon Ratchasima
Ubon Ratchathani
Hue
Da Nang
BANGKOK
Chon Buri
Qui Nhon
Nha Trang
Phnom Penh
Bien Hoa
Long Xuyen
HO CHI MINH CITY
Can Tho
My Tho
Nakhon Si Thammarat
Hat Yai
Songkhla
Kota Baharu
George Town
Kuala Trengganu
Taiping
Ipoh
Medan
Kuantan
Pemantangsiantar
Kuala Lumpur
Kelang
Seremban
Johore Baharu
Singapore
Pakanbaru
Padang
Jambi
Palembang
Tanjungkarang-Telukbetung
JAKARTA
Bogor
Bandung
Cirebon
Pekalongan
Tegal
Semarang
Magelang
Surabaya
Yogyakarta
Surakarta
Madiun
Kediri
Malang
Jember
Pontianak
Balikpapan
Banjarmasin
Ujung Pandang
Manado
Ambon
Baguio
San Carlos
Tarlac
Cabanatuan
Angeles
San Fernando
Olongapo
MANILA
Calamba
San Pablo
Lucena
Lipa
Batangas
Calbayog
Silay
Cadiz
Tacloban
Iloilo
Ormoc
Cebu
Bacolod
Butuan
Cagayan de Oro
Iligan
Zamboanga
Davao
General Santos

major share of the wealth, financial and cultural activity, national political institutions, manufacturing establishments, and commercial activities have remained in these primate, port cities. Given such circumstances it is not surprising that so many people migrate to these places seeking jobs and other opportunities. Such cities cannot support the vast numbers of mostly poor who come to them, and new migrants are often forced to reside with relatives and friends before moving out on their own. When they do start their own households, it is most often in the ubiquitous slum and squatter communities which account for up to one-third, and occasionally over one-half, of the city population. Such residential communities are built where vacant land exists and today this usually means on land in the periphery of metropolitan areas. Such land use has proliferated in the region since World War II, when heavy population increases began. Ideally, new arrivals in the city hope to reside near potential jobs, like those that exist in the port zones and the "central business districts," but usually land is not available in such areas. As Southeast Asian cities have expanded geographically new industrial and commercial land uses have emerged in peripheral areas, as is suggested by one model of the Southeast Asian port city (see diagram on page 41).

Oftentimes of course jobs are not found and migrants are either forced to return to their homeplaces, join the long list of unemployed, or secure work in what is called the urban "informal" sector or petty commodity production. The informal sector includes many different types of service-related jobs for which the worker does not earn a regular wage or salary. People who work as vendors in public markets or on streets, beggars, drivers of certain types of vehicles like the pedicab in Indonesia and the jeepney in the Philippines, itinerant stevedores, and prostitutes are but a few examples of informal sector workers. Such workers are often described as underemployed (as opposed to unemployed),

Squatter settlement, Cebu, the Philippines (R. Ulack)

MODEL OF URBAN LAND USE IN THE MAJOR SOUTHEAST ASIAN PORT CITIES

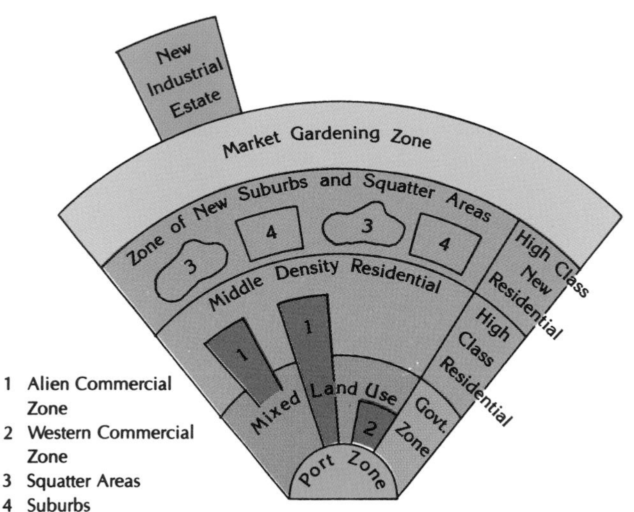


Source: T. G. McGee, The Southeast Asian City (N.Y.: Frederick A. Praeger, 1967). Reprinted with permission.

that is, they do not work full-time but rather only when work is available. On the other hand, many informal sector workers do work full-time and quite frequently earn more than those in the "formal" sector. Today in many Third World cities informal jobs account for a greater share of urban employment than do those in the formal sector. The latter jobs include those in which employees receive a regular wage or salary, as for example government workers, clerks in department stores and supermarkets, professionals, and factory workers. In short, the urban informal sector plays a very important role in cities in that it provides employment for the many low-income, often poorly educated migrants who come from the nation's densely populated rural areas.

## INTERNATIONAL MIGRATION AND REFUGEES

Since 1975 it is estimated that nearly two million refugees have fled Vietnam, Laos, and Kampuchea. Many have traveled over land from Laos and Kampuchea to nearby border camps in Thailand, and hundreds of thousands more have fled by boat from Vietnam to other nations of first asylum in the region. Boat refugees are often subject to attack by pirates, especially in the Gulf of Thailand (see map), where many have lost their lives. The majority of Indochinese refugees enter Thailand as their country of first asylum. Most of the other nations in the region also permit such temporary asylum for refugees but few accept significant numbers for permanent resettlement, if any at all. In 1985 it was estimated that there were some 300,000 Indochinese refugees in temporary camps and transit centers in Southeast Asia. Since 1975 the largest number of Indochinese refugees have been permanently resettled in the United States, which has claimed approximately 800,000 such people. China, with over 250,000 resettled refugees, and Canada, France, and Australia with over 100,000 each, rank after the United States in terms of the number of refugees permanently resettled.

Not all refugees in the region originate in Vietnam, Laos, and Kampuchea. Continuing Communist or minority insurgencies or problems in Burma, Thailand, Malaysia, Indonesia, and the

Making a peacock chair, informal employment sector, Cebu City, the Philippines (R. Ulack)

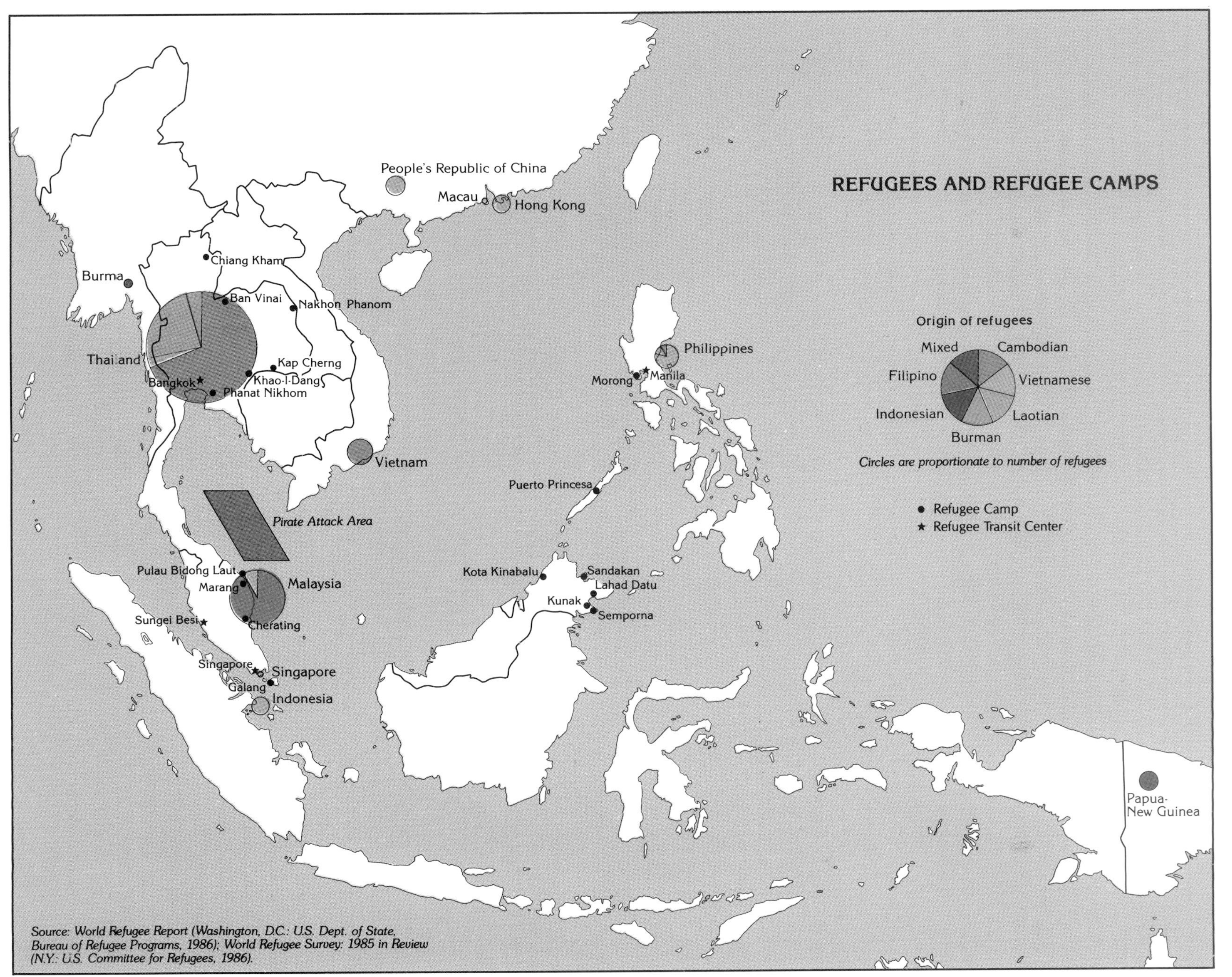
REFUGEES AND REFUGEE CAMPS
Origin of refugees
Mixed
Cambodian
Filipino
Vietnamese
Indonesian
Laotian
Burman
Circles are proportionate to number of refugees
● Refugee Camp
★ Refugee Transit Center
People's Republic of China
Macau
Hong Kong
Burma
Chiang Kham
Ban Vinai
Nakhon Phanom
Thailand
Kap Cherng
Bangkok
Khao-I-Dang
Phanat Nikhom
Vietnam
Pirate Attack Area
Pulau Bidong Laut
Marang
Malaysia
Sungei Besi
Cherating
Singapore
Singapore
Galang
Indonesia
Philippines
Morong
Manila
Puerto Princesa
Kota Kinabalu
Sandakan
Lahad Datu
Kunak
Semporna
Papua-
New Guinea
Source: World Refugee Report (Washington, D.C.: U.S. Dept. of State,
Bureau of Refugee Programs, 1986); World Refugee Survey: 1985 in Review
(N.Y.: U.S. Committee for Refugees, 1986).

Philippines have led to the flight of refugees to nearby havens. Thus, it is estimated that 90,000 Filipino Muslims have fled to Sabah in eastern Malaysia, and some 11,000 Indonesians have left Irian Jaya Province (on New Guinea) for Papua-New Guinea.

## POPULATION AND THE FUTURE

The United Nations estimates that by the year 2000 there will be 520 million people in Southeast Asia, or more than 25% more than the number living in the region today. Given the economic, social, and political differences between and within nations it can be expected that the international and internal migration trends of the recent past will continue, at least for the next decade or so. In short, continued population growth means that both urban and rural areas will become more densely populated, although the rate of growth will be greater in the urban areas. In addition, refugee movements will continue

# PART TWO

# *The Nation-States*

The ten "nation-states" that comprise the Southeast Asian region are a product of the colonial period. The national boundaries were drawn by the colonizers and do not reflect the pre-European history or cultural realities of this complex region. Part I presented an overview of the entire Southeast Asian region. It is the purpose of Part II to examine the political and economic realities that exist today in the ten national units. Those nations of insular and peninsular Southeast Asia, which include the vast majority of people who speak Malayo-Polynesian languages, are discussed in Chapters 5–9. In Chapters 10–14 we examine the physical environment, history, economy, and population characteristics of the five nations that comprise the mainland part of Southeast Asia.

# 5

# *Republic of Indonesia*

*Area:* 741,100 sq mi (1,919,450 sq km); about the size of Alaska and California combined

*Population:* 169,482,000 (1986)

*Population Density:* 229 persons per sq mi (88 persons per sq km)

*Urban Population:* 22.3%

*Annual Average Rate of Population Increase:* 1.8%

*Crude Birth Rate:* 29.8 per 1,000 population

*Crude Death Rate:* 11.7 per 1,000 population

*Infant Mortality Rate:* 77 infant deaths per 1,000 live births

*Life Expectancy:* Male—53.9 years; Female—56.7 years

*Official Language:* Bahasa Indonesia

*Currency:* Indonesian Rupiah (US$ = Rp 1,550 in 1988)

*Capital:* Jakarta

*Form of Government:* Unitary multiparty republic with two legislative houses

*Head of State and Government:* President

*Armed Forces (1985):* 278,050 (army—78%; air force—9%; navy—13%)

## HISTORICAL OVERVIEW

7th–14th centuries: Maritime empire of Srivijaya, centered on Palembang, preeminent.

11th century: Islam enters northern Sumatra.

14th–15th centuries: Kingdom of Majapahit ascends to power.

1513: Portuguese reach the "Spice Islands."

1595: First Dutch ships arrive in East Indies.

1602: Dutch United East India Company founded; Dutch decisively defeat Portuguese in naval battle near Bantam.

1618: Jan Pieterszoon Coen appointed governor-general.

1619: Batavia established as capital of Netherlands East Indies (predecessor of modern Jakarta)

1811–1816: British defeat Dutch and occupy Java; Thomas Stamford Raffles appointed Lieutenant-Governor to administer Java.

1824: Anglo-Dutch Treaty of London defines spheres of influence in archipelago; British exchange Bencoolen (on Sumatra) for Dutch-held Malacca (on Malaya).

1825–1830: Dutch defeat Javanese in Java War.

1830: Dutch introduce the "culture system" (system of forced cultivation).

1870: Agrarian Law of 1870 ends "culture system."

1942–1945: Japanese occupation.

1945: Sukarno proclaims independence.

1949: Dutch agree to independence for the new Republic of Indonesia.

1963: Irian Jaya (West New Guinea) incorporated into Indonesia.

1965: Abortive military coup by some army sections; thousands of Communists subsequently massacred.

1966: The military assumes emergency power under General Suharto.

1968: Suharto inaugurated as president of the republic.

1976: East Timor becomes the twenty-seventh province of Indonesia.

BURMA
KAMPUCHEA
VIETNAM
Ho Chi Minh City
GULF OF
THAILAND
ANDAMAN
SEA
SOUTH
CHINA
SEA
THAILAND
Balabac
We
Sabang
Banda Aceh
Lhokseumawe
George Town (Penang)
MALAYSIA
Kota Kinabalu
Bandar Seri Begawan
BRUNEI
Great Natuna Besar
Natuna Islands
Anambas Islands
Belawan
Medan
Pemantangsiantar
Kuala Lumpur
Strait of Malacca
Simeulue
Melaka (Malacca)
MALAYSIA
Sibolga
Dumai
SINGAPORE
Paloh
Kuching
BORNEO
Bintan
Riau Islands
Nias
Natal
Pakanbaru
KALIMANTAN
Kapuas
Batu Islands
Kampar
Lingga
Pontianak
Sintang
SCHWANER MOUNTAINS
Bukittinggi
Singkep
Inderagiri
Padang
7,470
Bukit Raja
Telukbatang
Samarinda
Balikpapan
SUMATRA
BARISAN RANGE
Siberut
12,480
Gunung Kerinci
Jambi
Mentawai Islands
Sipura
North Pagai
South Pagai
Bangka
Palembang
Musi
Belitung
Karimata Strait
Kendawangan
Palangkaraya
Banjarmasin
Laut
Bengkulu
JAVA SEA
Enggano
Krui
Tanjungkarang-Telukbetung
JAKARTA
Sunda Strait
Bogor
Cirebon
Pekalongan
Madura
Kangean Islands
Sukabumi
Bandung
Tegal
Semarang
Pamekasan
Magelang
Madiun
Surabaya
BALI SEA
Borobodur (Buddhist temples)
Surakarta
Yogyakarta
Kediri
Malang
Gunung Semuru
12,050
Jember
Mataram
Denpasar
Bali
Lombok
JAVA
INDIAN OCEAN
Christmas Island (Australia)
SCALE 1:12,600,000
0 100 200 300 400 Miles
0 100 200 300 400 500 600 Kilometers
96°
104°
112°
8°
0°

PHILIPPINES
Cebu
Davao
SULU SEA
CELEBES SEA
PACIFIC OCEAN
Palau Islands
Talaud Islands
Sangihe Islands
Morotai
HALMAHERA
Manado
Ternate
Cape Mangkalahit
Gorontalo
Gulf of Tomini
MOLUCCA SEA
MOLUCCAS
Halmahera Sea
Waigeo
Dampier Strait
Sorong
Doberai Peninsula
Biak
Schouten Islands
Gulf of Cenderawasih
Japen
Palu
Poso
Lake Poso
Banggai Islands
SULAWESI (CELEBES)
Gulf of Tolo
Lake Towuti
Sula Islands
Obi
Salawati
Misool
CERAM SEA
Gulf of Berau
Fakfak
Mamberamo
Jayapura
11,330
Bulu Rantekombola
Buru
CERAM
Ambon
Highest point in Indonesia
16,500 Puntiak Jaya
MAOKE RANGE
NEW GUINEA
(Irian Jaya)
Kendari
Kolaka
Gulf of Bone
Muna
Butung
Kai Islands
BANDA SEA
Aru Islands
Digul
SEA
Sunda
Islands
Wetar
Jamdena
Tanimbar Islands
Kolepom
Rutong
Flores
Alor
Dili
TIMOR
Babar Islands
Merauke
Waingapu
SAVU SEA
ARAFURA SEA
Sawu
Kupang
Roti
TIMOR SEA
Darwin
AUSTRALIA
120°
128°
136°
8°
0°

Indonesia, the world's fifth most populous nation with 170 million people, contains over two-fifths of the region's total population. An archipelago of over 12,000 islands (the vast majority of which are uninhabited), the country stretches for over 3,000 miles (4,800 km) from east to west and 1,250 miles (2,000 km) from north to south. Most of the area within these limits, however, consists of water and the nation ranks only fourteenth in the world in total land area. Indonesia also comprises about two-fifths of the total land area of Southeast Asia.

As would be expected of such a large, fragmented nation, there are a myriad of ethnic groups who speak several hundred languages and dialects. Nearly all languages belong to the Malayo-Polynesian family of languages; the official language is Bahasa Indonesia, which is based on Malay. There is less diversity in terms of religion in that the vast majority of the population adheres to Islam, which was introduced to Indonesia in the eleventh century. Economically, the country is typical of most developing nations in that the livelihood of most people is based on agriculture and fishing and nearly four-fifths of the population live in rural areas. Indonesia's export economy is dominated by oil and natural gas; over three-quarters of export revenues consist of these fossil fuels and their by-products.

In part because of its large population, Indonesia, unlike most other countries of the region, supports several metropolitan areas with a population of over one million. The largest city in the country and the region is Jakarta, with over seven million people. Three other cities on Java—Surabaya, Bandung, and Semarang—also have at least one million people, and Bandung is among the most rapidly growing cities in the world. Medan, in northern Sumatra, also has over one million people.

## THE PHYSICAL ENVIRONMENT

Although a land of thousands of islands and islets, the five largest islands account for over four-fifths of the total land area. In order by size these are: Kalimantan (the Indonesian portion of Borneo), Irian Jaya (the western half of New Guinea), Sumatra, Sulawesi (formerly Celebes), and Java. Java and nearby Madura, the most fertile and least rugged or swampy of the larger islands, are intensively cultivated and heavily populated. About two-thirds of the nation's population are found on these two islands, which together comprise less than 7% of the total land area. Rural population densities are among the highest in the world, in some parts of Java attaining levels over 2,000 persons per square mile (775 per sq km).

The archipelago is geographically divided into four regions: the Greater Sunda Islands (Sumatra, Java, Kalimantan, Sulawesi); the Lesser Sunda Islands (including Bali and those islands east through Timor); the Moluccas (Maluku), between Sulawesi and New Guinea; and the western half of New Guinea, or West Irian (Irian Jaya). Eastern New Guinea consists of the independent nation of Papua-New Guinea, considered a part of the Pacific region.

Indonesia is characterized as being geologically active in that two major sections of the earth's crust (tectonic plates) meet where the Indo-Australian plate subducts beneath the Eurasian plate (see map in Chapter 1). Near this boundary, which lies west and south of Sumatra and Java, are located a series of deep oceanic trenches including the Java Trench, and a series of volcanic mountain chains. In the eastern part of Indonesia is the extension of yet another crustal boundary, which separates the Eurasian and Philippine plates. Indonesia is one of the most active volcanic zones in the world with over 200 active volcanoes and many more that are extinct. Volcanic eruptions are not uncommon and in recent years Java has had the greatest concentration of eruptions. The best-known eruption was that on Krakatoa (a small island between Sumatra and Java) in 1883, so violent that it destroyed all life nearby and carried ash into the upper atmosphere that circled the earth, decreasing the amount of solar radiation that entered the lower atmosphere for several years. English paintings of the period are noted for their colorful "Chelsea sunsets," thought to have been brought about by the Krakatoa explosion. One positive effect of vulcanism in this area is that the ash and lava ultimately yield very fertile soils and the relationship between the rich volcanic soils of Java and intensively cultivated land is no accident.

Most of western Indonesia including Sumatra, Java, and Kalimantan are a part of the Sunda Shelf where oceanic depths are relatively shallow. This area was a part of the Asian land mass during the Ice Age, which lasted for several million years until about 10,000 years ago. The land bridges that once existed facilitated the migration of flora and fauna, including man, from the large Asian land mass. It is thought that "Java man," among the earliest of man's ancestors to inhabit the region, came to Java over these land bridges some 500,000 years ago.

The relief in that part of Indonesia that is farthest from the plate boundaries is relatively low and is not volcanic; rarely on Kalimantan do elevations exceed 4,000 feet (1,200 m), although in the Malaysian portion of Borneo elevations are higher, and one isolated peak, Mt. Kinabalu, is nearly 13,500 feet (4,100 m) high. Outward from this center the relief becomes more rugged, and higher. On Sumatra the Barisan Range is a north-south trending mountain spine near the west coast with elevations that approach 12,500 feet (3,800 m). There are several scenic lakes, the best known of which is beautiful Lake Toba at nearly 3,000 feet (900 m). Indonesia's highest peak, Puntiak Jaya at 16,500 feet (5,000 m), is located in the rugged heartland of West Irian.

Indonesia has no great rivers; the longest is the Kapuas (715 mi; 1,150 km) in Kalimantan. The many short rivers of Kalimantan, Sumatra, and Irian Jaya descend rapidly from the interior uplands to the sea. Transportation on these rivers is restricted since they are narrow and fast-flowing, and near the sea their courses shift. The relatively wide eastern coastal plain of Sumatra is very swampy and not well suited to ports or settlement, as is also the case for much of the West Irian and Kalimantan coastal plains.

The equator bisects Sumatra and Kalimantan, and Indonesia's climatic characteristics reflect this equatorial position. Except in highland areas, the monthly average temperature does not vary much from 80°F (27°C). Places near the equator generally have heavy rainfall in all seasons whereas locations north or south of the equator experience the effects of the monsoons and thus there is seasonal variation in rainfall amounts. For example, Jakarta, at 6° S. latitude, receives about two-thirds of its rainfall between November and March, whereas precipitation at Pontianak, located on the equator in western Kalimantan, is quite evenly distributed throughout the year (total of 125 in, or 315 cm, with no month receiving less than 6 in, or 15 cm). Eastern Java and the Lesser Sunda Islands, which lie nearer the more arid climates of Australia, experience a marked dry season and lower annual amounts of rainfall.

In terms of natural vegetation, Indonesia still has extensive forests and it is estimated that it contains perhaps 10% of the world's remaining tropical rainforests (Brazil with one-third, and Zaire with 10%, are the other two major rain-

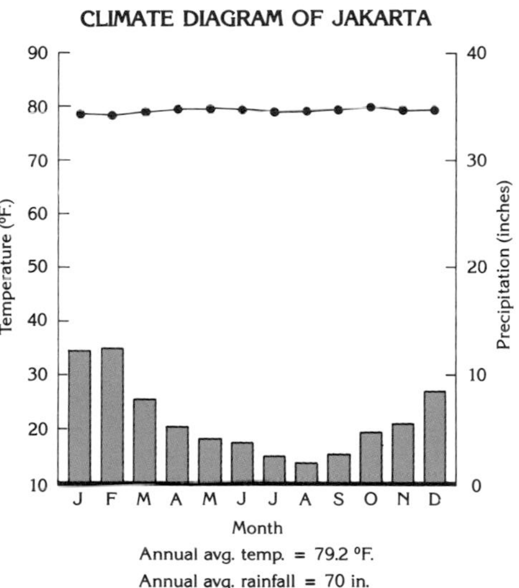


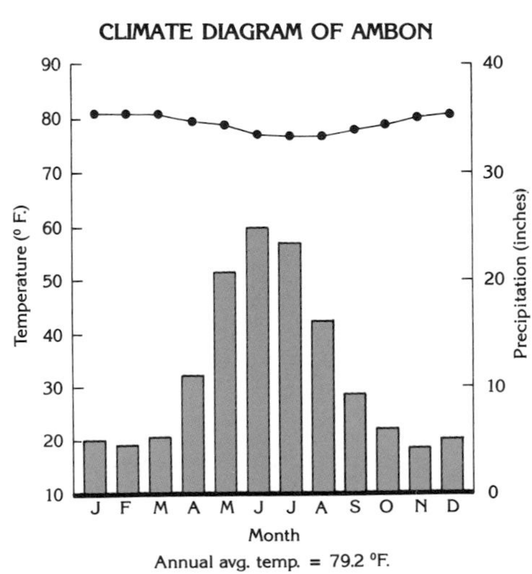

forested nations). As is characteristic of other tropical areas, there is tremendous variety including over 3,000 species of trees. Rattan, ironwood, and teak are among the more valuable commercial forest products. Indonesia's forests are also noted for orchids, of which there are about 5,000 species. Other types of forests include the temperate upland forests found at elevations of over 5,000 ft (1,500 m) and the vast mangrove forests along the swampy coasts of Kalimantan and Sumatra.

Indonesia's fauna include species from two great realms: the Oriental and the Australian. The boundary between the two, called Wallace's Line, is located in eastern Indonesia (see map in Chapter 1). The Lesser Sunda Islands, Sulawesi, the Moluccas, and Irian Jaya are to the east of the line. In eastern Indonesia are found animals related to the marsupials of Australia, such as bandicoots, as well as birds such as the group known as birds-of-paradise. In western Indonesia the best-known animals of the Oriental realm are the orangutan, tapir, tiger, leopard, and single-horned Javan and Sumatran rhinoceros. Many species are endangered; in the case of the Javan rhinoceros perhaps a dozen still exist in the wild, all restricted to a nature preserve in extreme western Java. The Javan and Balinese tigers are extinct and today perhaps 600 Sumatran tigers remain in Indonesia. As is so in tropical climates there is a tremendous variety of insects and reptiles, many of which are endemic (i.e., found locally and therefore subject to extinction as habitats are lost). A well-known endemic creature is the giant Komodo dragon (monitor lizard), which reaches a length of 12 feet (3.6 m), found only on two small islands of the Lesser Sunda group.

## HISTORICAL BACKGROUND

Certainly the maritime situation and monsoon characteristics of the archipelago have greatly influenced its history. While the very earliest human inhabitants in Indonesia arrived during the Pleistocene epoch, it is the more recent southerly migrants from mainland Asia who are the ancestors of the majority of Indonesians. As is so for the history of most of the region, the successive waves of migrants took over the best coastal and valley locations and pushed the earlier, less-sophisticated peoples to interior and upland locations, or to remote islands. Considerable intermixing also occurred, which has brought about the variety of distinctive, albeit predominantly Mongoloid, human physical (racial) characteristics of the contemporary Indonesian.

The era of recorded history in Indonesia begins about 2,000 years ago with the beginning of the period of Indianization. It was Sumatra and Java that were earliest influenced by India but from about the sixth century A.D. Indian cultural influence had diffused to the Lesser Sundas and Moluccas as well. The imprint of this first great cultural influence is still strongly evident throughout the archipelago and includes the Indian-style script, political organization, and architectural evidence such as Hindu and Buddhist temples. Today the majority of Balinese on Bali still adhere to Hinduism, the only major non-Indian population anywhere in the world that is predominantly Hindu.

During this period two great "Indianized" kingdoms emerged. From the seventh to the thirteenth centuries A.D. the great maritime power of Srivijaya controlled much of what is today western Indonesia. Its capital was located near present-day Palembang and at its greatest extent it controlled most of Sumatra, eastern Java, western coastal Kalimantan, and the Malay Peninsula. During this time a variety of agriculturally based or maritime kingdoms rose and fell in eastern Java, among them Mataram and Singhasari. Srivijaya was succeeded by Majapahit in the 1300s which, for a brief time, at least nominally unified the whole of contemporary Indonesia from northern Sumatra in the west to the Spice Islands (the Moluccas) in the east. During this time Java became the focal point for the entire archipelago and has remained so ever since. Certainly other kingdoms thrived in Indonesia during the Majapahit period and one of the best known of these was the Hindu-Malay kingdom of Minangkabau in northern Sumatra. Today the Minangkabaus and the nearby Batak peoples are among the most advanced agriculturally, and are the most highly educated people in Sumatra.

Hindu shrine at foot of Mount Agung, Bali (courtesy W. L. Thomas)

By the fifteenth century the sultanate of Malacca, centered on the western coast of the Malay peninsula, came to dominate most of insular Southeast Asia and geopolitically it replaced Srivijaya and Majapahit. Although Islam had arrived in Indonesia earlier, it was during the time of Malacca that Islam diffused most rapidly throughout the archipelago. By the nineteenth century, Islam had been embraced by the majority of Indonesians.

One of the major reasons for early European interest in the archipelago was the spices associated with the Moluccas, collectively referred to as the Spice Islands. The Portuguese and the Spanish were the first to enter the area and in the Treaty of Saragossa of 1529 Spain sold its claim over the islands to Portugal. By the late sixteenth century the English had also sailed to the Spice Islands, but it was the Dutch who were ultimately to control what became known as the East Indies. From 1602 until 1799 Dutch power in the area was represented by the mercantilist United East Indies Company. In 1799 control passed to the Dutch government and from that time on the colonialists played a much more active role in the development of the resources of interior Java, as well as of the "Outer Islands" (and especially Sumatra). Except for a brief period of British control under Thomas Stamford Raffles (who later founded Singapore) from 1811 to 1816, Dutch rule prevailed until the Japanese occupation during World War II. In 1830 the Dutch introduced their "Culture System" of forced labor and exploitation. In 1870 this was replaced by a more humane Agrarian Law. Also beginning in the 1870s private enterprise was allowed. The period 1870 to 1910 witnessed the conquest by the Dutch of the rest of present-day Indonesia and the consequent diffusion of plantation agriculture. The Dutch interacted less with the indigenous population than perhaps any other colonizer in Southeast Asia, preferring to rule indirectly through local elites loyal to the Dutch. As a result, fewer lasting Dutch cultural and social impacts remain than is the case elsewhere in the region.

In the early twentieth century a nationalistic movement, partly Islamic and partly secular in nature, emerged among some urban intellectuals and elites. One of the important early leaders of this movement was Sukarno. Immediately following the end of the Japanese occupa-

Large Minangkabau palace and museum built in 1980, western Sumatra (courtesy W. L. Thomas)

tion in 1945 independence was proclaimed. The Dutch, however, did not recognize this independence and it was not until 1949, after several military confrontations and subsequent negotiations, that independence was achieved.

President Sukarno, Indonesia's first leader, was initially an extremely popular and charismatic ruler. His influence declined as inflation and political corruption increased, and as he acquired an increasingly non-aligned and pro-Marxist stance. In 1963 West Irian was incorporated and also in 1963, in opposition to what he saw as the neocolonialist establishment of the Federation of Malaysia, Sukarno began a period of confrontation with Malaysia. It was at this time that the president also approved the takeover of foreign businesses and the inclusion of Indonesian Communist leaders in government. A coup d'etat by some military elements, purportedly including Communists, occurred in 1965. The coup failed and there followed a mass slaughter of tens of thousands of alleged members of the Communist Party (PKI) and their supporters, many of whom were ethnic Chinese. Described as one of the worst single massacres in Southeast Asian history, the entire left wing and Communist party was eliminated. In 1966 Sukarno was forced to transfer emergency powers to the military, led by General Suharto, the army chief of staff, who banned the PKI. Confrontation with Malaysia also ended and in 1967 full powers were transferred to Suharto and thus officially began the period dubbed the "New Order." In 1967 diplomatic relations with the People's Republic of China were ended and Indonesia returned to a pro-Western stance. In 1967 Indonesia also became a charter member of ASEAN and reestablished links with Malaysia. In 1975 the era of colonialism in the archipelago finally ended when the Portuguese withdrew from East Timor. In 1976, against the wishes of those who advocated independence, Indonesian forces set up a provisional government and soon integrated East Timor as the twenty-seventh province of the republic.

Opposition to Suharto and the central government has manifested itself in a variety of ways since 1967. Certainly some of this opposition, in spite of the oil revenues, is sparked by economic difficulties and spatial inequalities, and some is based on the cultural-historical differences among the diverse groups. Examples include the ongoing separatist rebellions that persist in East Timor and in West Irian. In the latter, the Free Papua Movement advocates unification with Papua-New Guinea. Fighting there between Indonesian troops and the insurgents has led to the flight of some 11,000 refugees to Papua-New Guinea. One way in which the Indonesian government is seeking to quell such divisiveness is to encourage Javanese to migrate to the more sparsely populated and remote regions, such as West Irian, thereby ultimately decreasing the population of minorities. This policy, known as "Transmigration," was begun in the early twentieth century by the Dutch and was designed to alleviate population pressures on Java and to develop economically the more remote Outer Islands. At best, most critics agree that the program has met with only limited success as only a few million persons have thus far migrated.

Indonesia is a unitary multiparty republic with two legislative houses, the 920-member People's Consultative Assembly and the 460-member House of Representatives. Executive power is vested in the president, who is elected by the Assembly for a five-year term (President Suharto was elected in 1973, 1978, and 1983). The Cabinet is the top executive body and is chaired by the president. In Indonesia, most of the highest positions are held by senior armed forces officers. Administratively, the country is divided into 24 provinces (*propinsi*) and 3 provincial-level special territories: Jakarta, Yogyakarta, and Aceh. Provinces are divided into districts, or regencies (*kabupaten*), and municipalities. These are further subdivided into subdistricts (*kecamatan*) and villages.

## THE ECONOMY

The majority of the labor force, about 55%, is comprised of agricultural laborers, and agriculture contributes over one-quarter of the gross domestic product. Some two-fifths of the total cultivated land is planted with rice and other important subsistence crops, including maize (14% of the cultivated area) and cassava (6%), from which tapioca is made. The major commercial crops are rubber, coconuts, sugar, and coffee. Indonesian agriculture, especially on densely populated Java, is characterized by a high degree of landlessness, underemployment, and heavy indebtedness. In the case of the Javanese peasant, well over 50% are landless and over 60% are heavily in debt. In short, a generally inefficient agricultural system has meant low crop yields and extensive poverty. Nonetheless, Java seemingly has always been able to support increased numbers, a phenomenon described as "agricultural involution" by the anthropologist Clifford Geertz. Java's rich soils, the introduction of new rice cultivation techniques, and the higher-yielding varieties and new technologies associated with the Green Revolution have meant that ever greater population densities could be supported, at least at bare subsistence levels. Between 1969 and 1984 rice production doubled both by increasing cultivated area outside of Java, and through an increase in yields. National self-sufficiency in rice has been a goal of the Indonesian government but as late as 1982 Indonesia was still the world's largest importer. By 1984 Indonesia had neared

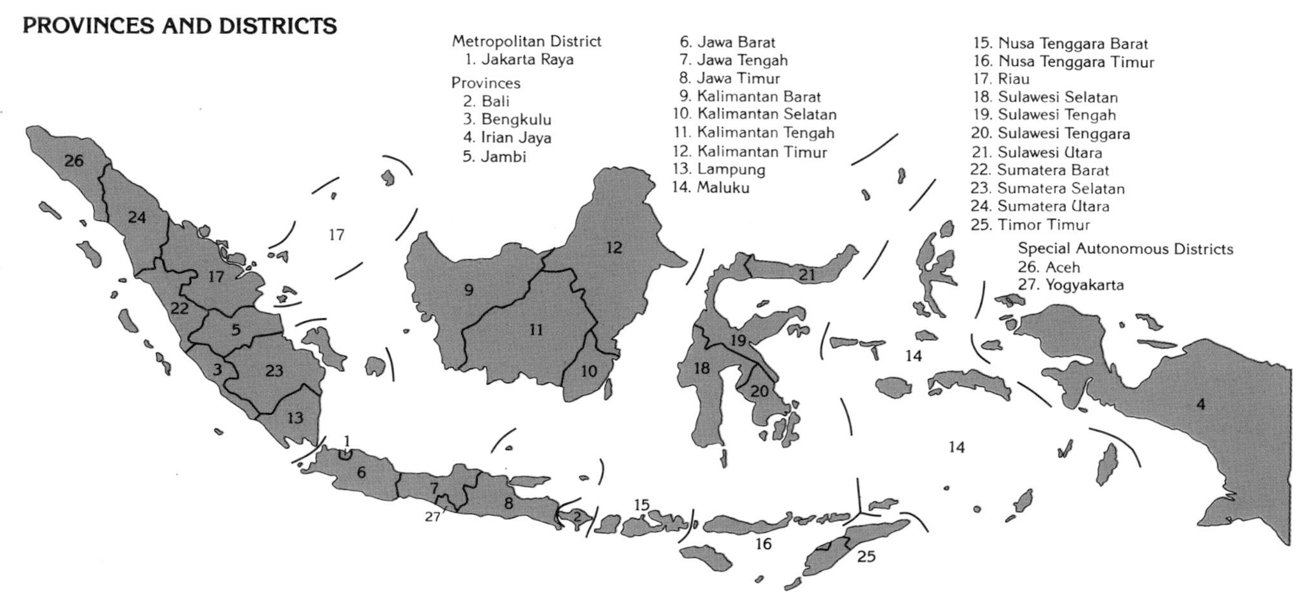

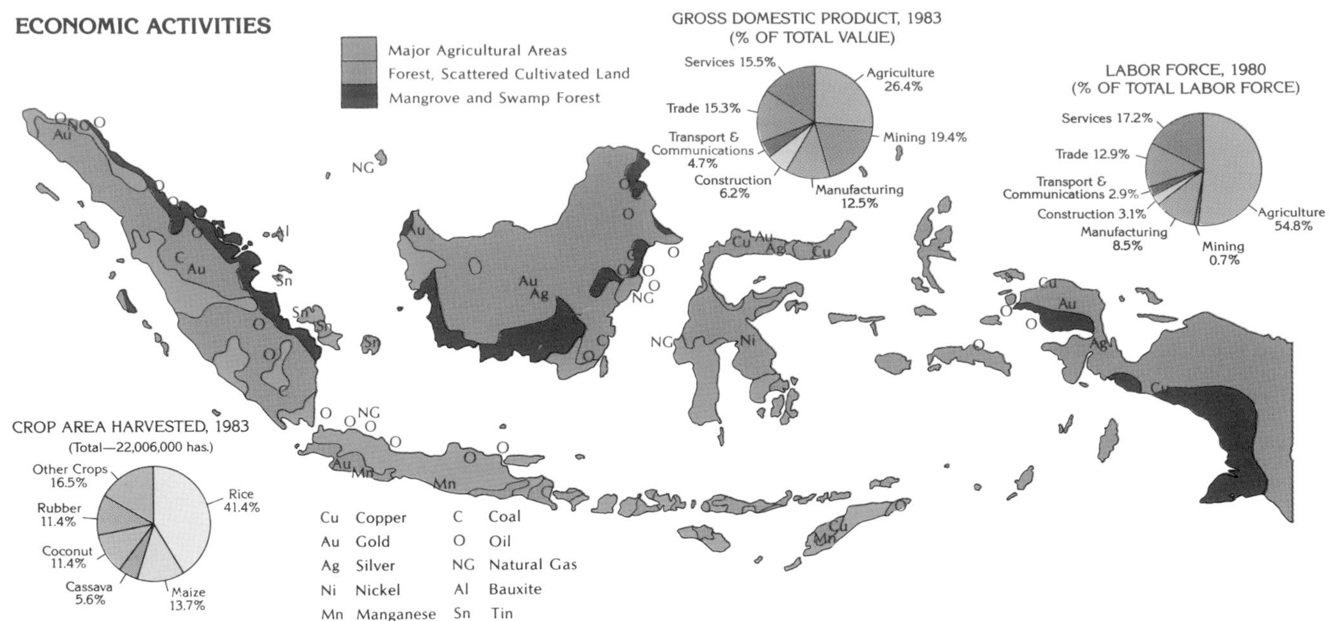


self-sufficiency but, like many other countries, it was now becoming dependent upon another grain import: wheat.

Indonesia has an abundance of mineral resources but since the 1970s the most important by far has been crude petroleum. Fully three-fifths of all exports by value were accounted for by crude petroleum in 1983, and another 15% were derived from exports of other fuel products. As recently as 1969 over two-thirds of exports by value came from the agricultural sector but by 1983 less than one-tenth came from this economic sector. Since 1968 petroleum production has been under the management and control of Pertamina, a government-owned company. Much of the petroleum and natural gas

Balikpapan oil refinery, Kalimantan (courtesy W. Wood)

lies in offshore oilfields, many of which have not been tested. American companies have the greatest investment in Indonesian petroleum and pump some 90% of all crude. The potential for further offshore discoveries prompted Indonesia in 1979 to declare an exclusive offshore economic zone, extending 200 nautical miles (370 km) from the coast. This has lead to offshore boundary problems with other nations, notably Australia, Vietnam, and Malaysia. Other minerals of importance include tin, copper, nickel, and bauxite.

Manufacturing is underdeveloped, accounting for only 12% of the gross domestic product and 5% of the export value. Consumer goods account for about four-fifths of the value added in manufacturing. The most important industries include food processing, textiles, lumber processing, rubber processing, and handicrafts, including batik.

Because of energy exports, Indonesia has had a trade surplus, estimated at four billion dollars (US) in 1983. More recently, however, export earnings have declined because of the fluctuations in world oil prices and because of the cutback in import-substituting industries. Further economic problems are related to the country's increasing foreign indebtedness. Japan is Indonesia's major trading partner and Japan, together with the United States and the rest of

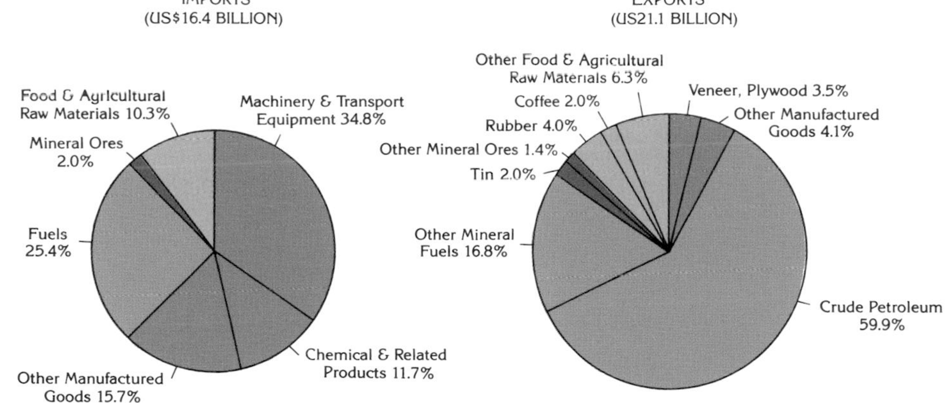


Source: *1983 International Trade Statistics Yearbook (N.Y.: U.N., 1985)*

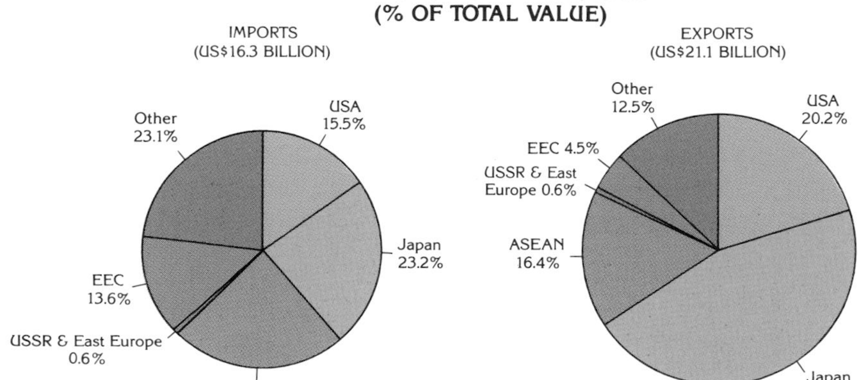


Source: *1983 International Trade Statistics Yearbook (N.Y.: U.N., 1985)*

ASEAN, accounted for nearly three-quarters of Indonesia's total trade in 1983.

## TRANSPORTATION AND TOURISM

There are some 83,000 miles (134,000 km) of road in the country, mostly on Java, of which about two-fifths are paved. Two major road-building projects of recent years have been the Trans-Sumatra and Trans-Sulawesi highways. Nearly three-fourths of the more than 4,000 miles (6,400 km) of railways in the country are on Java. In general, the railways have been neglected and are still predominantly narrow-gauge. As with any nation of islands, interisland shipping is a major form of transportation for both passengers and cargo; unfortunately, the interisland merchant fleet is old and poorly developed. There are some 46 ports considered to be major, and the two largest, Tanjung Priok near Jakarta and Tanjung Perak near Surabaya, have been modernized. Indonesia's airline, Garuda, has the second largest Asian fleet after Japan Airlines and links major cities throughout the nation, as well as providing international service. Major airports are located at Medan, Denpasar (Bali), and Cengkareng, the site of Jakarta's new international airport.

When traveling between cities on one of the major islands, one can take the frequent and cheap busses which are usually overcrowded. Within cities, in addition to taxis, travel can be made in the ubiquitous and inexpensive *bemo* (minivan) or *becak* (pedal trishaw).

Tourism is not as well developed in Indonesia as in Thailand or the Philippines but the government is hoping to achieve increased visitors through programs that encourage tourism. In 1984 nearly 700,000 foreign visitors arrived. The vast majority visited Jakarta and other parts of Java, which is noted for its volcanoes and historic and architectural sites such as that at Borobudur. Bali, well known for its dancing, handicrafts, religious festivals, and beach resorts, is another popular tourist destination. Occasionally, trekkers or naturalists will visit the forests and nature preserves wherein are found Indonesia's vanishing wildlife, such as the orangutans of northern Sumatra and Kalimantan.

Container facilities at harbor at Tanjung Priok, Java (courtesy T. Leinbach)

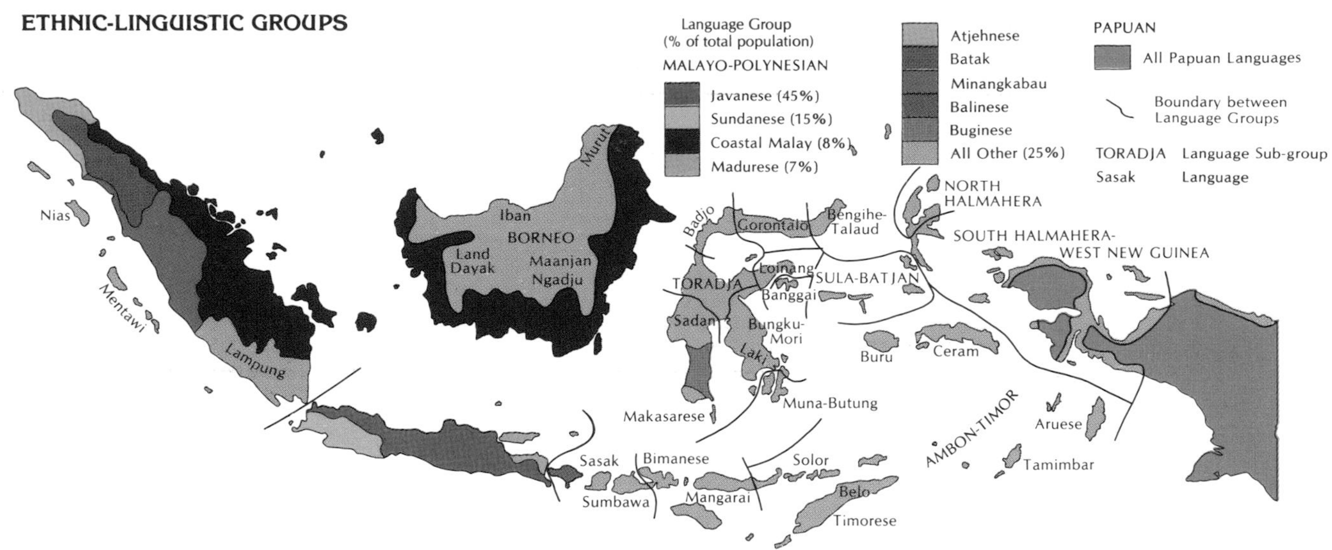


## PEOPLE AND CULTURE

Whereas Bahasa Indonesia is the official language, over 25 languages and 250 dialects are spoken. The vast majority belong to the Malayo-Polynesian family of languages and of these the principal languages are Javanese (spoken by 40% of the population), Sundanese (15%), coastal Malay (12%), and Madurese (5%). In the eastern archipelago and in West Irian, languages of the Papuan family are spoken. There are possibly two million ethnic Chinese in Indonesia, most of whom are citizens and who comprise one of the larger Chinese communities in Southeast Asia. As is so elsewhere, most Chinese live in cities and are involved in retail activities.

About four-fifths of all Indonesians are Muslim but there are often considerable variations in the degree of adherence to Islam. The second major religion is Christianity, adhered to by about 7.5% of the population. Christianity has made inroads among interior populations throughout the arichipelago, and a major segment of the Batak group of northern Sumatra subscribes to Christianity. Hinduism, practiced among the Balinese, is the major religion on Bali. Animism is the belief system of most of the interior minority groups.

The art and architecture of the archipelago reflects Malay, Indian, and Islamic influences. Extensive temple complexes, for example, were built in central Java from about the eighth to tenth centuries. Among the best-preserved of these are the Indian Buddhist monument of Borobudur and the Hindu temple complexes of Prambanan (see photo in Chapter 2). The Javanese literary tradition began around the tenth century and has since flourished; Javanese is today the language of literature. Cultural life is also reflected in the Indian legends popularized by the "shadow plays" (*wayang kulit*); their puppets are found throughout the rural areas of Java and Bali. Dance is also widely popular and there are as many dance styles as there are ethnic groups; Balinese and Javanese dance troupes are world-renowned. Many decorative art forms are practiced and perhaps the best known is that of batik-making. Batik is a dyed cloth produced through a complex process whereby wax is applied to those parts of the cloth not to be dyed. When handmade, it is a very time-consuming process that can produce extremely intricate patterns.

Much of the art and culture of Indonesia is represented in the extensive collections held at the National Museum in Jakarta. As the region's largest city, Jakarta holds many other attractions for the visitor, including Merdeka Square (the city's most central landmark), the massive National Mosque, many markets (and foodstalls!), and a park known as Tamin Mini Indonesia Indah (Beautiful Indonesia in Miniature), similar

JAKARTA METROPOLITAN AREA
JAVA SEA
TANJUNG PRIOK
SUNDA KELAPA (OLD PORT)
Kel. Penjaringan
PENJARINGAN
TAMAN IMPIAN JAYA ANCOL (AMUSEMENT COMPLEX)
Laksamana E. Martadinata Rd.
Kota Railway Station
JAKARTA CITY MUSEUM
KOTA
Kemayoran Domestic Airport
CHINATOWN
TAMAN SARI
TAMBURA
SAWAH BESAR
GROGOL
PETAMBURAN
KEMAYORAN
Daan Mogot Rd.
Kiyai Tapa Rd.
K.H. Hasyim Asyari Rd.
MARKET
CENTRAL POST OFFICE
PRESIDENTIAL PALACE
to Soekarno-Hatta International Airport (Cengkareng)
GAMBIR
Bus Station
ISTIQLAL MOSQUE
Let Jen Suprapto Rd.
Perintis Kemerdekaan Rd.
SLIPI ORCHID GARDEN
MERDEKA NATIONAL MONUMENT
NATIONAL MUSEUM
MERDEKA SQUARE
MARKET
CEMPAKA PUTIH
PULOMAS RACETRACK
Merak Superhighway
CITY HALL
U.S. EMBASSY
SENEN
TAMAN ISMAIL MARZUKI CULTURAL CENTER
Pramuka Rd.
Pemuda Rd.
UNIVERSITY OF INDONESIA
MENTENG
MATRAMAN
PULO GADUNG
TANAH ABANG
PARLIAMENT HOUSE
SETIA BUDI
SENAYAN STADIUM
JATINEGARA
TEBET
KEBAYORAN BARU
Let Jendral Haryono Rd.
MAMPANG PRAPATAN
Halimperdanakusuma Airport
SCALE 1:75,000
0 .5 1 1.5 2 Miles
0 1 2 3 Kilometers
TO RAGUNAN ZOO

to parks near Bangkok and Manila which show Thailand and the Philippines in miniature, respectively.

Jakarta was originally settled as a trading center by Indians in about the fifth century. In 1619 the Dutch under Jan Pieterszoon Coen captured the city, fortified it, and named it Batavia. Kota, or the Old Town, still has a Dutch flavor, with narrow residential structures and canals. Otherwise the city has the characteristics of large cities throughout Southeast Asia: a port zone, huge traffic jams, nondescript shopping areas, a Chinatown, luxury hotels, plush residential districts for the local elite and foreign diplomats and businessmen, all amidst extensive slum and squatter settlements, estimated to house at least one-third of the city's population.

The cultural hearth of Java is represented by the city of Yogyakarta, in central Java, with its Kraton (palace) of the Sultan, its "bird market," batik factories, silversmiths, and the temples of Prambanan and monument of Borobodur in close proximity.

# 6

# *Republic of the Philippines*

*Area:* 115,831 sq mi (300,000 sq km); about the size of Arizona or Italy

*Population:* 56,460,000 (1986)

*Population Density:* 487 persons per sq mi (188 persons per sq km)

*Urban Population:* 36.2%

*Annual Average Rate of Population Increase:* 2.5%

*Crude Birth Rate:* 33.8 per 1,000 population

*Crude Death Rate:* 8.2 per 1,000 population

*Infant Mortality Rate:* 59 infant deaths per 1,000 live births

*Life Expectancy:* Male—60.9; Female—64.1

*Official Languages:* Pilipino; English

*Currency:* Philippine peso (US$ = 20.8 pesos in 1988).

*Capital:* Manila

*Form of Government:* Federal republican and democratic state with two legislative houses (Senate and House of Representatives)

*Chief of State:* President

*Armed Forces (1985):* 114,800 (army—61%; navy —24%; air force—15%)

## HISTORICAL OVERVIEW

1521: Ferdinand Magellan lands in the central Philippines and is killed by Chief Lapu-Lapu, ruler of Mactan Island.

1565: Miguel Lopez de Legaspi lands in Cebu and soon establishes first Spanish settlement there.

1570: Spanish land in Manila and soon after proclaim their settlement as capital.

1896: Filipinos begin revolution against Spain.

1896: José Rizal executed.

1898: Independence proclaimed with General Emilio Aguinaldo as head of the government.

1898: United States defeats Spain in Spanish-American War and Philippines is ceded by Spain to the United States.

1899–1902: Filipino-American War, which ends in U. S. Victory.

1935: Commonwealth status approved; Manuel Quezon elected president.

1942–1945: Japanese occupation.

1946: Independence; Manuel Roxas becomes president.

1965: Ferdinand Marcos elected president.

1972: President Marcos declares martial law.

1983: Benigno Aquino assassinated.

1986: Corazon Aquino elected president; Marcos forced to leave Philippines.

A former colony of both Spain and the United States, the Philippines is today the region's third, and the world's seventeenth, most populous nation. Whereas the Mongoloid racial and Malayo-Polynesian ethnolinguistic characteristics of Filipinos are similar to that of other insular and peninsular Southeast Asians, distinct Filipino cultural traits, sometimes similar to those found in Latin America, can be attributed in part to a unique colonial history. There is considerable evidence of the impact of both colonizers. Whereas spoken Spanish is not significant today in the Philippines (it is spoken by less than 1% of the population), the fact that about 85% of the population is Roman Catholic, the predominance of Spanish place names and surnames, and the pattern of land tenancy and ownership are but a few legacies that attest to Spain's former presence. The United States colonial period

Batan Islands
Luzon Strait
Babuyan Islands
Babuyan Channel
SOUTH CHINA SEA
Laoag
Vigan
CORDILLERA CENTRAL
CAGAYAN VALLEY
SIERRA MADRE
Ilagan
LUZON
Mt. Pulog 9,625
Lingayen Gulf
Baguio
Dagupan
San Carlos
ZAMBALES MTS
CENTRAL PLAIN
Tarlac
Cabanatuan
Clark Air Base (U.S.)
Angeles
Olongapo
San Fernando
Polillo Islands
Subic Bay Naval Base (U.S.)
MANILA
Quezon City
Corregidor Island
Manila Bay
Laguna de Bay
Lamon Bay
Calamba
San Pablo
Daet
Catanduanes
Lipa
Lucena
Lubang
Batangas
Tayabas Bay
Ragay Gulf
Naga
Lagonoy Gulf
8,075
MINDORO
Calapan
Marinduque
Mayon Volcano
Legaspi
Burias
Sibuyan
Mindoro Strait
Tablas Strait
Sibuyan Sea
Ticao
Catarman
Busuanga
Culion
Tablas
MASBATE
Calbayog
Samar Sea
SAMAR
Roxas
Visayan Sea
PHILIPPINE SEA
PANAY
Tacloban
Ormoc
Cadiz
Leyte Gulf
Cuyo
Iloilo
Silay
Bacolod
CEBU
LEYTE
PHILIPPINE TRENCH
32,995
Dumaran
8,087
Canlaon Volcano
Camotes Sea
Mandaue
Cebu
Guimaras
Panay Gulf
Dinagat
Siargao
PALAWAN
Puerto Princesa
Surigao Strait
Surigao
NEGROS
BOHOL
Bohol Sea
Lake Mainit
Dumaguete
Siquijor
Camiguin
Butuan
SULU SEA
Dipolog
Iligan Bay
Cagayan de Oro
AGUSAN VALLEY
Iligan
Ozamis
Marawi
Lake Lanao
Bislig
Balabac
Pagadian
Balabac Strait
Illana Bay
MINDANAO
Tagum
Davao
Cotabato
Samal
Cagayan Sulu
Moro Gulf
9,690
Mt. Apo
Mati
Highest point in the Philippines
COTABATO VALLEY
Digos
Davao Gulf
Zamboanga
Basilan
Kota Kinabalu
Sandakan
Jolo
Jolo
CELEBES SEA
General Santos
MALAYSIA (SABAH)
Sulu Archipelago
Tawitawi
Sarangani Islands
SCALE 1:7,686,000
0 50 100 150 200 250 Miles
0 50 100 150 200 250 300 350 400 Kilometers
117° 119° 121° 123° 125° 127°
19° 17° 15° 13° 11° 9° 7° 5°

left the Philippines with a mixed blessing: an educational system that emphasized Western culture and values, political institutions that sometimes did not work very well, a dependency on but a few primary agricultural and mineral commodities, and the English language. Today, English is spoken as a second language by over two-fifths of the population and is one of the nation's two official languages. Philippine educational levels today are higher than those of most other Third World nations because of the American influence and the high value Filipinos place upon formal education. It is estimated that three-quarters of Filipino adults, both male and female, are literate. Elementary education, beginning at seven years of age and lasting for six years, is compulsory.

As has been the case for many Third World nations since political independence, the Philippines have been beset with social and economic problems. Today, the nation suffers from a serious trade deficit, a huge foreign debt, heavy dependence on external aid, and civil disobedience all related to a variety of political, social, and economic difficulties.

## THE PHYSICAL ENVIRONMENT

The Philippines consist of an archipelago of over 7,100 islands and islets. The eleven largest islands comprise over 92% of the nation's land area and the two largest, Luzon and Mindanao, account for about two-thirds of the total.

The islands began to form some 50 million years ago with the volcanic eruptions caused by the collision of two tectonic plates (see map in Chapter 1). Today the islands are still experiencing mountain-building and volcanic activity since they lie near the juncture of two such plates. Thus the islands can be characterized as having rugged topography. The highest individual peak is Mindanao's Mount Apo at 9,690 feet (2,954 m), but the Cordillera Central on northern Luzon is the largest and most rugged mountain system. There are a number of active volcanoes. The most famous, and one of the world's best known because of its nearly perfect symmetry, is Mayon Volcano (8,075 ft; 2,462 m), located on the Bicol Peninsula of southern Luzon. Another well-known attraction is Lake Taal and its Volcano Island, a crater lake located south of Manila.

Manila is typical of the sea-level climate found in a nation that lies just north of the equator: hot and humid throughout most of the year. Some relief from the heat occurs at night, when average temperatures in Manila are 15°F (−9.5°C) lower than during the daytime. Relief from the heat can also be found by traveling to highland areas, the best known of which is the upland resort of Baguio (called the "City of Pines"), located 150 miles (240 km) north of Manila. At an elevation of 5,000 feet (1,500 m), average temper-

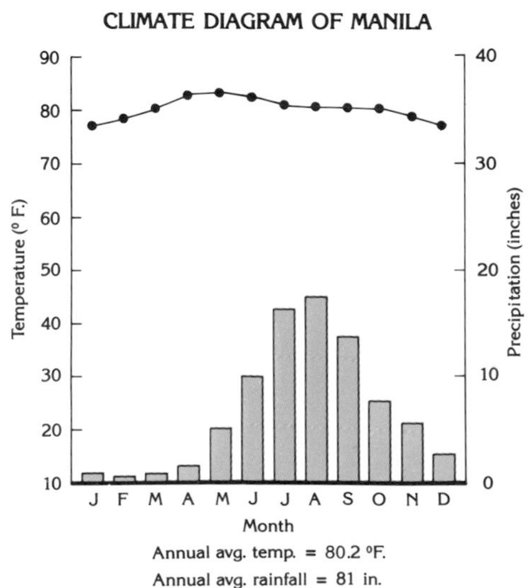


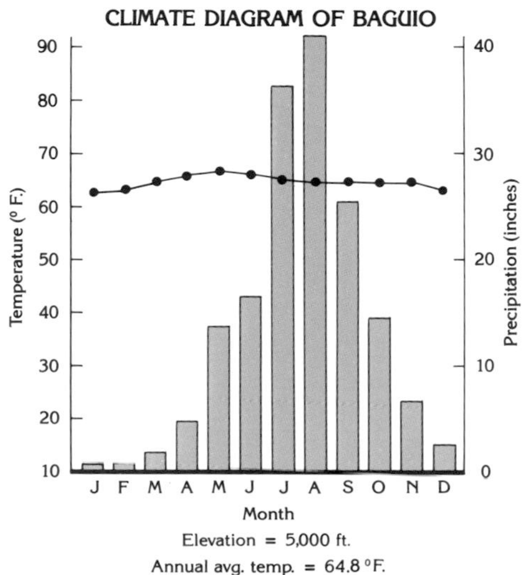

atures in Baguio are 15°F (−9.5°C) below those at sea level.

The Philippines experience the effects of the Asian Monsoon. Manila and the western coastal regions of the nation receive the bulk of their rainfall from June through September as a result of the Southwest monsoon, whereas the eastern coast receives most of its precipitation between December and February. North of 9° N. latitude, the Philippines are prone to severe typhoons that originate to the east in the western Pacific Ocean. One such typhoon in 1911 deposited 46 inches (117 cm) of rainfall on Baguio in a 24-hour period, a world record.

Natural vegetation and animal life, where it still exists, is typical of that in a tropical environment. Monsoon forests include many species of trees and other plant life. Commercially, Philippine mahogany (or *lauan*) is a major source of revenue for the economy. Numerous species of small mammals, birds, and reptiles live in the forests. However, the extensive deforestation that has resulted from commercial exploitation, human population growth, and conversion of land to agriculture has brought about the extinction of many life forms. Others, such as the buffalo-like tamaraw of Mindoro Island and the Philippine (monkey-eating) eagle, are nearly extinct.

## HISTORICAL BACKGROUND

Of the major land areas of Southeast Asia, the Philippines were one of the last to witness the arrival of man. The earliest such archeological evidence, fossilized bone found in the Tabon Caves on Palawan Island, can be dated to over 20,000 years ago. However, it is generally believed that the first movement of man to Palawan occurred some 50,000 years ago during the last major period of glaciation (the Pleistocene epoch) when Palawan, a part of the shallow Sunda Shelf, was connected by land to the Indonesian archipelago, and thus to mainland Southeast Asia. These earliest peoples were the ancient ancestors of today's Negritos, black-skinned people of short stature. Very few people of this racial stock remain in the Philippines, where today they are found only in the most remote, upland areas. The present-day Aetas, ancestors of these early Negrito groups, are located in a few remote interior areas on the islands of Luzon, Mindanao, and Panay.

The first seafarers probably arrived in the northern Philippines from China and Tonkin over 10,000 years ago. These were the forebears of the present-day Bontoc and Ifugao peoples (the "Igorots," or mountain people) of interior, upland northern Luzon. These groups were sedentary wet-rice farmers who built magnificent terraced fields into the steep mountain slopes of the Central Cordillera. Such practices were probably learned from the Chinese and today such terraces are found only in northern Luzon.

Beginning about 2,000 years ago significant numbers of Malay-speaking peoples of Mongoloid racial stock began to migrate to the islands from the Indonesian archipelago and Malay Peninsula. These early migrants orga-

Ifugao rice terraces and hamlet (foreground), Banaue, northern Luzon (courtesy W. L. Thomas)

nized themselves into small, independent communities called *barangays,* each ruled by a *datu.* Unlike Indonesia and other areas of Southeast Asia, there were no great unified kingdoms that existed when more recent outsiders, like the Spanish, arrived. Approximately 500 years before the arrival of the Europeans, commercial relations with China, Indochina, Malaya, India, and the Arab lands intensified. These seafarers brought their porcelain wares, silk, cotton, gold, and jewelry and traded for bird's nests (for soup), pearls, shells, rattan, and other primary products from the sea and forest.

The pre-European period witnessed the arrival of another important impact: Islam. Beginning about the fourteenth century, Muslim traders brought Islam to the southern Philippines and although Islamic influence reached as far north as Luzon (early Manila, called Maynilad, was a Muslim settlement before the Spanish arrived), Islam was never a very significant religious force in the central and northern portions of the archipelago. Today, about 5% of the population are Muslim and virtually all reside on Mindanao Island and on the smaller islands, such as those of the Sulu Archipelago, between Mindanao and Borneo. Because of the continuing conflict between Philippine Muslims and the Philippine government, it is estimated that perhaps 90,000 Muslims from the southern Philippines have sought and been granted temporary refuge in nearby Sabah, a part of Islamic Malaysia. The refugee situation and the long-standing dispute over the boundary between Sabah and the Philippines, continue to be sore points between these two ASEAN nations.

In 1521 Ferdinand Magellan, Portuguese by birth but a citizen of Spain, opened the colonization of the Philippines. Magellan landed in the central Philippines near Leyte, and soon after successfully converted the *datu*s of Cebu to Christianity. He met resistance only on nearby Mactan Island where he was killed by Lapu-Lapu, the ruler of Mactan. In 1565 other Spanish vessels arrived and Spanish settlements quickly began to appear. Among the earliest was Cebu, settled by Miguel Lopez de Legaspi, today the second largest metropolitan area in the nation. In 1570, after the defeat of the forces of the Muslim ruler Rajah Soliman, Manila was settled by the Spanish and proclaimed the capital of the colony. By the early 1600s Spain's control of the Philippines was complete. Roman Catholicism soon replaced the pantheistic beliefs of most Filipinos and, except in the Muslim south, it became the predominant religious belief nearly everywhere.

The nearly 350 years of Spanish rule greatly altered the Philippines. In addition to the introduction of Roman Catholicism and all that that implied, other important legacies of the Spanish period were the *encomienda* system (whereby the colony was divided into parcels, each assigned to a deserving Spanish national), payment of tribute and forced labor for the production of agricultural commodities such as sugar cane, and the Galleon Trade. This latter legacy was beneficial to Manila, a stopover port for the Manila galleons, sailing ships whose owners profited greatly from the trade between China and Mexico between the sixteenth and early nineteenth centuries. Economic development within the Philippines suffered during this period since so much money was invested in the voyages of the galleons. Another legacy of the Spanish period was the intermixing of the native Filipino population and the Spanish (and later American and other Caucasians), which produced the population known as *mestizo.*

Discontent among the Filipino clergy and unrest throughout the Philippines became especially significant during the latter half of the nineteenth century. José Rizal, a national hero, was perhaps the best known of a number of Filipinos who advocated reform and change. His execution by the Spanish in 1896 sealed his martyrdom and facilitated the revolt against Spain. The people's revolution began in 1896 under the leadership of Andres Bonifacio, who headed the Katipunan, or the Association of Sons of the People. After the American victory over Spain in 1898, Emilio Aguinaldo declared independence from Spain with himself as president. The Philippines, however, were ceded to the United States by Spain for $20 million and thus became an American colony. Filipinos opposed this and war ensued between them and their new colonizers; Filipino forces were finally subdued by 1902. In 1935 a self-governing commonwealth was approved for the Philippines which was to end after ten years, when the Islands were to become fully independent. World War II intervened; the Japanese occupied Manila in 1942 and soon afterward the entire country was under Japanese occupation. American forces, under General Douglas MacArthur, were forced to surrender. MacArthur left the Philippines from Corregidor Island where he made his famous vow, "I shall return." American forces under MacArthur did return in October 1944 to defeat the Japanese. Many Filipino and American lives were lost at the hands of the Japanese. Certainly, the infamous "Death March" will be remembered for the atrocities and deaths that occurred. Final independence from the United States came in 1946, with Manuel Roxas inaugurated as the republic's first president.

The Philippines and the United States have maintained close political and economic ties since 1946, although beginning in the 1970s the Marcos government moved toward a policy of nonalignment and established diplomatic relations with its Communist neighbors. To the dismay of at least some Filipinos, the United States continues to maintain its huge naval and air bases at Olongapo City (Subic Bay) and Angeles City (Clark Air Base), respectively.

PROVINCES

1. Abra
2. Agusan del Norte
3. Agusan del Sur
4. Aklan
5. Albay
6. Antique
7. Aurora
8. Basilan
9. Bataan
10. Batanes
11. Batangas
12. Benguet
13. Bohol
14. Bukidnon
15. Bulacan
16. Cagayan
17. Camarines Norte
18. Camarines Sur
19. Camiguin
20. Capiz
21. Catanduanes
22. Cavite
23. Cebu
24. Davao del Norte
25. Davao del Sur
26. Davao Oriental
27. Eastern Samar
28. Ifugao
29. Ilocos Norte
30. Ilocos Sur
31. Iloilo
32. Isabela
33. Kalinga-Apayao
34. La Union
35. Laguna
36. Lanao del Norte
37. Lanao del Sur
38. Leyte
39. Maguindanao
40. Marinduque
41. Masbate
42. Misamis Occidental
43. Misamis Oriental
44. Mountain
45. Negros del Norte
46. Negros Occidental
47. Negros Oriental
48. North Cotabato
49. Northern Samar
50. Neuva Ecija
51. Nueva Vizcaya
52. Occidental Mindoro
53. Oriental Mindoro
54. Palawan
55. Pampanga
56. Pangasinan
57. Quezon
58. Quirino
59. Rizal
60. Romblon
61. Samar
62. Siquijor
63. Sorsogon
64. South Cotabato
65. Southern Leyte
66. Sultan Kudarat
67. Sulu
68. Surigao del Norte
69. Surigao del Sur
70. Tarlac
71. Tawi-Tawi
72. Zambales
73. Zamboanga del Norte
74. Zamboanga del Sur

Metro Manila

The head-of-state and commander-in-chief of the armed forces is the president, elected for a six-year term. The president governs with the assistance of an appointed cabinet. Legislative power is vested in the Congress of the Philippines, which consists of a Senate (24 members elected to 6-year terms) and a House of Representatives (no more than 250 members elected to 3-year terms). There is a supreme court, which is comprised of a chief justice and 14 associate justices.

Provinces are the largest geographical political units. The 74 provinces and Metro Manila are subdivided into 1,513 municipalities, 60 chartered cities, and 21 municipal districts. These are further subdivided into more than 40,000 *barangays* (formerly *barrios*), the basic unit of the Philippine political system.

## THE ECONOMY

Like most Third World nations, the Philippine economy historically has been dependent upon the production and export of the primary products derived from agriculture, mines, forests, and the sea. Since the Spanish period, the commodities that have been the most important commercially are sugar, coconuts and coconut products such as copra and coconut oil (today the Philippines are the world's largest producer and exporter), lumber, abaca (Manila hemp), gold and silver, and copper. Not all of these remain important but primary products still account for nearly one-half of Philippine export earnings and employ over one-half of the labor force. Production and earnings for such commodities are highly dependent on international demand and competition. When there is an ample supply of a commodity, or demand is low, then prices decline. Such has been the case with both sugar and coconut products in recent years. For example, between 1981 and 1984 Philippine export earnings for sugar alone declined by nearly 75%.

Bringing in the early morning catch, Ilana Bay, western Mindanao (R. Ulack)

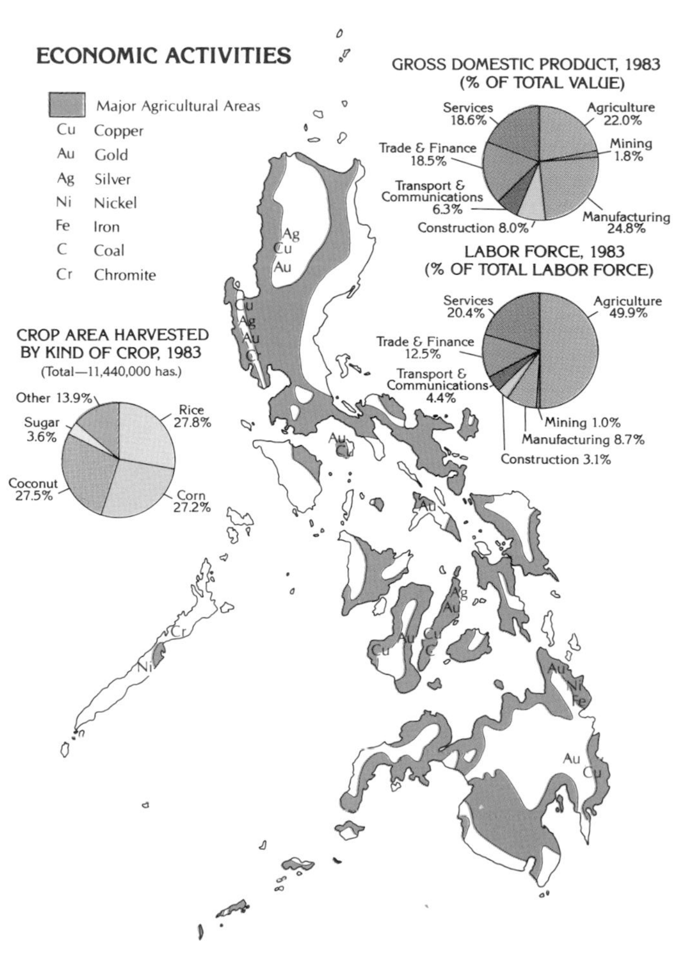


The vast majority of workers in the primary sector are in agriculture, most of whom are poor, subsistence tenant farmers producing rice or corn which together account for over one-half of the harvested crop area. The major rice-producing areas in the nation are located in the lowland portions of Luzon, most notably the Central Plain north of Manila. It is on Luzon, at Los Baños in Laguna Province, that the International Rice Research Institute was established. This is the world center for rice research and it has been here that many of the Green Revolution's modern high-yielding varieties of rice have been developed. Such varieties often yield three times that of the traditional varieties and thus where they are grown production has increased. Adoption of these new varieties by many Filipino farmers has enabled the nation to become nearly self-sufficient in rice. Land reform, though an espoused policy of recent Philippine leaders including presidents Ferdinand Marcos and Corazon Aquino, is not yet widespread and the issue of tenancy remains a major problem for Philippine development. Given that the political elites are also the nation's principal landowners, it would seem that real land reform will be difficult, if not impossible, to put into effect without radical change.

**TRADE BY COMMODITY GROUP, 1982**
**(% OF TOTAL VALUE)**

IMPORTS
(US$8.3 BILLION)
Food & Agricultural Raw Materials 12.5%
Machinery & Transport Equipment 21.4%
Mineral Ores 1.8%
Fuels 26.5%
Chemical & Related Products 10.1%
Other Manufactured Goods 27.9%

EXPORTS
(US$5.0 BILLION)
Other Food & Agricultural Raw Materials 14.8%
Textiles & Apparel 8.5%
Manufactured Wood Products 4.1%
Timber 4.2%
Sugar 8.9%
Other Manufactured Goods 36.7%
Coconut Oil & Copra 10.4%
Other Mineral Ores 2.2%
Gold & Silver 3.4%
Copper 6.2%
Fuels 0.7%

*Source: 1983 International Trade Statistics Yearbook (N.Y.: U.N., 1985)*

Since independence, industrialization has been underway and in terms of value added to gross domestic product (GDP) and export earnings, the nation is more industrialized than other nations in the region, with the exception of Singapore. Philippine industrialization, however, has not been the panacea for the nations' problems as had been hoped. Industry is largely capital intensive (rather than labor intensive) and has thus not directly affected a large number of people. Further, the majority of industries are located in the metropolitan Manila area and therefore most benefits derived from the manufacturing sector are concentrated in the primate city. In recent years the Philippines, like some other developing nations, has established export-processing zones (EPZ) in order to attract industries from abroad. Such zones provide the infrastructure for industry as well as exemptions from payment of most taxes and export fees. The benefits derived from the multinational corporations that have located in such zones, except for the limited employment and training they provide, have thus far been minimal to the host nation.

Political and military events in recent years have further caused the economy to suffer. Political corruption and increased inequities during the Marcos era, the escalation of activity by the Communist guerrilla insurgency and its New People's Army (NPA), and the assassination of Benigno Aquino in 1983 discouraged investment and caused a substantial flight of capital from the country. The total foreign debt today exceeds $25 billion and the Philippines is unfortunately among the world's leaders in

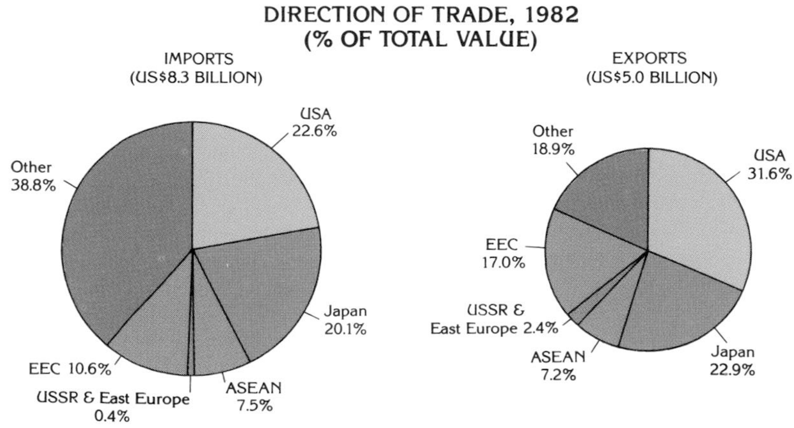


*Source: 1983 International Trade Statistics Yearbook (N.Y.: U.N., 1985)*

INSURGENT ACTIVITY, EARLY 1980s

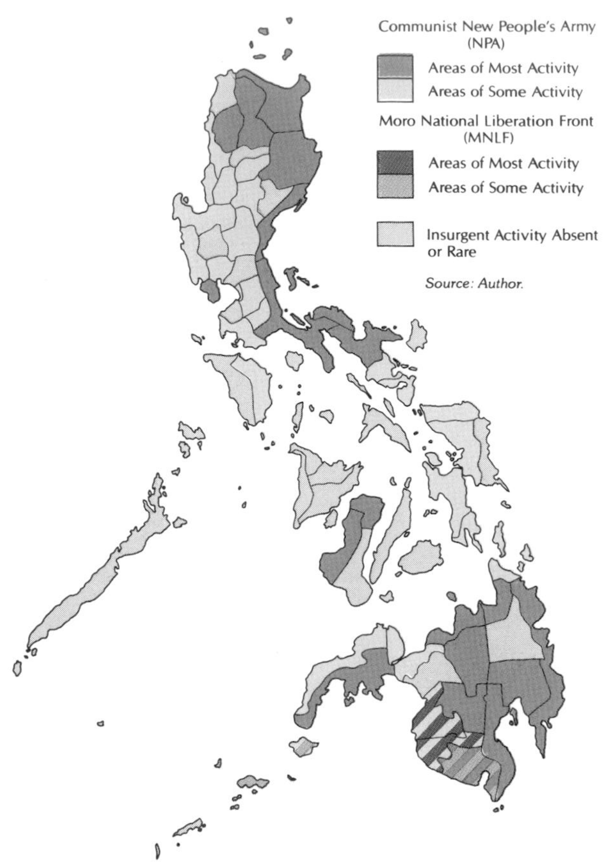


this category. Since 1974, the Philippines have recorded a balance of payment deficit; in 1982 the deficit was in excess of $3.2 billion. The tremendous excesses of the years that the Marcoses were in power are one explanation for the current economic difficulties. President Corazon Aquino's ascendancy to power in 1986 and her popularity have given Filipinos new hope that their situations will improve. But without major structural transformations it is the feeling of many in the Philippines that the status quo will be maintained.

## TRANSPORTATION

As is so for any archipelagic nation, interisland shipping plays a considerable role in domestic passenger and cargo traffic. Over 11 million passengers embarked or disembarked at the 22 major ports throughout the Philippines in 1982. Because of its central location, the leading port for domestic sea passenger traffic was Cebu. Philippine Airlines has both domestic and international air service and there are two major international airports, at Manila and on Mactan Island, which serves metropolitan Cebu. There are over 96,000 miles of roads in the nation (two-thirds of which are macadam, concrete, or asphalt) serving 1.2 million motor vehicles. Busses provide the most widely used form of intercity transportation but within cities the famous and colorful jeepney is usually most important. The several hundred miles of railway that exist are limited to the islands of Luzon and Panay. In 1984, a Light Rail Transit (LRT) system began operation in Manila. The LRT is electricity-driven, with light cars running on rails some 20 feet above street level. Built at great expense, its purpose is to decongest the streets, lessen pollution and accidents, decrease commuter travel time, and conserve energy. This latter point has been a policy of the government for years since the Philippines is highly dependent upon outside sources for its petroleum (over one-quarter of the value of all imports is for energy).

Jeepneys in Quiapo, Manila (R. Ulack)

## PEOPLE AND CULTURE

The Philippines are very diverse ethnically. Some 75 languages and dialects are spoken throughout the country and six of them have at least 1 million speakers each. This diversity of languages, together with the introduction of an alien educational system during the American colonial period, facilitated the adoption and use of English as the major secondary language. English is also the medium of instruction in schools throughout the nation. Tagalog and Cebuano (or Visayan) are most widely spoken of the native languages. They, and all other native languages and dialects, belong to the Malayo-Polynesian family of languages.

Although the Philippines are still a rural nation, about one-third of the population today resides in urban areas. By far the largest metropolitan area is Manila, where there are well over six million people, accounting for 12% of the national total. The second largest metropolitan area is Cebu, but its population is only one-tenth that of Manila. As befits most such large cities, Manila is the major destination for tourists who visit the islands—about 800,000

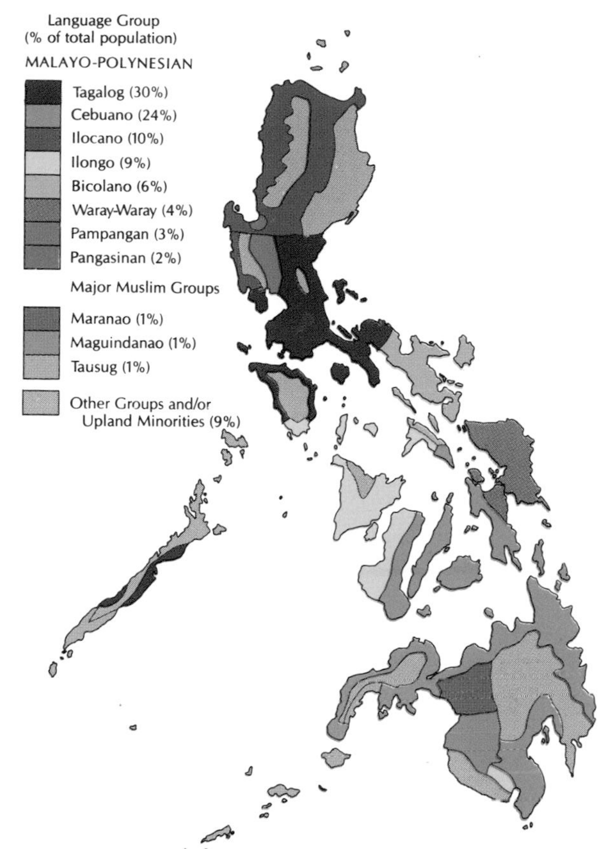

Ayala Avenue, Makati, Metro Manila (R. Ulack)

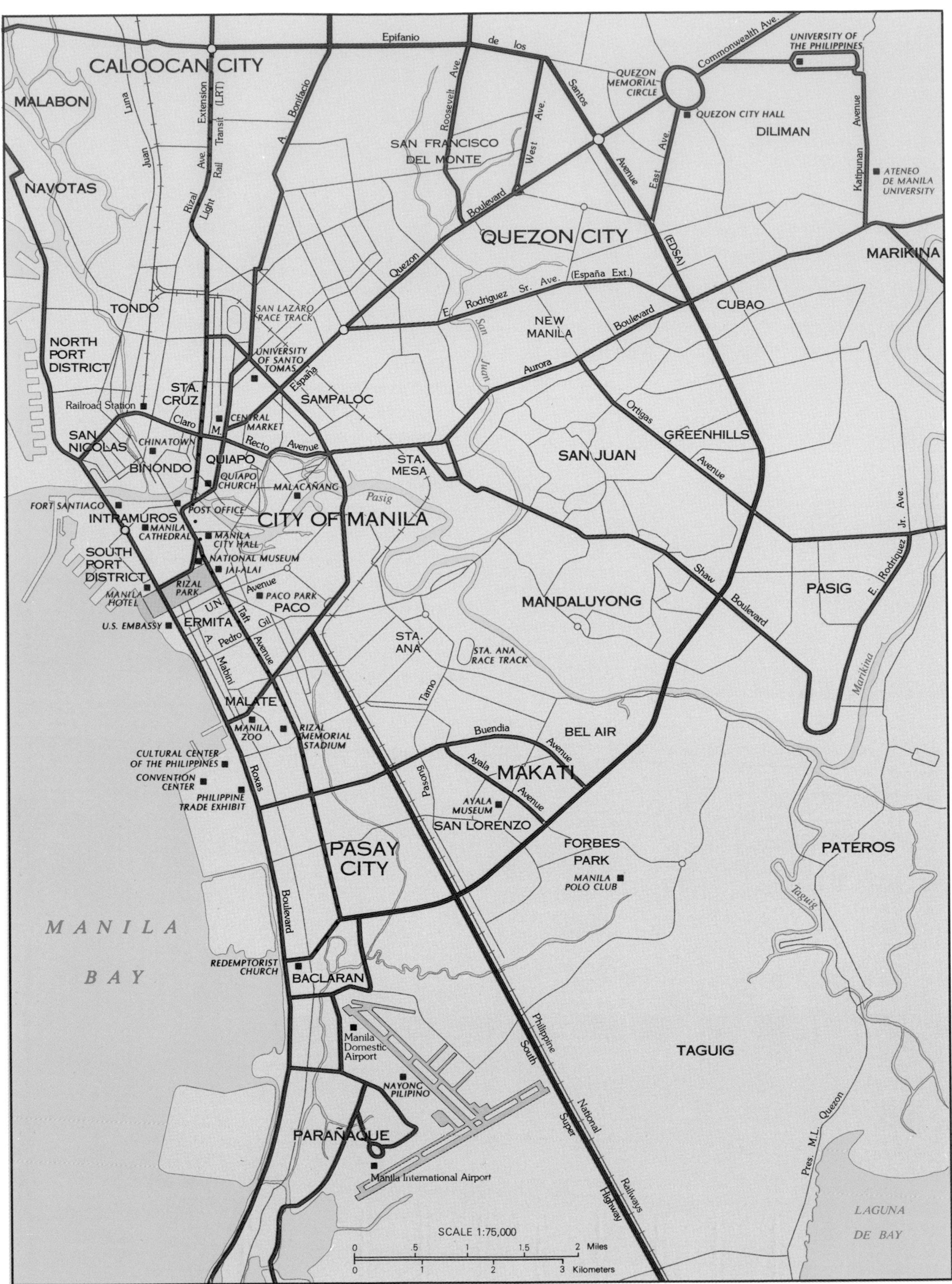


MANILA METROPOLITAN AREA

annually. Numerous points of interest throughout the Philippines and in Manila coupled with the well-known Filipino hospitality attract visitors from all over the world. The port zone, Rizal Park, older government buildings, a number of embassies (including that of the United States), hotels including the famous Manila Hotel, and the city's famous night clubs are still found in the old downtown area of Manila and along Roxas Boulevard, which parallels Manila Bay. But the "new" Manila is found in peripheral areas. Thus, Makati is the modern center for finance and business, the area where wealthy Filipinos and international businessmen and government bureaucrats reside. Quezon City, for a few years the national capital, is the area where the new government buildings, medical centers, and universities are located. And interspersed throughout these areas are found the poor of Manila who live in the numerous slum and squatter areas typical of cities throughout the developing world.

The varied cultural overlays that are represented in the Philippines are expressed in art, architecture, literature, and food. For example, the folk arts introduced from Indonesia have been altered by the subsequent impacts of the Chinese, Arabs, Spanish, and Americans; the Moros (Muslims) of the South produce a decorative art in which Islamic influences are combined with those from China. Such decoration is applied to fabric, brass, weapons (the *kris,* or knife, carried by Muslims), and metal boxes that hold the betel nut, which is chewed for its narcotic effect throughout many parts of Asia. Following the Spanish conquest, churches, sculptures of religious figures, and paintings began to reflect heavily the Catholic religious influence. Food, too, has been greatly modified and altered by the Chinese, Spanish, and Americans, and today most "native" dishes are a combination of several influences. Although there is some variation among regions in the Philippines, generally Philippine foods are not as spicy or distinctive as the dishes of most other Southeast Asian nations.

# 7

# *Malaysia*

*Area:* 127,581 sq mi (330,435 sq km); slightly larger than Norway or New Mexico

*Population:* 16,087,000

*Population Density:* 126 persons per sq mi (49 persons per sq km)

*Urban Population:* 34.2%

*Annual Average Rate of Population Increase:* 2.5%

*Crude Birth Rate:* 30.6 per 1,000 population

*Crude Death Rate:* 5.7 per 1,000 population

*Infant Mortality Rate:* 27 infant deaths per 1,000 live births

*Life Expectancy:* Male—67.0; Female—71.2

*Official Language:* Malay

*Currency:* Malay dollar (US$ = M$2.55 in 1988)

*Capital:* Kuala Lumpur

*Form of Government:* Federal constitutional monarchy with two legislative houses

*Head of Government:* Prime minister

*Chief of State:* Yang di-Pertuan Agong (king)

*Armed Forces (1985):* 110,000 (army—82%; navy—8%; air force—10%)

## HISTORICAL OVERVIEW

c. 1400: Malacca (Melaka) sultanate founded.

1511: Malacca captured by Portuguese.

1786: British acquire Penang Island.

1800: British acquire Province Wellesley.

1819: Singapore established by Thomas Stamford Raffles.

1824: Malacca ceded to British.

1826: Straits Settlements, consisting of Singapore, Malacca, Penang, Province Wellesley, and Dindings, established.

1832: Singapore made capital of Straits Settlements.

1841: James Brooke made Rajah of Sarawak by Sultan of Brunei.

1844: Labuan Island made part of Straits Settlement.

1896: Federated Malay States, consisting of Perak, Negeri Sembilan, Selangor, and Pahang, organized with capital at Kuala Lumpur.

1909: British-Siamese treaty brings Unfederated Malay States (Terengganu, Kedah, Perlis, and Kelantan) into British sphere.

1941–1945: Japanese occupation.

1946: Malayan Union proposal; Sarawak and North Borneo made crown colonies.

1948: Federation of Malaya established with Singapore separate.

1957: Federation of Malaya becomes independent.

1963: Federation of Malaysia (Malaya, Sarawak, Sabah, and Singapore) established.

1965: Singapore becomes independent.

Malaysia is centrally located in Southeast Asia and the peninsular portion sits astride the region's most strategic waterway, the Strait of Malacca. For these reasons Malaysia has historically been one of the more important maritime areas in the region. It was on peninsular Malaya's west coast, at the port of Malacca (Melaka) in 1511, that the Portuguese established the region's first European fort and set-

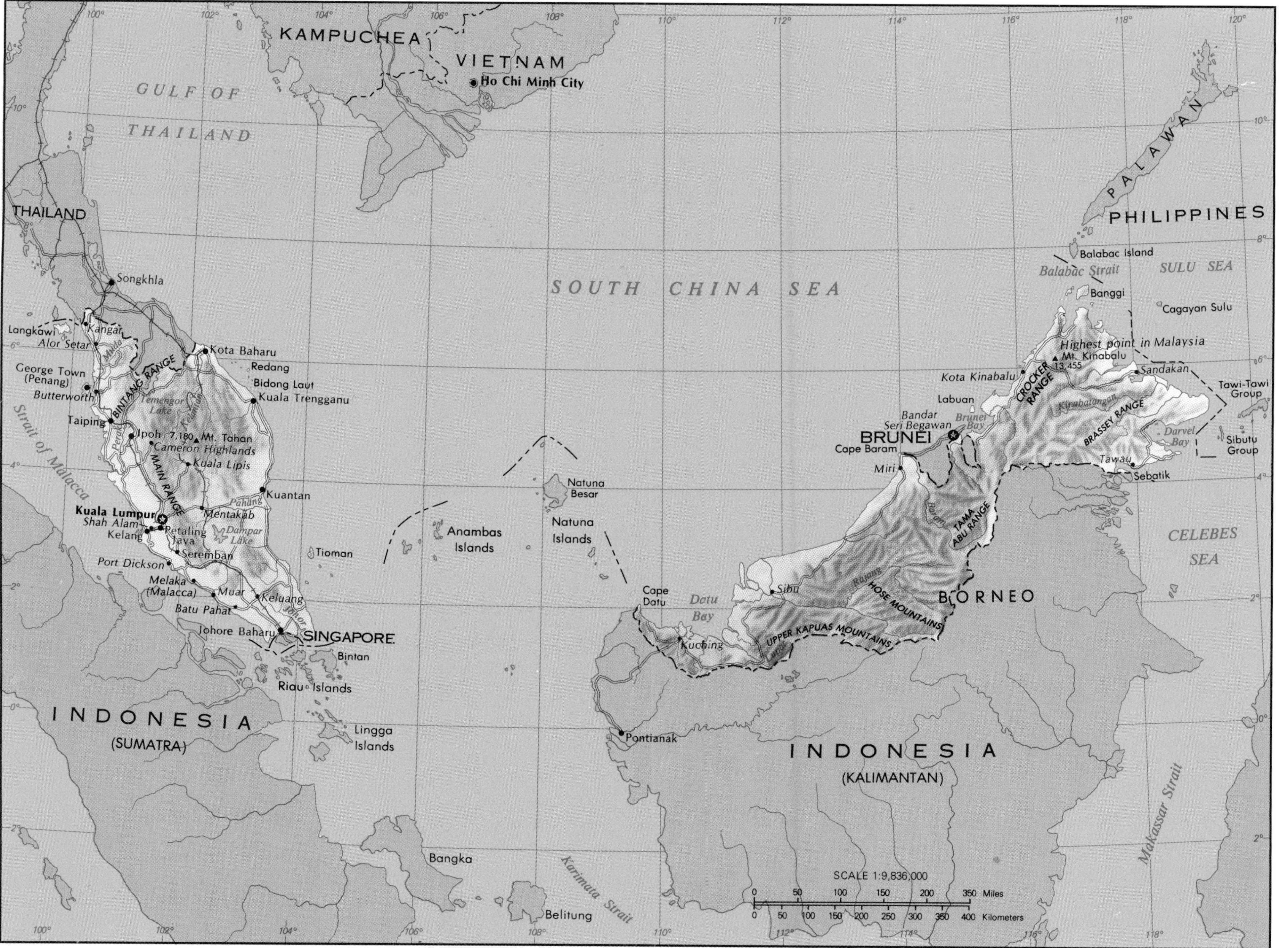

KAMPUCHEA
VIETNAM
Ho Chi Minh City
GULF OF THAILAND
THAILAND
Songkhla
Langkawi
Kangar
Alor Setar
George Town (Penang)
Butterworth
Taiping
BINTANG RANGE
Temengor Lake
Ipoh
7,186 Mt. Tahan
Cameron Highlands
MAIN RANGE
Kuala Lipis
Kota Baharu
Redang
Bidong Laut
Kuala Trengganu
Kuantan
Pahang
Mentakab
Dampar Lake
Kuala Lumpur
Shah Alam
Petaling Jaya
Kelang
Seremban
Port Dickson
Melaka (Malacca)
Muar
Keluang
Batu Pahat
Johor
Johore Baharu
SINGAPORE
Bintan
Riau Islands
Lingga Islands
Tioman
Strait of Malacca
INDONESIA
(SUMATRA)
Bangka
Belitung
Karimata Strait
SOUTH CHINA SEA
Anambas Islands
Natuna Besar
Natuna Islands
Cape Datu
Datu Bay
Kuching
Pontianak
Sibu
Rajang
UPPER KAPUAS MOUNTAINS
HOSE MOUNTAINS
BORNEO
TAMA ABU RANGE
Baram
Miri
Cape Baram
BRUNEI
Bandar Seri Begawan
Brunei Bay
Labuan
Kota Kinabalu
CROCKER RANGE
Highest point in Malaysia
Mt. Kinabalu 13,455
Kinabatangan
BRASSEY RANGE
Sandakan
Darvel Bay
Tawau
Sebatik
Tawi-Tawi Group
Sibutu Group
CELEBES SEA
PALAWAN
PHILIPPINES
Balabac Island
Balabac Strait
Banggi
SULU SEA
Cagayan Sulu
INDONESIA
(KALIMANTAN)
Makassar Strait
SCALE 1:9,836,000
Miles
Kilometers

tlement. The Portuguese, Dutch, and British all fought over this important area, and it was the British who finally gained control. Although now an independent nation, Singapore (established in 1819 by the British) was once politically part of colonial Malaya and was the capital of the Straits Settlement. Today both Malaysia and Singapore are members of the Association of Southeast Asian Nations (ASEAN) and have close economic ties. Since the Federation of Malaysia was established in 1963, Malaysia has been a fragmented nation consisting of two separate parts: peninsular Malaya and the northern part of Borneo, comprised of Sarawak and Sabah. Population is distributed very unevenly in the country. About 2.5 million, or only 17% of the total population, live in Sabah and Sarawak, which account for 60% of the land area. The vast majority of the population in peninsular Malaya reside near its west coast. A greater share of Malaysia's population, over one-third, live in urban areas including the national capital, Kuala Lumpur (or KL).

Malaysia, like the other nations of the region, has been dependent on primary commodities for revenues, in this case tin and rubber. With the exception of Singapore, Malaysia today has a more highly developed economy than the other nations of the region because it has diversified its production, lessened its dependency on imported foodstuff (especially rice), and begun exporting recently discovered offshore oil.

## THE PHYSICAL ENVIRONMENT

Geologically both parts of Malaysia are a part of the Sunda Shelf and are therefore older than that part of Southeast Asia undergoing active mountain-building activity. Peninsular Malaysia has a long, narrow, and rugged Main Range of mountains that trend roughly north–south. The maximum elevations are over 7,000 feet (2,100 m) and it is in this area that Malaysia's famous upland resorts are located, the best known of which are Fraser's Hill, Cameron Highlands, Genting Highlands, and Maxwell Hill (Bukit Larut). Such resorts served the colonialists and local elites in an earlier era and today they are popular among tourists as well as Malaysian citizens. Like peninsular Malaysia, Sabah and especially Sarawak have a flat coastal plain rising to rugged uplands toward the interior. Malaysia's highest mountain, Kinabalu, located in Sabah, is 13,455 feet (4,100 m).

Nowhere in Malaysia are there any great rivers like those of the mainland; rather, drainage consists of many short, rapidly flowing, flood-prone rivers that begin in the interior mountain ranges. The alluvial materials carried by the rivers on the western side of peninsular Malaysia's Main Range include tin, which is deposited at the break-in-slope; it was in these foothills that the country's first tin mines were established. The discovery of tin, coupled with access to the Strait of Malacca, are the major reasons for the intensive development of the western part of the peninsula.

Malaysia, which lies between 1° and 7° N. latitude, has an equatorial wet climate with no distinct dry season. Both the southwest (summer) and northeast (winter) monsoons affect the country and because of its position near the equator the marked seasonal rainfall differences of other areas in Southeast Asia are generally not found in Malaysia. For example, while the eastern coast of peninsular Malaysia is affected by the winter monsoon, with the greatest rainfall in November and December, rarely does any month receive less than 4 inches (10 cm). Throughout Malaysia, annual average precipitation amounts are between 80 (200) and

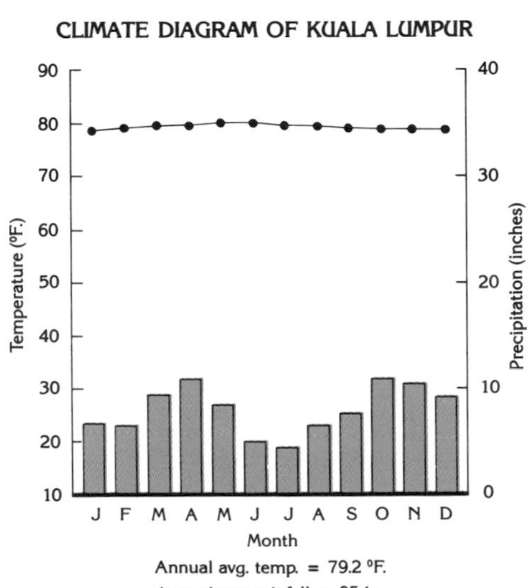

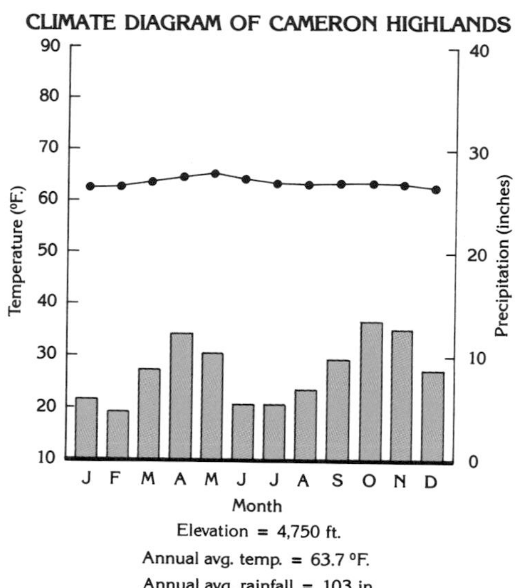


120 inches (300 cm). Also because of the country's position near the equator, average monthly temperatures are nearly always between 75°F (24°C) and 85°F (30°C). The exceptions of course are the highland areas where temperatures are lower. Average annual temperatures at the upland resorts are sometimes less than 65°F (18°C).

Among Malaysia's varied and abundant natural resources are its tropical forests, estimated to cover over two-thirds of the land area. Malaysian forests have among the world's greatest variety of flora and fauna. Among the thousands of species of plants that exist are over 2,000 kinds of trees. A single hectare (2.47 acres) may have more than 100 species of trees. As elsewhere in the region, much of the original (primary) forest has disappeared as a result of human activity. Mountain tribes clear land as shifting cultivators and other forests are cleared as a result of new settlement, expansion of agricultural lands, and lumbering activities. Indeed, lumber and wood products account for over one-tenth of the country's export value. Six major national parks have been established to preserve some of Malaysia's natural beauty and endangered flora and fauna. The largest of these, over 1,600 square miles (4,100 sq km), is Taman Negara in the central part of peninsular Malaysia. Located within the park is the peninsula's highest peak, Gunung (Mount) Tahan. In the parks and in other parts of the country are hundreds of species of birds, mammals, insects, and reptiles. Among Malaysia's more famous wildlife are tigers, elephants, tapirs, many species of deer including the tiny mouse deer, Sumatran rhinoceros, Malayan gaur (a large wild ox), hornbills, crocodiles, and cobras. Orangutans are forest dwellers in Sarawak.

## HISTORICAL BACKGROUND

The very earliest inhabitants of peninsular Malaysia were Negrito peoples who traveled overland from South Asia. There are several thousand descendents of these early travelers living in upland areas, among them the present-day Semang and Senoi. It was, however, the much larger migrations of Mongoloids who originated in southern China and came via mainland Southeast Asia who were the ancestors of the majority of lowland-dwelling Malays.

There are differences of opinion as to when large-scale settlement and the first states emerged among this group in the peninsula. One of the early states was coastal Langkasuka, which, according to Chinese records, was established as early as the first or second century A.D. By the eighth century an important kingdom was centered on Kedah, in the northwest corner of modern peninsular Malaysia. Certainly the peninsular area, like most of the rest of the region, was influenced by early Indianized kingdoms including those of the Mon, Khmer, and Thai on the mainland, and by Srivijaya and Majapahit in the archipelago.

The founding of the Islamic sultanate of Malacca around the beginning of the fifteenth century is usually considered the starting point in the history of present-day Malaysia. Malacca soon became the leading maritime power in the entire region and was the emporium of the spice trade and the major center for the diffusion of Islam, which had been adopted by Malacca's ruler in 1414. The strategic importance of Malacca brought the Portuguese initially in 1509, and in 1511 Malacca was conquered. Portuguese domination and control of the Strait of Malacca lasted for 130 years until 1641 when the Dutch, aided by the independent Malay state of Johore, defeated the Portuguese. Malacca remained under Dutch control until 1824 when the Anglo-Dutch

Dutch colonial *stadthuys* (administrative buildings), Melaka (courtesy R. Reed)

Treaty of London was signed and the English exchanged Bencoolen in Sumatra for Malacca.

The first English ship to arrive in Malay waters was in 1592 at Penang Island but it was not until 1786, when Francis Light founded Penang for the East India Company, that Britain's territorial advance began. In 1819 Thomas Stamford Raffles founded Singapore, soon to become the largest port in all of Southeast Asia. In 1826 Penang, Malacca, and Singapore, along with two small areas of coastal land (the Dindings and Province Wellesley) became known as the Straits Settlements. This colony was established to control maritime trade in the Strait of Malacca; at this time England had no intention of extending its control into the peninsula. In 1841 James Brooke, an English adventurer, became rajah of Sarawak, thereby establishing English supremacy in Borneo, and in 1881 the British North Borneo Company took control of the area that was named Sabah in 1963. Meanwhile, major deposits of tin had been discovered on the peninsula in the 1840s, which led to heavy mining activity. Internal disorder in the tin mining areas brought about, in part, by a large influx of Chinese immigrant labor caused England to expand its control over the peninsula. By 1896 British administration had been accepted in the Federated Malay States which consisted of Perak, Negeri Sembilan, Selangor, and Pahang, with the capital at Kuala Lumpur. In 1909 the Unfederated Malay States were established bringing Terengganu, Kedah, Perlis, and Kelantan into the British sphere of influence, and in 1914 Johore, the last territory, joined the Unfederated Malay States thus bringing British suzerainty over the area that encompasses present-day Malaysia.

As is so of all former colonies, colonial legacies in Malaysia included many that were problematic. At independence in 1957, for example, the country was faced with a heavy dependence on just two primary export commodities, tin and rubber. Also, large inequalities between urban and rural populations, a high rate of natural population increase, and a polyglot society which included large minorities of Chinese and Indians were all a result of the colonial period.

The move toward independence in Malaya

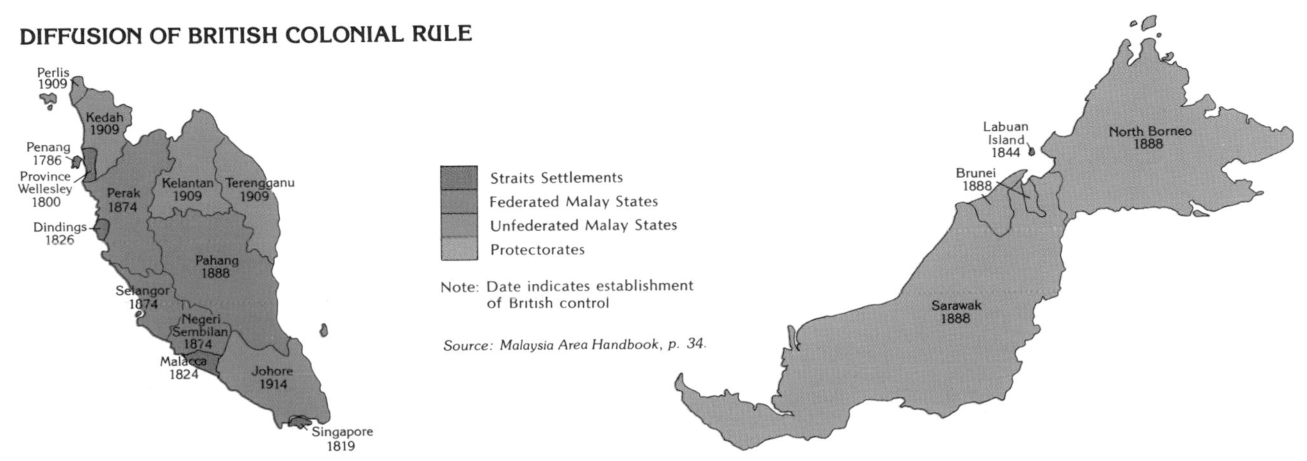

was much less vocal than in other former colonies. Although Malaysian nationalism and desire for self-rule was discussed as early as the 1930s, no radical party or group, with the important exception of the Malayan Communist Party founded in 1930, emerged as a rallying point for support. The British policy of accommodation with both wealthy Chinese and the local elite played an important role in keeping nationalistic fervor low-key. The eleven states of Malaya were united as the Malayan Union in 1946 and in 1948 they became the Federation of Malaya, still under British protection. Following World War II, an armed Communist revolt known as the "Emergency" commenced in 1948 and was not completely put down until 1960. Final independence for the eleven states of peninsular Malaya, within the Commonwealth, was achieved in 1957. Malaysia was established in 1963 when Singapore, Sarawak, and Sabah (formerly North Borneo) joined the Federation. In 1965 Chinese-dominated Singapore withdrew and became an independent nation, although Malaysia and Singapore maintain close economic ties. In the mid-1970s the Communist insurgency again threatened Malaysia along its border with Thailand but military cooperation between the two nations has at least temporarily quelled the revolt. Malaysia has had border disputes with Indonesia and the Philippines but these have been largely resolved and today Malaysia is a member of ASEAN, as well as the British Commonwealth, the Colombo Plan, and many other international organizations.

Malaysia is a parliamentary democracy based on universal suffrage. There are two legislative houses, the 68-member Senate (Dewan Negara) and the 176-member House of Representatives (Dewan Rakyat). The supreme head of state is His Majesty the Yang di-Pertuan Agong, a constitutional monarch elected for a five-year term by the Conference of Rulers. The head of government is the prime minister. Malaysia is a federation of thirteen states, each headed by a hereditary ruler. The capital, Kuala Lumpur, is a separate Federal Territory. Each of the eleven peninsular states is divided into administrative districts, Sabah is divided into four residencies, and Sarawak is divided into five divisions.

## THE ECONOMY

Malaysia is more developed economically than most of its Southeast Asian counterparts and this is indicated by the fact that it has a much higher per capita income, higher life expectancy, and only slightly more than one-third of its labor force is employed in agriculture; only one-fifth of its gross domestic product is derived from agriculture. There remain, however, the urban and rural inequalities, dependence on primary commodities, and the high rate of natural population increase typical of developing nations.

The most important agricultural commodities are rubber and palm oil, and Malaysia is the world's leading producer of both. Together they account for about one-fifth of the coun-

1. Johore
2. Kedah
3. Kelantan
4. Melaka (Malacca)
5. Negeri Sembilan
6. Pahang
7. Penang
8. Perak
9. Perlis
10. Sabah
11. Sarawak
12. Selangor
13. Trengganu
14. Federal Territory

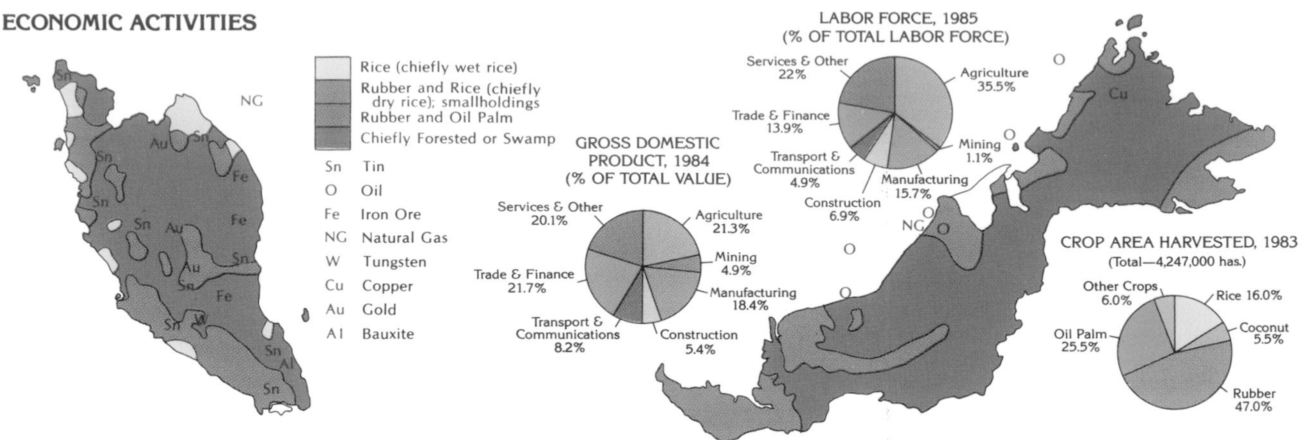


try's export revenues. Most of the rubber and oil palm, as well as rice, is produced in the western portion of the peninsula. Only about 16% of Malaysia's total cultivated area is in rice and the country has never been self-sufficient in this major subsistence crop. Even since the introduction of the high-yielding varieties of the Green Revolution and land development projects such as that at Muda River in the north, Malaysia has not been able to meet its needs, and in recent years it has produced only about three-fifths of its requirements. The majority of its rice needs are met by imports from Thailand. Other agricultural crops of commercial importance include cocoa (Malaysia is among the world's top 10 producers) and pepper, produced mainly in Sarawak.

The nation has abundant and varied natural resources. In addition to timber, another resource is tin, of which Malaysia is the world's leading producer, even though this commodity accounts for only 5% of the country's export earnings. Far more important to the economy is offshore oil, discovered in the 1960s. Although it is only a small portion of total world production, crude petroleum accounts for about one-quarter of the nation's export earnings. Copper, bauxite, and iron ore are the country's other important minerals. Production of all these commodities has fluctuated from year to year with the vagaries of world commodity markets.

Since the 1960s the industrial sector has been a major source of growth and today accounts for the employment of over 15% of the national labor force and nearly one-fifth of the gross domestic product. In its infancy indus-

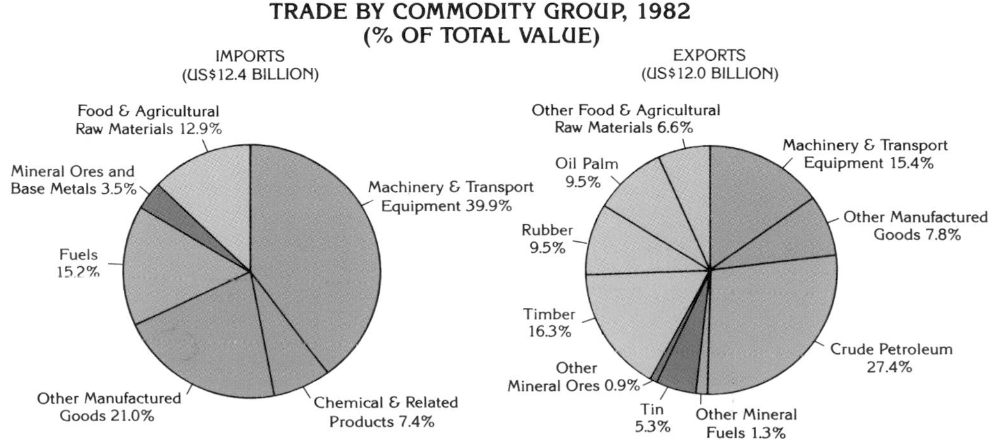


*Source: 1983 International Trade Statistics Yearbook (N.Y.: U.N., 1985)*

trial development followed the import substitution strategy but this has changed to one of export-oriented industrialization based on local resources. Today its most rapidly expanding industries are those based on the processing of timber, rubber, and palm oil, in addition to electronics and textiles; nearly one-quarter of Malaysia's export revenues are derived from manufactured products. Uncharacteristic of many developing nations Malaysia has in recent years enjoyed a trade surplus; in 1983 that surplus was nearly US$1 billion. Over three-fifths of the total trade was with Japan, the United States, and ASEAN.

## TRANSPORTATION

Peninsular Malaysia, and especially the western portion, has benefited from heavy development of the road, rail, and port systems during the British colonial period. Sarawak and Sabah, much more remote, have much less developed transportation networks. There is a total of some 1,600 miles (2,500 km) of railway and 24,000 miles (38,000 km) of roads. The vast majority are located in the peninsular portion of the country and most of these run north to south. In recent years Malaysia has begun to improve east–west transportation on the peninsula to better link the major urban areas of the west with the much less-developed eastern part.

The major ports are George Town (Penang) and Port Kelang on the Strait of Malacca and Kuching and Labuan in Sarawak and Sabah, respectively. The major international airport is at Kuala Lumpur and it is served by the Malaysian Airways System (MAS), as well as by most major international carriers. MAS also serves domestic airports and there are daily flights from Kuala Lumpur to Kuching and Kota Kinabalu, the capitals and largest cities of Sarawak and Sabah, respectively.

Malaysia's tourist industry is among the most rapidly growing in the region and over 2.5 million tourists have arrived annually during the 1980s. Attracted by upland resorts, miles of beautiful beaches and beach resorts, the scenic beauty of the national parks, wildlife, a variety of cultures, and Islamic architecture, the Tourist Development Corporation (TDC) is doing much to attract greater numbers of visitors. Tourists should be careful to avoid bringing illegal drugs into the country since in 1983 the government mandated the death penalty for persons convicted of drug offenses.

## PEOPLE AND CULTURE

The nation's original settlers were augmented during the British colonial period by Europeans, Chinese, Indians, and other Asian immigrants. Many Asian males arrived in the nineteenth century as laborers for the tin mines and rubber plantations. These immigrants, and especially the Chinese, have since become leading mercantilists and control a disproportionate share

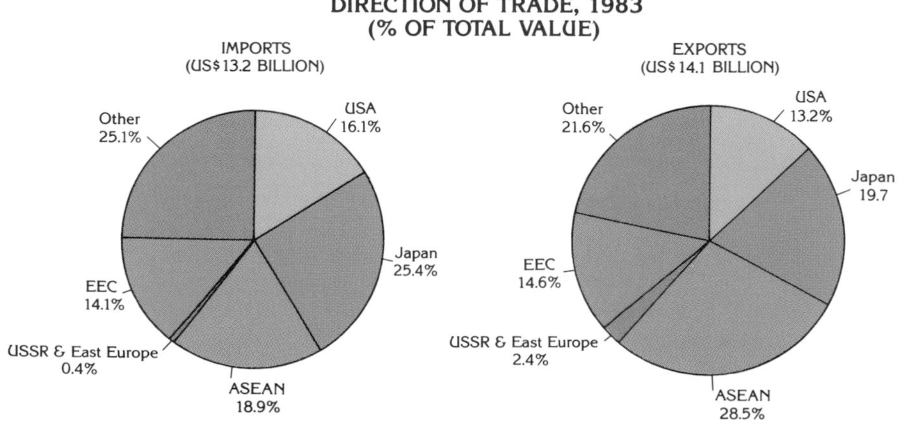


*Source: 1983 International Trade Statistics Yearbook (N.Y.: U.N., 1985)*

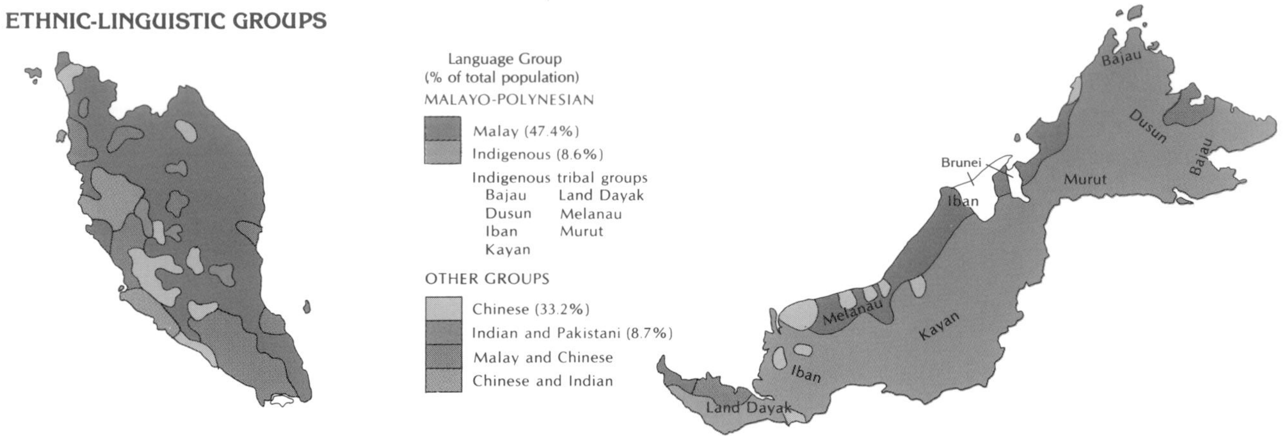


the retailing and wholesaling, shipping, and financial institutions. According to the Malaysian government estimates, Malays and "other indigenous groups" accounted for 59% of the population in 1983, Chinese accounted for 31%, 8% had their origins in South Asia (mostly Indians, but also included are those from Pakistan and Bangladesh), and 2% were listed as "other." Malays actually comprise less than the 59% (probably about 50%) indicated if "other indigenes" are subtracted from the total. In Sarawak, for example, such peoples, who include Iban and Melanau, comprise about one-half of the total. In addition to the large minorities of Chinese and tribal groups in Sabah, there is also a large contingent (nearly 100,000) of Philippine Muslim refugees who have settled there.

Iban dancers wearing batik cloth, Sibu, Sarawak (courtesy T. Leinbach)

The official language is Bahasa Malaysia, based on Malay, but English is also widely used and is a compulsory second language in all schools. A variety of Chinese dialects, Tamil and other languages from the Indian subcontinent, and Iban are also spoken widely.

Islam is the official religion, adhered to by about 53% of the population and by virtually all Malays. Nearly one-fifth of the population, mostly Chinese, are Buddhists, and a further 10% belong to one or a combination of other Chinese religions, including Confucianism and Taoism. About 7% are Hindu, 6% are Christian, and the remaining 5% are animists.

Thus Malaysia is a melting pot of different cultural traditions including that of China, India, the Middle East, and Europe, as well as that of the Malay Archipelago. A collective, distinctively Malay cultural pattern has emerged out of these many influences and artistic manifestations are best represented in literature, music, dance, and the decorative art forms. A distinctive example of such a form is the colorful batik cloth, eagerly sought by locals and visitors alike,

TO BATU CAVES
TO ZOO NEGARA AND AQUARIUM
Pahang Road
TITIWANGSA LAKE GARDENS
Batu
Gombak
Ipoh Road
Kuching Road
Tun Razak Road
GENERAL HOSPITAL
Tuanku Abdul Rahman Rd.
Gurney Road
Bunus
Raja Muda
KAMPUNG BAHARU
Raja Laut Road
Raja Abdullah Road
Tun Ismail Road
Kelang
SUNDAY MARKET
Sultan Ismail
Ampang Rd.
MEDAN TUANKU
KAMPUNG CHENDANA
RACE COURSE (PADANG LUMBA KUDA)
TAMAN FREEMAN
U.S. EMBASSY
(proposed)
Mahameru Road
PRIME MINISTER'S RESIDENCE
BUKIT NANAS (PINEAPPLE HILL)
Mahameru Rd.
Tun Perak
Raja Chulan
Parlimen
NATIONAL MONUMENT
OLD TOWN
JAME MOSQUE
SELANGOR CLUB
KARYANEKA HANDICRAFT CENTER
PARLIAMENT HOUSE
Sultan Hishamuddin Rd.
PADANG PARK
Pudu Raya Bus Station
LAKE GARDENS
CENTRAL MARKET
CHINATOWN
Railway Station
Pudu Rd.
Kebun Bunga Rd.
GENERAL POST OFFICE
SRI MAHAMARIAMMAN TEMPLE
Imbi Rd.
Damansara Road
Lake Perdana
NATIONAL MOSQUE
Bus Station
CHINWOO STADIUM
STADIUM NEGARA
NATIONAL MUSEUM
Railway Station
MERDEKA STADIUM
Hang Tuah Rd.
PUDU
Maharajalela Road
Travers Rd.
Brickfields Rd.
ISTANA NEGARA (ROYAL PALACE)
Istana Rd.
Loke Yew
PUDU MARKET
INTERNATIONAL BUDDHIST PAGODA
Syed Putra Rd.
Cheras Road
Bangsar Road
Sungai Besi Road
Kelang
to Airport and Petaling Jaya
SCALE 1:37,500
0 .5 1 Miles
0 .5 1 1.5 Kilometers

and articles made of pewter, an alloy of tin with lead.

The diversity of Malaysia's people as expressed in its variety of culinary experiences and the varied artistic expressions can perhaps best be witnessed in Kuala Lumpur, the nation's capital and largest metropolitan area. As one guide book states, "Malaysia is a veritable paradise for food lovers" (*All-Asia Guide,* p. 333) and in Kuala Lumpur one can obtain the full range of foods from rich and spicy Malay dishes (which are similar to Indonesian dishes) to the full range of Chinese regional specialties. One need not seek out a lavish restaurant to try the various dishes but would, in fact, be better off experimenting at the ubiquitous food-stalls such as those found at the Sunday Market. While Kuala Lumpur was established only in 1859 as a settlement of Chinese tin miners, the city offers an array of attractions representing the cultural diversity and history of the country. For example, the National Mosque (Masjid Negara) is one of the largest in all of Southeast Asia; there is also an international Buddhist pagoda as well and a major Hindu temple, Sri Mahamariamam. Not far north of the city are the famous Batu Caves, the location of an important Hindu shrine. In January or February on the festival day called Thaipusam, participating Hindus work themselves into a deep trance and climb to the caves while supporting a large wooden altar attached by steel hooks pierced through their skin. Other places worth visiting are art galleries, museums, a zoo, and handicraft centers; all offer a look at the rich and varied past of the nation.

Hindu penance festival, Batu Caves, near Kuala Lumpur (courtesy T. Leinbach)

# 8

# *Republic of Singapore*

*Area:* 239 sq mi (618 sq km); one-fifth the size of Rhode Island

*Population:* 2,586,000 (1986)

*Population Density:* 10,820 persons per sq mi (4,184 persons per sq km)

*Urban Population:* 100%

*Annual Average Rate of Population Increase:* 1.1%

*Crude Birth Rate:* 15.9 per 1,000 population

*Crude Death Rate:* 5.0 per 1,000 population

*Infant Mortality Rate:* 9 infant deaths per 1,000 live births

*Life Expectancy:* Male—69.9 years; Female—76.2 years

*Official Languages:* Chinese; Malay; Tamil; English

*Currency:* Singapore dollar (US$ = S$2.05 in 1988)

*Capital:* Singapore

*Form of Government:* Unitary multiparty republic with one legislative house

*Chief of State:* President

*Head of Government:* Prime minister

*Armed Forces (1985):* 55,500 (army—81%; air force—11%; navy—8%)

## HISTORICAL OVERVIEW

1819: British, under Thomas Stamford Raffles, establish trading post.

1824: Local Malay chiefs cede Singapore Island to British East India Company.

1826: Singapore, along with Penang and Melaka (Malacca), become part of Straits Settlements under East India Company.

1867: Straits Settlements become a Crown Colony.

1942–1945: Japanese occupation.

1946: Singapore becomes a separate Crown Colony.

1959: Internal self-government granted; Lee Kuan Yew becomes prime minister.

1963: Federation of Malaysia formed a constituent state with Singapore.

1965: Singapore separated from Malaysia and becomes fully independent; Singapore joins Commonwealth.

Singapore is really the smallest nation in Southeast Asia and is unique in the region in that it is a city-state; nearly the entire population is urban. Singapore is also unique in the region in that it can be classified as a developed nation. It has, except for oil-rich Brunei, the highest per capita gross national product of any Southeast Asian nation and its economy is based on manufacturing and services, rather than the production of primary commodities. Culturally the nation is also atypical in that the majority of its population, over three-quarters, is ethnically Chinese.

## THE PHYSICAL ENVIRONMENT

Singapore is comprised of one main island, which accounts for over 90% of its total territory, and more than fifty smaller islands and islets. Singapore Island has low relief; only one elevation, Bukit Timah, exceeds 500 feet (150 m). Geologically, the island is a continuation of the mountains of the Malay Peninsula and consists of a granitic core. Much of the land near the coast is mangrove swamp but there has been considerable reclamation of such land. One major reclamation area is the extensive region in the southwestern part of Singapore Island that comprises the Jurong Industrial Estate.

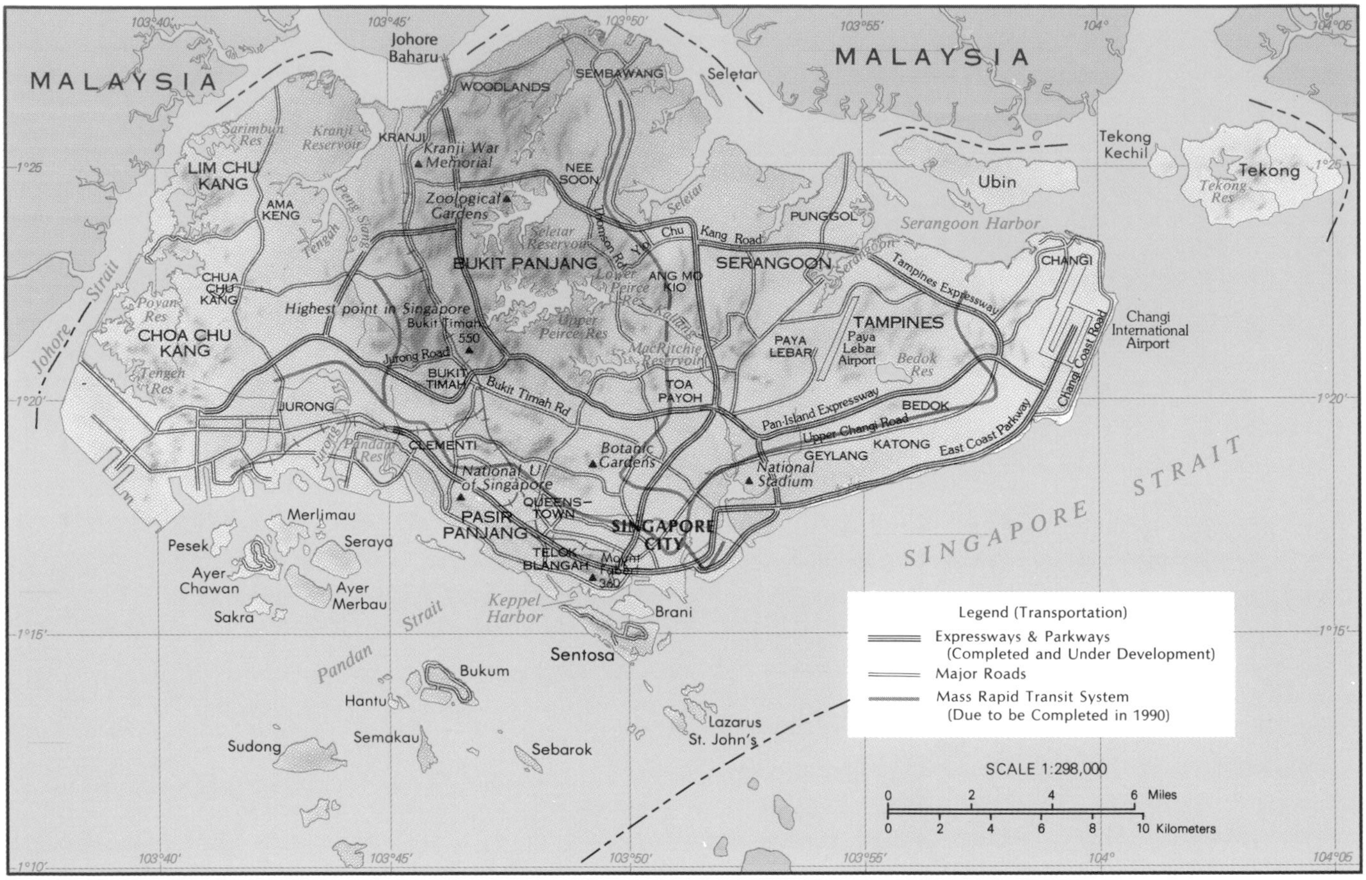

Since Singapore lies almost on the equator, its climate is of course equatorial. The annual average rainfall is 95 inches (240 cm) and is distributed quite evenly throughout the year, although November, December, and January receive the greatest monthly amounts. The annual average temperature is 80°F (27°C) and no single month averages more than 2°F higher or lower than that.

Singapore has very little in the way of natural resources. A small area of forest remains at the higher elevations in the central part of the main island. There is an inadequate supply of fresh water and Singapore depends upon piped water from nearby Malaysia, to which it is linked by a causeway across the Johore Strait. The most important natural resources are the country's location and its sheltered, deepwater harbor. Singapore is centrally located in Southeast Asia and sits astride the major shipping lanes, and for these reasons it has become the world's busiest port in terms of total tonnage.

CLIMATE DIAGRAM OF SINGAPORE

Annual avg. temp. = 80.0 °F.
Annual avg. rainfall = 95 in.

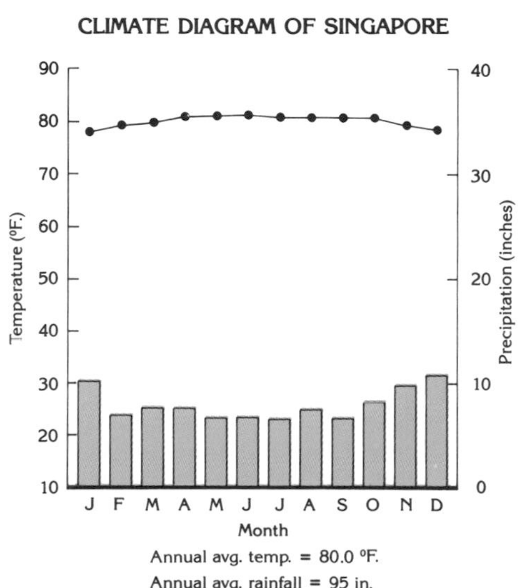

## HISTORICAL BACKGROUND

Long before the arrival of the Europeans in the region, Singapore (from the Sanskrit Siṁhapura, meaning Lion City) was a major trading center known as Temasek. Subservient to Srivijaya, Majapahit, and Ayutthaya at various times, the trading port flourished until the fourteenth century, when it was destroyed by war. Its rulers fled to Melaka which soon became a renowned trading empire. For the next four centuries Singapore was a very minor fishing village populated by a handful of boat people (*orang laut*).

Singapore's rebirth came about in 1819 when Thomas Stamford Raffles of the British East India Company, realizing the strategic importance of the location, established a trading post at the mouth of the Singapore River. Five years later Singapore Island was ceded to the Company by the local chiefs. In 1826 Singapore was joined with Penang and Melaka to form the Straits Settlements and after 1832 the Straits Settlements were administered from Singapore. From the very beginning, Singapore under Raffles had a policy of unrestricted immigration and free trade. Under such a policy traders and settlers of all backgrounds came to the port, among them were Malays, Chinese, Indians, and maritime groups from many parts of the East Indies.

In 1867 the Straits Settlements became a Crown Colony and therefore under direct British rule. Two years later, in 1869, the Suez Canal was opened and Singapore developed even more rapidly. Events in the Malay states in the late nineteenth century, most notably the exploitation of the rich tin mines and the development of commercial agriculture based largely on rubber, further enhanced Singapore's economic position since it became the commercial center for these operations.

After the three-year Japanese occupation ended in 1945 the British returned, and by the following year civil rule had been restored. However, the British no longer maintained the Straits Settlements; rather, Singapore was established as a Crown Colony separate from the Malayan Union, which comprised all the Malay states and Penang and Malacca. This did not please everyone in Singapore and the first political party was formed, the Malayan Democratic Union (MDU), which favored joining a socialist Malayan Union. The MDU became heavily leftist and in 1948 after the outbreak of the Communist-led Emergency in Malaya, the Communist Party and the MDU were outlawed in Singapore.

In 1955 a new constitution was adopted which gave some measure of self-government to Singapore. In 1959 complete internal self-rule was achieved, and Lee Kuan Yew, who led the left-wing People's Action Party (PAP), became prime minister. The new government was committed to a program of rapid industrialization and social reform. Under an impressive Master Plan, one of the more visible evidences of social change has been the massive public housing developments that replaced slum and squatter areas. Under Lee Kuan Yew's leadership, the PAP has been in power ever since and Singapore has moved forward economically, its residents enjoying a standard of living well above that of other Southeast Asians.

In 1963 the independent Federation of Malaysia came into being with Singapore as a constituent state. Two years later in 1965, because of major differences between Malaysia and Singapore, Singapore became a fully independent nation. Later in the same year Singapore joined both the British Commonwealth and the United Nations and in 1967 Singapore was one of the founding members of ASEAN.

Singapore is a democratic republic with one legislative body, the 79-member Parliament, elected by universal suffrage. Although Singapore is a multiparty state, 77 of the members of Parliament in 1984 belonged to the People's Action Party. The president is elected by Parliament and executive authority is vested in the Cabinet, headed by the prime minister, who is appointed by the president.

## THE ECONOMY

Singapore has an industrial and services-oriented economy and depends upon imports of natural resources to meet its basic requirements. Over one-quarter of its gross domestic product is derived from manufacturing and a similar proportion of the labor force is em-

Public housing, Singapore (courtesy T. Leinbach)

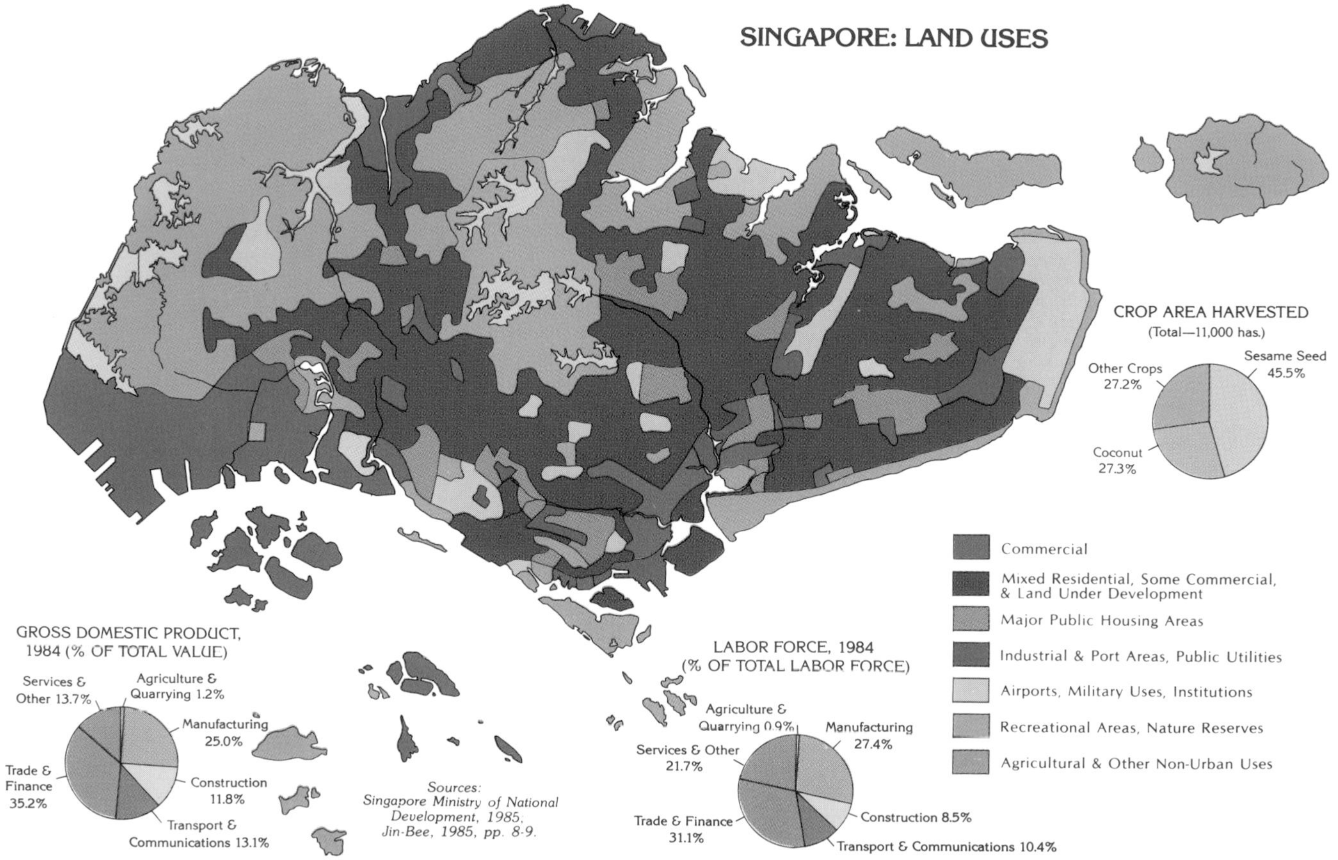

## SINGAPORE: LAND USES

CROP AREA HARVESTED
(Total—11,000 has.)

Sesame Seed 45.5%
Other Crops 27.2%
Coconut 27.3%

Commercial
Mixed Residential, Some Commercial, & Land Under Development
Major Public Housing Areas
Industrial & Port Areas, Public Utilities
Airports, Military Uses, Institutions
Recreational Areas, Nature Reserves
Agricultural & Other Non-Urban Uses

GROSS DOMESTIC PRODUCT, 1984 (% OF TOTAL VALUE)

Services & Other 13.7%
Agriculture & Quarrying 1.2%
Manufacturing 25.0%
Construction 11.8%
Transport & Communications 13.1%
Trade & Finance 35.2%

LABOR FORCE, 1984 (% OF TOTAL LABOR FORCE)

Agriculture & Quarrying 0.9%
Manufacturing 27.4%
Services & Other 21.7%
Construction 8.5%
Transport & Communications 10.4%
Trade & Finance 31.1%

*Sources:*
*Singapore Ministry of National Development, 1985.*
*Jin-Bee, 1985, pp. 8-9.*

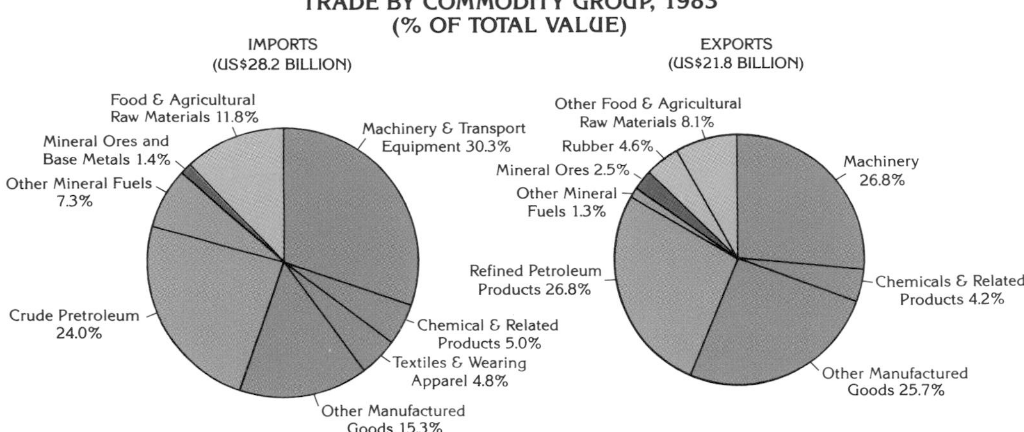


*Source: 1983 International Trade Statistics Yearbook (N.Y.: U.N., 1985)*

ployed in this sector. Services, including transportation and communications, trade, and finance, account for over three-fifths of the GDP and labor force. In terms of finances, Singapore is the world center of the tin and rubber markets. It is also a major port, served by more than 500 shipping lines. The principal manufacturing industry is petroleum refining and the city-state has the third largest refining complex in the world with a capacity of well over one million barrels daily. Other important industries include shipbuilding, textiles, electronics, and sawmilling. Most industry is located on estates, the largest of which is the Jurong Industrial Estate. Labor shortages in manufacturing and in construction have necessitated the importation of foreign labor, mostly from other ASEAN nations. There were estimated to be about 150,000 foreign workers in 1985.

Singapore experiences a trade deficit, but one that has narrowed in the 1980s. The major import is petroleum, which is used to produce the major export, refined petroleum products. The main source of crude petroleum is Saudi Arabia (which accounted for 11% of Singapore's imports in 1983). Malaysia is the second major source of raw materials for Singapore's economy, accounting for nearly 15% of imports by value, and Singapore handles the majority of peninsular Malaysia's external trade. Three countries, the United States, Japan, and Malaysia, together account for about one-half of Singapore's total trade.

There is very little land available for agricul-

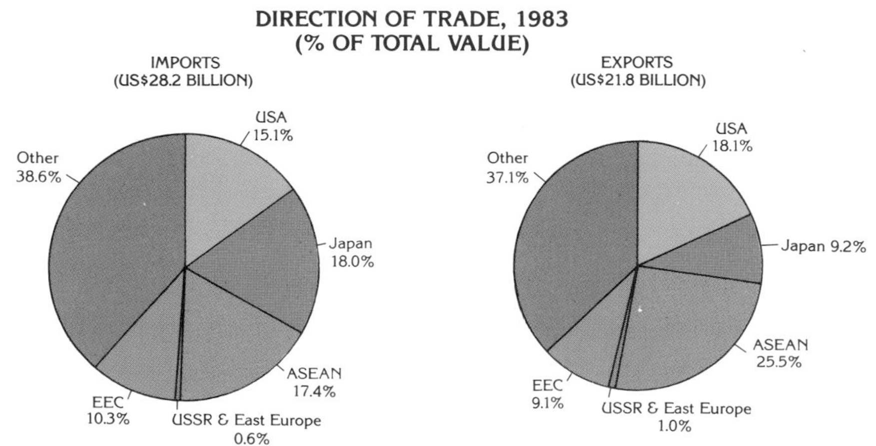


*Source: 1983 International Trade Statistics Yearbook (N.Y.: U.N., 1985)*

ture, and the farming that exists is devoted to truck farming (vegetables), pig and poultry raising, and egg and fish production. The city is not self-sufficient in any agricultural products and food and food products and beverages account for about 8% of the value of imports.

## TRANSPORTATION AND TOURISM

Singapore is the world's busiest port; in 1984 over 63 million metric tons of cargo were discharged and over 40 million tons were loaded. The port includes modern container terminal facilities, as well as conventional wharves. Over 25,000 vessels dock at Singapore each year.

There are about 16 miles (26 km) of railway and over 1,600 miles (2,500 km) of road in the country. The Malaysian Railways network extends into Singapore; there are several trains daily to Kuala Lumpur and it is possible to travel by train all the way to Bangkok and beyond. Nearly 500,000 motor vehicles were registered in 1984, nearly half of which were privately owned cars. A cross-island expressway system is nearing completion and the Metropolitan Rapid Transit (MRT) system, when completed in 1990, will further facilitate mobility in the city-state. A new international airport was completed at Changi in 1981 and some 35 international airlines operate over 80 flights daily from all over the world.

In 1984 nearly three million tourists visited Singapore. The country is a major tourist destination for the elite from other ASEAN nations (as well as for those from Europe, Japan, and North America) because of its excellent shopping facilities and low prices for imported goods. Singapore is a relatively free port, with protective duties on only a few locally made items such as garments and furniture. This, in addition to the blend of cultures and varied culinary ex-

Docks near Jurong industrial area (courtesy T. Leinbach)

**SINGAPORE METROPOLITAN AREA**

periences, helps to keep most of the more than fifty tourist hotels occupied. In all, Singapore has over 16,000 hotel rooms, a figure that by 1990 is expected to increase by 80%.

## PEOPLE AND CULTURE

Since as early as 1827, the Chinese have been the largest single community in Singapore. By 1900 they constituted over three-quarters of the total population and their proportion has since remained at that level. Most Chinese are descendents of those who came from southern China. They speak a number of different dialects including Hokkien, Cantonese, Teochew, Hakka, and Hainanese. The vast majority of Chinese who arrived in the nineteenth and early twentieth centuries were males and only later did women arrive to settle, marry, and raise families. The peak year for immigration was 1927, when 360,000 Chinese arrived. The Great Depression brought about the first restrictions on immigration in Singapore. A quota was imposed on the entry of Chinese men, but it did not affect Chinese women, who were still greatly in the minority.

Other major groups in Singapore include Malays, who comprise nearly 15% of the total, and descendents of immigrants from India, Pakistan, Bangladesh, and Sri Lanka, who together account for nearly 7%. As in the case of the Chinese, persons whose ethnic origin is the Indian subcontinent speak a wide variety of languages and dialects including Tamil (an official language), Urdu, Hindi, Telugu, and Bengali. Europeans and other groups account for the remaining 2% of the population.

Primary and secondary education is available in all four of the official languages of Chinese, Malay, Tamil, and English. A 1978 policy of bilingualism made it mandatory for students who wanted to enter secondary schools to pass examinations in Mandarin Chinese and English. Beginning in 1987 English was to be the medium of instruction in all schools. There are a number of technical and vocational institutes. The National University of Singapore is the principal institution of higher education.

The religious composition of the population is reflected in its ethnic make-up. According to the 1980 census 24% of the population were Taoist or Confucianist, 22% Buddhist, 13% Muslim, 8% Christian, 3% Hindu, and the remainder were followers of other beliefs or were nonreligious.

Cultural characteristics, including art, architecture, the fine arts, dress, and food, are reflected in the various cultures represented—Chinese, Indian, Malay, British, among the more important. British colonial architecture is well-represented by the Parliament Building and City Hall. The old, colonial Raffles Hotel, where Somerset Maugham stayed on his visits, is another relic of the colonial period, and still quite popular among old-timers and romantics. Most tourists today, however, stay in the dozens of new, fancy but rather sterile, high-rise chain hotels located in the vicinity of the Orchard Road shopping areas. Chinese, Indian, and Muslim religious shrines are scattered throughout the city and are perhaps best represented in the architecture of the Shuang Lin Temple, Sri Mariamman Temple, and Sultan Mosque, respectively. Culinary delights abound in Singapore and the city can hold its own with any city in the region in terms of variety and quality of offerings. Among the many possibilities, one can experience lavish traditional Chinese dining, exquisite seafood, dishes which combine Malay and Chinese styles (for example, *nonya* food, which is southern Chinese cooking blended with the spices of the Malay), or outdoor eating at foodstalls such as those at the Satay Club or the Newton Circus car park. Artistic representations of the various cultural groups can be seen at the National Museum and Art Gallery and purchased at the Handicraft Centre. Flora and fauna are well represented and displayed in the Jurong Bird Park, Botanic Gardens, Zoological Gardens, Orchid Farm, and Crocodile Farm.

# 9

# *Negara Brunei Darussalam*

*Area:* 2,226 sq mi (5,765 sq km); slightly larger than Delaware

*Population:* 241,000 (1986)

*Population Density:* 108 persons per sq mi (42 persons per sq km)

*Urban Population:* 80.8%

*Annual Average Rate of Population Increase:* 2.6%

*Crude Birth Rate:* 29.8 per 1,000 population

*Crude Death Rate:* 3.5 per 1,000 population

*Infant Mortality Rate:* 12 infant deaths per 1,000 live births

*Life Expectancy:* Male—70.1 years; Female—72.7 years

*Official Language:* Malay

*Currency:* Brunei dollar (US$ = B$2.05 in 1988)

*Capital:* Bandar Seri Begawan

*Form of Government:* Monarchy

*Chief of State:* Sultan

*Head of Government:* Prime minister

*Armed Forces:* 4,050 (army—89%; navy—9%; air force—2%; all services are part of the army); in addition, a British army Gurkha battalion is stationed in Brunei.

## HISTORICAL OVERVIEW

15th century: Brunei becomes independent sultanate.

1842: James Brooke appointed rajah of Sarawak by Brunei sultan.

1846: Labuan Island ceded to Britain.

1888: Brunei becomes a British protectorate.

1929: Oil discovered at Seria.

1983: Brunei becomes fully independent.

Brunei is the last of the nations of Southeast Asia to achieve independence. Today, the economy of this tiny nation revolves almost wholly around oil and gas production and the great oil wealth means that Brunei has one of the world's highest per capita Gross National Products ($20,520 in 1983). Predominantly Muslim, Brunei is one of the few remaining monarchies in the world and supreme authority rests with the sultan, the twenty-ninth ruler in the present line.

## THE PHYSICAL ENVIRONMENT

Brunei is a fragmented nation on northern Borneo, surrounded by the Malaysian state of Sarawak. Except for its narrow coastal plain it is mostly rugged and hilly. Maximum altitudes of around 3,000 feet (915 m) are in the southern, inland portion of the two separate parts of the nation. Drainage is toward the north and the Belait River is the country's longest.

Located 5° north of the equator, Brunei's climate is governed by the monsoons. Annual total rainfall is over 100 inches (250 cm) near the coast and approaches 200 inches (500 cm) in some parts of the hilly interior. Most of the rain falls between November and March when the low-sun (northeast) monsoon occurs. Some three-quarters of the country is covered by tropical rainforests and lumber, notably hardwoods, is a resource of some importance. Fauna include monkeys (such as the rare proboscis monkey) and a large variety of reptiles, insects, and birds, such as the hornbill, once in great demand by Chinese traders for its hornbill-ivory. Early Chinese traders also sought edible birds' nests for soup from Brunei and other parts of archipelagic Southeast Asia.

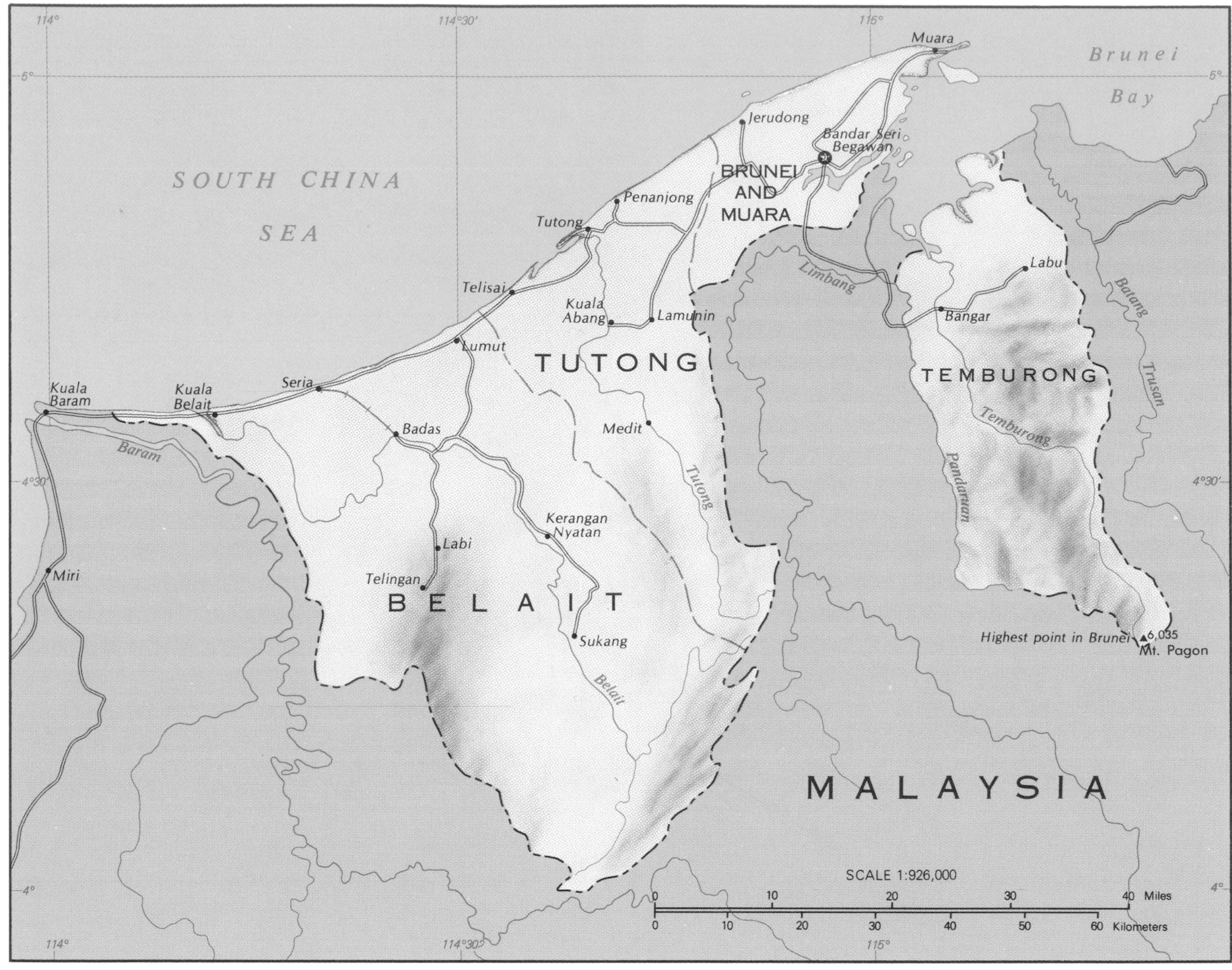


## HISTORICAL BACKGROUND

Not much is known about Brunei's early history but it is clear that Chinese influence had entered the area at least as early as the sixth century. After being ruled by the Javanese Majapahit empire, the sultanate of Brunei became independent about the fifteenth century. At about the same time, Sultan Mohammed, the first in the present line of sultans, embraced Islam. By the sixteenth century Brunei had extended its power to include most of the coastal areas of present-day Sarawak and Sabah as well as much of the rest of Borneo and the Sulu Archipelago. In the seventeenth century internal strife gradually brought about a decline of power.

European intervention in the area began in the nineteenth century with the coming of the English adventurer, James Brooke. In 1841 Sarawak was ceded to Brooke and in the next year he was appointed rajah of Sarawak by the sultan. In 1846 Labuan Island, at the mouth of Brunei Bay, was ceded to Britain and became part of the Straits Settlement. Gradually the rest of northern Borneo came under British rule and in 1888 Brunei was declared a protectorate.

Following World War II and the Japanese occupation (1941–1945) Brunei gradually attained a greater degree of autonomy and in 1959, the year that Brunei's first written constitution was promulgated, the country was declared a "protected state" with Great Britain retaining responsibility for Brunei's defense and foreign relations. Following this the sultan indicated that Brunei might eventually join the proposed Malaysian Federation, but in 1962 a bloody revolt opposing entrance into the Federation ensued. British forces were called in, the rebellion was put down, and the sultan subsequently decided against joining. Both Indonesia and Malaysia assured the sultan that they would recognize an independent Brunei. This allayed fears that one of its larger neighbors might take over the micro-state, and at the end of 1983 Brunei achieved full independence. There is a defense agreement with Great Britain, and a battalion of British Gurkhas is stationed in Brunei, with the specific role of guarding the onshore oil and gas fields. In 1984 Brunei became the 159th member of the United Nations and the 6th member of ASEAN.

As of the 1959 constitution, supreme executive authority has been vested in the sultan, although since the 1962 revolt some of the provisions of the constitution have been suspended and the sultan has ruled by decree. There is a Privy Council which advises the sultan, a Council of Ministers, and a 20-member elected legislative council. The nation is divided into four administrative districts, each presided over by a district officer.

## THE ECONOMY

The economy is almost wholly dependent upon the petroleum and natural gas discovered in 1929. Nearly all export earnings are derived from these fossil fuels. Today, most of the oil is produced in offshore wells and whereas some is refined within Brunei, the majority of the oil is piped to the Lutong refinery in nearby

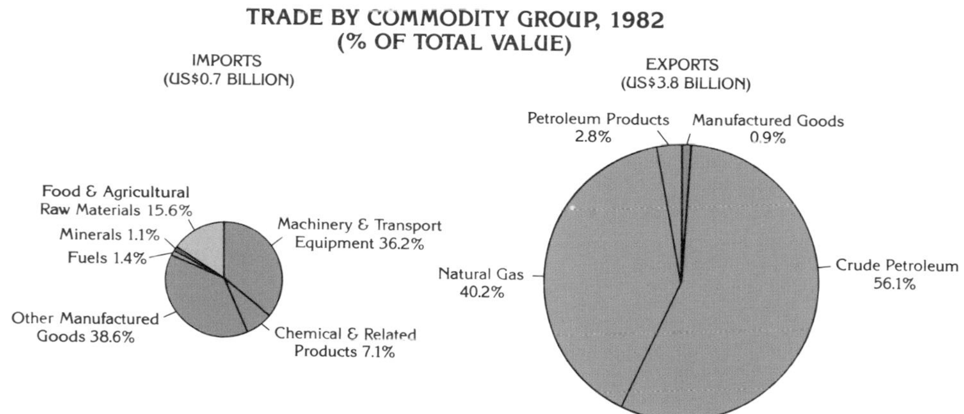


*Source: 1983 International Trade Statistics Yearbook (N.Y.: U.N., 1985)*

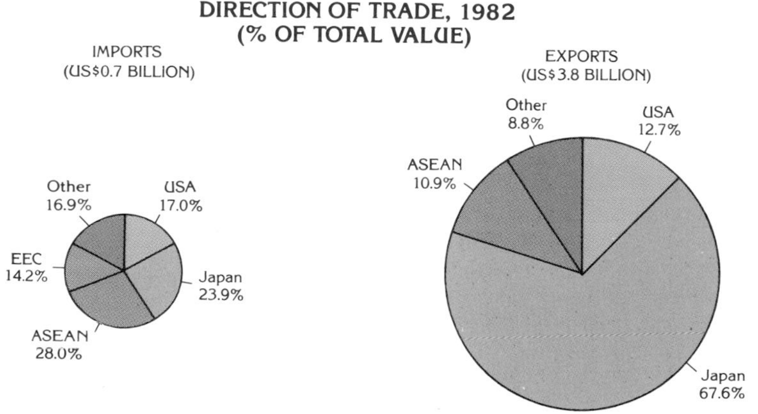


*Source: 1983 International Trade Statistics Yearbook (N.Y.: U.N., 1985)*

and medical services for its citizenry, and there is a non-contributory pension plan for the aged and disabled, as well as financial assistance for the poor.

The capital is noted for its elaborate Islamic architecture including the Omar Ali Saifuddin Mosque, one of the largest mosques in Southeast Asia. Completed in 1958, the mosque is linked to an elegant concrete royal barge constructed in the middle of a lagoon. Other places of interest in the capital include a large memorial museum to Sir Winston Churchill (who never visited Brunei but was held in high esteem by the sultan); one of the region's largest aquariums; the Royal Ceremonial Hall; and the Brunei Museum, located about four miles from the city. Just south of the city on a bluff overlooking the Brunei River and the capital is the recently completed Royal Palace, the Istana Nurul Imam, with two domes covered with 22-karat gold leaf. Containing nearly 1,800 rooms and built at a cost of perhaps US$500 million, the palace is by far the largest and costliest royal residence ever constructed anywhere. The palace is generally closed to the public but sometimes visits can be arranged.

# 10

# Kingdom of Thailand

*Area:* 198,114 sq mi (513,115 sq km); about the size of Spain or almost twice the size of Colorado

*Population:* 52,442,000 (1986)

*Population Density:* 265 persons per sq mi (102 persons per sq km)

*Urban Population:* 19.5%

*Annual Average Rate of Population Increase:* 1.8%

*Crude Birth Rate:* 25.3 per 1,000 population

*Crude Death Rate:* 7.4 per 1,000 population

*Infant Mortality Rate:* 52 infant deaths per 1,000 live births

*Life Expectancy:* Male—61.3 years; Female—67.3 years

*Official Language:* Thai

*Currency:* Thai baht (US$ = B24.7 in 1988)

*Capital:* Bangkok (Krung Thep)

*Form of Government:* Constitutional monarchy with a National Assembly comprised of a Senate and House of Representatives

*Chief of State:* King

*Head of Government:* Prime minister

*Armed Forces (1985):* 235,300 (army—68%; navy—14%; air force—18%)

## HISTORICAL OVERVIEW

Mid-1200s: First Thai kingdoms (Sukhothai and Chiang Mai) established.

1350–1767: Ayutthaya period.

1767–1782: Thon Buri period.

1782–present: Bangkok (Rattanakosin) period.

1782: Capital moved from Thon Buri to Bangkok.

1851–1868: Reign of King Mongkut (Rama IV) who opened Siam to Western ideas yet preserved its independence.

1868–1910: Reign of King Chulalongkorn (Rama V).

1932: Bloodless coup d'etat ended absolute monarchy.

1939: Name changed from Siam to Thailand.

Thailand is unique in the region since it is the only nation that was never colonized by the West. That is not to say that Thailand has not been influenced by the West, or for that matter by other external powers. In part because of its position as a buffer state between the British in Burma and the French in Indochina, and partly because its rulers have followed a policy of accommodation toward powerful external influences in neighboring lands, Thailand has remained free from complete domination by a foreign power.

As with the other nations in the region, Thailand is ethnically diverse, but the vast majority of its people adhere to one major religion, in this case Theravada Buddhism. The nation's central position on the Southeast Asian mainland has meant that diverse groups from a variety of origins have migrated into, and through, Thailand and as a result the descendents of these early migrants today speak languages from four different language families.

Since the 1970s Thailand has been a haven for hundreds of thousands of refugees who have fled from the war-torn lands of Kampuchea, Laos, and Vietnam. Relations between Thailand and Vietnam have worsened in the 1980s following several Vietnamese incursions into Thailand.

Thailand, like other Southeast Asian na-

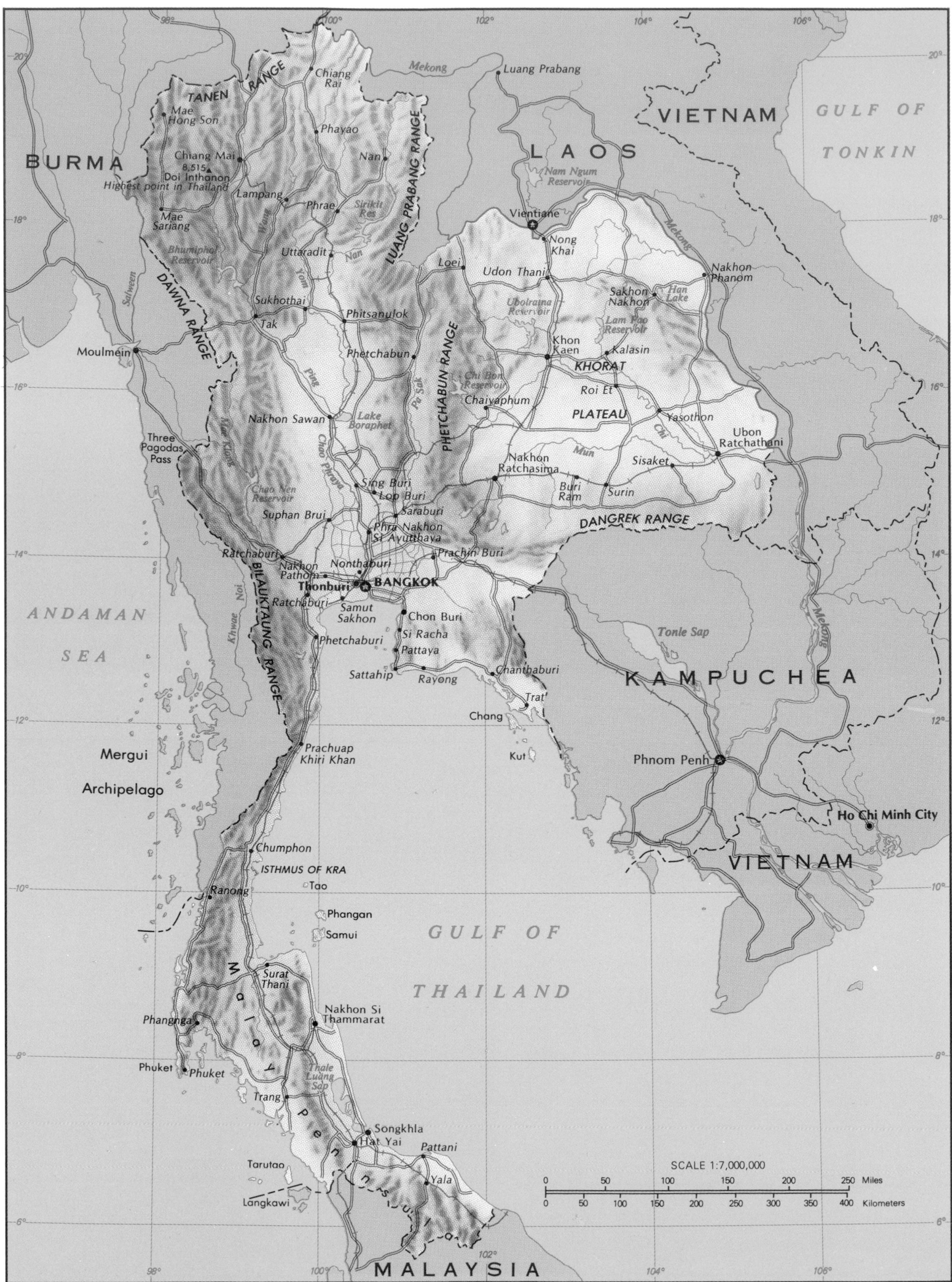
BURMA
LAOS
VIETNAM
GULF OF TONKIN
KAMPUCHEA
MALAYSIA
ANDAMAN SEA
GULF OF THAILAND
Mergui Archipelago
TANEN RANGE
LUANG PRABANG RANGE
DAWNA RANGE
PHETCHABUN RANGE
KHORAT PLATEAU
DANGREK RANGE
BILAUKTAUNG RANGE
ISTHMUS OF KRA
Malay Peninsula
Chiang Rai
Luang Prabang
Mae Hong Son
Chiang Mai
8,515
Doi Inthanon
Highest point in Thailand
Phayao
Nan
Lampang
Phrae
Sirikit Res
Mae Sariang
Nam Ngum Reservoir
Vientiane
Nong Khai
Bhumiphol Reservoir
Uttaradit
Loei
Udon Thani
Nakhon Phanom
Sakhon Nakhon
Han Lake
Ubolratna Reservoir
Lam Pao Reservoir
Sukhothai
Tak
Phitsanulok
Moulmein
Phetchabun
Khon Kaen
Kalasin
Chi Bon Reservoir
Roi Et
Chaiyaphum
Yasothon
Nakhon Sawan
Lake Boraphet
Ubon Ratchathani
Three Pagodas Pass
Nakhon Ratchasima
Sisaket
Buri Ram
Surin
Sing Buri
Lop Buri
Chao Nen Reservoir
Saraburi
Suphan Buri
Phra Nakhon Si Ayutthaya
Prachin Buri
Ratchaburi
Nakhon Pathom
Nonthaburi
BANGKOK
Thonburi
Samut Sakhon
Chon Buri
Si Racha
Tonle Sap
Phetchaburi
Pattaya
Sattahip
Rayong
Chanthaburi
Trat
Chang
Kut
Prachuap Khiri Khan
Phnom Penh
Ho Chi Minh City
Chumphon
Ranong
Tao
Phangan
Samui
Surat Thani
Nakhon Si Thammarat
Phangnga
Phuket
Thale Luang Sap
Trang
Songkhla
Hat Yai
Pattani
Yala
Tarutao
Langkawi
Mekong
Salween
Ping
Wang
Yom
Nan
Pa Sak
Chao Phraya
Mun
Chi
Mae Klong
Khwae Noi
SCALE 1:7,000,000
0 50 100 150 200 250 Miles
0 50 100 150 200 250 300 350 400 Kilometers

tions, is predominantly rural. Approximately two-thirds of the labor force is engaged in agriculture, principally the cultivation of rice, maize, and root crops. Rice has historically been Thailand's major crop and today the nation is the world's premier rice-exporting nation. In addition to rice, Thailand's other major exports are primary commodities such as tin, teak, and rubber. As is the case with many developing countries, Thailand's imports are predominantly manufactured products and fuel.

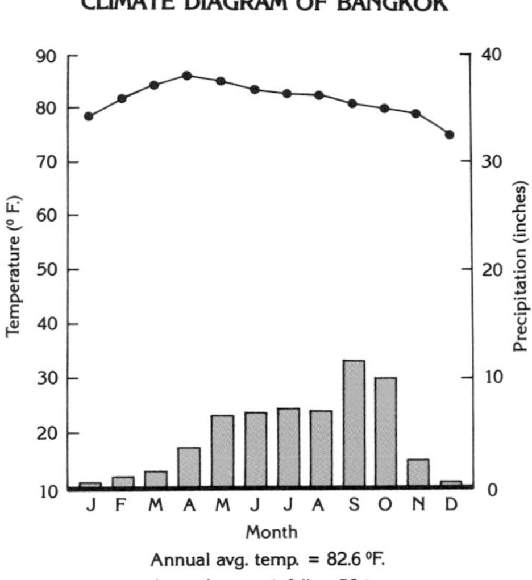


## THE PHYSICAL ENVIRONMENT

Physically, Thailand can be divided into five regions: the rugged Northern and Western ranges centered on the ancient city of Chiang Mai; the semi-arid Khorat Plateau, which corresponds to the administrative region called the Northeast; the Southeastern Upland and Coastal Plain, which include some of Thailand's well-known beaches; the southern extension, known as the Peninsular Region; and the rice-producing Central Plain, which includes the Chao Phraya delta and upper plain subregions. As is so throughout the region there are no mountains that attain the great heights of other parts of Asia, but most of the topography can be characterized as rugged. The highest peak is Doi Inthanon near Chiang Mai at 8,515 feet (2,595 m). Thailand is not on the boundary of tectonic plates and thus volcanoes and earthquakes are rare.

Nearly all of Thailand is drained by two north–south trending river systems: the Chao Phraya, whose drainage basin lies completely within Thailand; and the Mekong, which forms most of the boundary between Thailand and Laos. The former river drains the Central Plain and the North, and the Mekong drains the Khorat Plateau. A number of large dams have been constructed on rivers in both drainage areas, and these have created most of the nation's larger inland water bodies.

Thailand experiences the tropical monsoon climate found throughout the region but total rainfall amounts are less than elsewhere since most of the nation is sheltered from the moisture-laden winds by mountains in Burma on the west or Vietnam to the east. According to the Tourism Authority of Thailand, the country has three seasons: hot (from March to May), rainy (June to October), and cool (November to February). Climate diagrams for Bangkok and Chiang Mai tend to support this contention, although travelers from more temperate climates might disagree that there is a "cool" season. Chiang Mai is of course cooler than Bangkok since it is located at a more northerly latitude and a higher elevation. Much of interior Thailand, including parts of the Khorat Plateau, receive less than 50 inches (125 cm) of rainfall annually, amounts that are low for tropical environments. Rice grown in the Central Plain must be supplemented by irrigation water from the Chao Phraya. Peninsular Thailand receives the

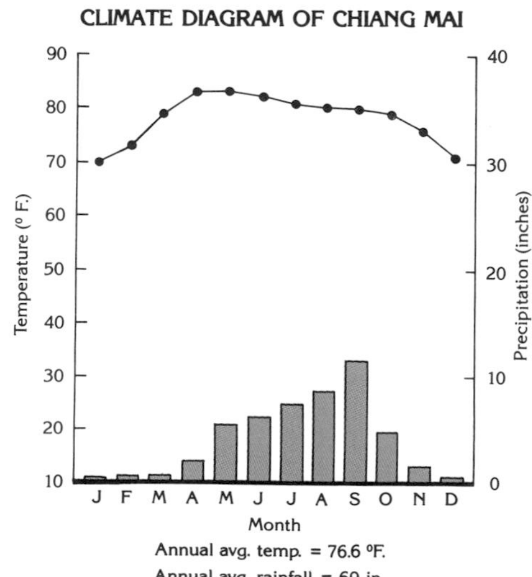

greatest amount of rainfall; in some areas annual amounts are in excess of 150 inches (380 cm). The lateritic soils associated with tropical climate regions are generally not fertile but the alluvial (water-deposited) soils of the Central Plain and mountain basin areas are very fertile and this has resulted in the intensive cultivation of rice and other crops.

Rapidly expanding populations and increasing cultivation have led to the deterioration of forested area, in Thailand estimated to cover about one-half of the nation. Thailand's natural vegetation includes a wide variety of forest types including tropical rainforests, coniferous pine forests, and deciduous forests. The best-known species is teak, which once thrived in the mountains of the north. While teak is still commercially cut and floated downriver for export, monsoon forests where teak is found are fast disappearing. Increased human activity in such forested areas also means eventual extinction or endangerment of wildlife species, the best known of which include the Asian elephant (widely used also as a domestic animal), rhinoceros, tapir, tiger, a variety of deer, Himalayan black bear, honey bear, and gaur and banteng (types of wild cattle). Many species of monkeys and gibbons, reptiles (including the king cobra and crocodile), and birds are also found.

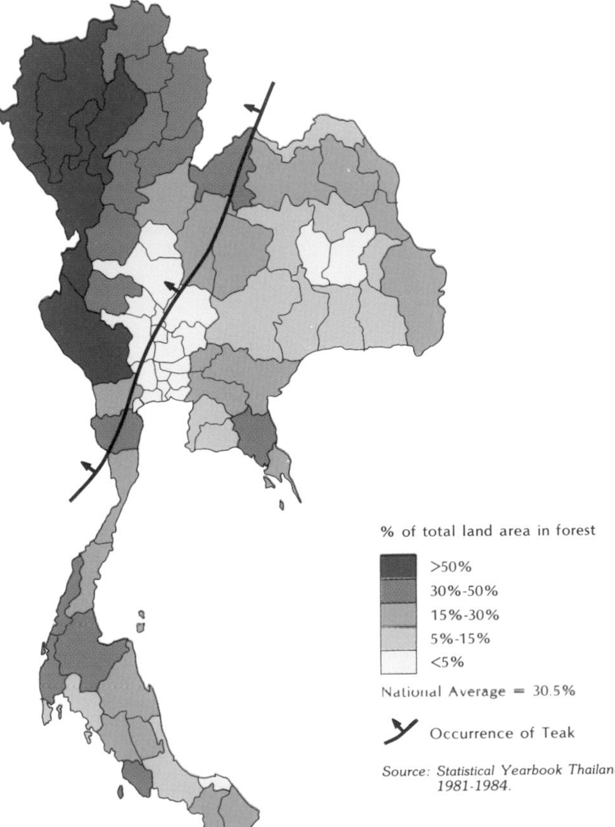


## HISTORICAL BACKGROUND

According to many historians, the ancestors of the present-day Thai peoples migrated south into the area from southern China beginning about 800 to 1,000 years ago. These migrants, pushed out of China by the more powerful Han Chinese from the north, traveled south through the river valleys and came into contact with indigenous groups, many of whom were under Indian cultural influence. These relatively recent arrivals in mainland Southeast Asia today make up the majority of lowland peoples in mainland Southeast Asia. Tribal groups and other ethnic minorities were gradually forced into the less desirable upland areas by the newly arrived interlopers. Today throughout much of Southeast Asia there is animosity between the lowland majority and upland minorities as a result of historic contact and conflict. In recent times, frequent moves by upland groups, who have ignored national boundaries as well as been involved in the production of opium poppies, have caused the lowland governments to view uplanders as security threats. This has sometimes brought about systematic efforts to undermine the cultures and lifestyles of the uplanders.

The earliest Thai states emerged in the thirteenth century following a decline of the power of the nearby Khmer empire and Mon state (in Burma and northern and central Thailand). Sukhothai was founded in the mid-thirteenth century following the Thai defeat of the Khmer, and Chiang Mai was founded toward the end of that century, after the defeat of the Mon in northern Thailand. It was during this period that the Thai began to subordinate their animistic beliefs to the Theravada Buddhism of the Mon. Other adoptions during this period included the alphabet, perhaps via monks from Sri Lanka, and writing system, as well as the Indianized art and architectural forms of the Khmer. However, not all art forms were borrowed, as exemplified by the distinctively Thai bronze sculptures of the Buddha from the Sukhothai period.

About 1350 a new Thai kingdom, Ayutthaya, emerged under the rule of King Rama Thibodi I. The capital was established at Ayutthaya, about 40 miles (65 km) north of present-day Bangkok. Whereas the more than four centuries of Ayutthayan rule was occasionally marked with internal dissension and external suzerainty (Burma controlled the area for 15 years), on the whole the period was marked by one of Thai domination over its neighbors. The period also witnessed the coming of the Europeans, who began to arrive in the sixteenth century. In 1767 the Burmese successfully invaded Thailand for a second time and thus ended the Ayutthayan period.

Phraya Tak Sin raised an army and successfully ousted the Burmese. Tak Sin was proclaimed king and he established a new capital, at Thon Buri on the west bank of the Chao Phraya. This capital was more accessible to foreign merchants and it was during this time that Europeans and, most notably, Chinese merchants began to arrive in greater numbers. In 1782 Tak Sin was succeeded by Chao Praya Chakkri; this began the period of the Chakkri dynasty (the Bangkok period), which continues to the present.

Whereas Thailand was never colonized, Western influence gradually became more evident and the Thai kings recognized that some adaptation to Western standards was necessary in order that Thailand, unlike the other Southeast Asian states, might survive as a free nation. Indeed, in order to maintain such a status much of Thailand's recent history has been marked by some accommodation with other, more powerful nations. For example, Thai concessions to the French in Indochina and to the British in Malaya led in 1896 to the recognition of Thailand as a free, neutral buffer zone. It was during the reign of King Chulalongkorn, or Rama V (1868–1910), that modern Thailand began to take form. The accommodationist policy, public education, the abolition of slavery, and the introduction of the railway were but a few of the programs continued or begun during the time of Rama V. A further example of Thai accommodationist policy was its alliance with Japan in 1941 after that powerful nation's expansionist policies in Southeast Asia were clearly directed toward the takeover of the entire mainland. Since the end of World War II Thailand's political and economic relations have been directed toward the West, and especially the United States, where the present king was born in Cambridge, Massachusetts.

Following the withdrawal of American forces from Vietnam in 1975, Thailand has sought closer ties with its Communist neighbors. Vietnam's invasion of Kampuchea in 1978, however, has caused a marked deterioration in relations between Thailand and Vietnam. Thailand, along with its ASEAN counterparts, has recognized the UN-supported coalition government-in-exile of Democratic Kampuchea and condemns the presence of Vietnamese armed forces in Kampuchea.

Since 1975 Thailand has been the sanctuary for over 800,000 refugees from Kampuchea, Vietnam, and Laos. Of these, nearly one-half have been resettled in other nations but over 115,000 remain in first asylum refugee camps (that is,

Laotian tribeswoman and child in Ban Vinai refugee camp (courtesy J. Hafner)

they are awaiting
tries) and over o
persons from Kan
camps. This group
resettlement and
turned gradually t
tially to further at
Whereas the kir
bol of the Thai n
d'etat in 1932 Thai
monarchy (the cc
1939 and from 19
land's governmen
under the control
1976 martial law v
The king is th
the armed forces
tional Assembly v
324-member Hou
by univeral suffra
which is appointe
mendation of the

**PROVINCES**

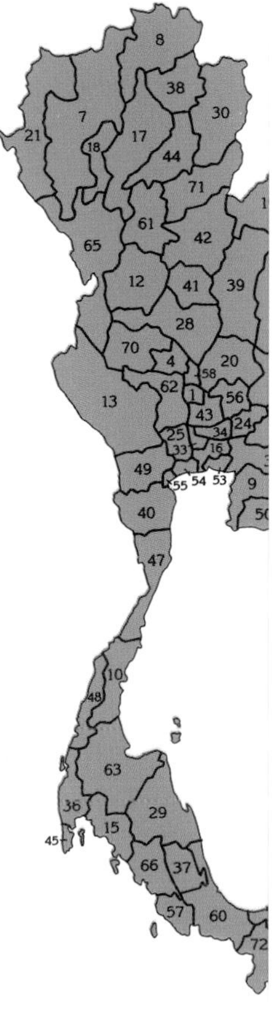




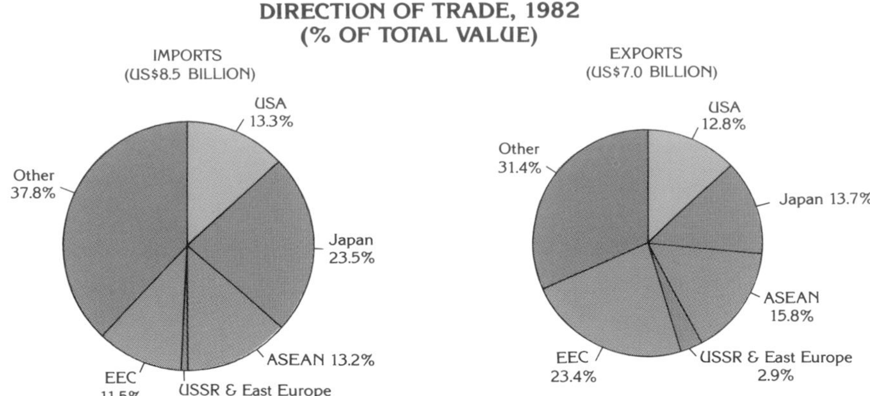


*Source: 1983 International Trade Statistics Yearbook (N.Y.: U.N., 1985)*

been forced to rely on external borrowing to meet this deficit which has in turn led to a large external public debt.

## TRANSPORTATION

Thailand's road and railway system connect Bangkok with the other major cities in the nation. The railway, begun in the nineteenth century, extends south from the northern city of Chiang Mai to Bangkok, and thence farther south along the peninsula where it connects with the Malaysian system. Another major railway line extends from Bangkok through the Northeast region to the Laotian border near Vientiane. Thailand has nearly 50,000 miles (80,000 km) of roads which serve over two million motor vehicles, about 60% of which are motorcycles, *samlor*s (three-wheeled motorized vehicles found in cities), and the like. In 1981 an overhead expressway was completed in Bangkok and additional expressways are planned.

Bangkok is not only the center of the nation's transportation system but Bangkok's Don Muang International Airport is also the hub for the entire Southeast Asian region and a major gateway to eastern Asia. Nearly 40 international airlines, including the state-owned Thai Airways International, serve Bangkok. The port of Bangkok, at Khlong Toei on the Chao Phraya, is the largest port in the nation and handles nearly all exports and imports. In addition to the Chao Phraya River, which divides Bangkok and Thon Buri, there is an extensive network of canals (*khlong*) which are transportation arteries for bulk goods, market products, commuters, and tourists.

Bangkok's temples and palaces, the unique Thai boxing, relatively inexpensive jewelry and silk items, the beautiful beaches of Pattaya and Phuket, the handicrafts of Chiang Mai, the highly-spiced Thai cuisine, and the warmth and hospitality of the Thai people are but a few of the reasons that have made tourism a major industry. More tourists visit Thailand than any other Southeast Asian nation, and tourism has become the nation's primary source of foreign exchange. In 1984, over 2.3 million persons visited the nation, nearly three times as many as visited the Philippines.

## PEOPLE AND CULTURE

Whereas Thailand's degree of ethnic diversity may be somewhat less than that of other Southeast Asian nations such as Burma and Indonesia, the nation is unique in that it is represented by languages of all four of the region's major language families: Malayo-Polynesian, Austro-Asiatic, Sino-Tibetan, and Tai. Thailand's central position in mainland Southeast Asia has meant that a great diversity of peoples have migrated through the area in historic times.

Thailand is characterized by the basic division and differences between lowland and upland peoples. That is, there is a lowland majority group which has come to dominate the national

Floating market, Bangkok (R. Ulack)

government and politics. In the case of Thailand the majority are those who speak Thai (one language of the Tai language family), and they account for over one-half of the population. Other Tai languages spoken in Thailand include Lao, spoken in the Northeast by about one-quarter of the population, and Yuan (Kammuang), spoken in the north. Upland groups who speak Sino-Tibetan languages include the Karen and Lolo groups. Ethnic Chinese account for 10% of Thailand's population and speak Chinese (Sino-Tibetan) languages. Of the nearly ten million ethnic Chinese in the Southeast Asian region about one-half reside in Thailand; only Singapore and Malaysia have a larger percentage of Chinese. The Malayo-Polynesian languages in Thailand are found in the extreme south, where Malay and Moken (the language of the sea gypsies) are spoken. Austro-Asiatic languages in Thailand are represented by Mon in the north and Khmer along the border with Kampuchea, the latter spoken by about 3% of the population. English is the most widely spoken Western language and one can get around in Bangkok and other tourist centers with English. It is

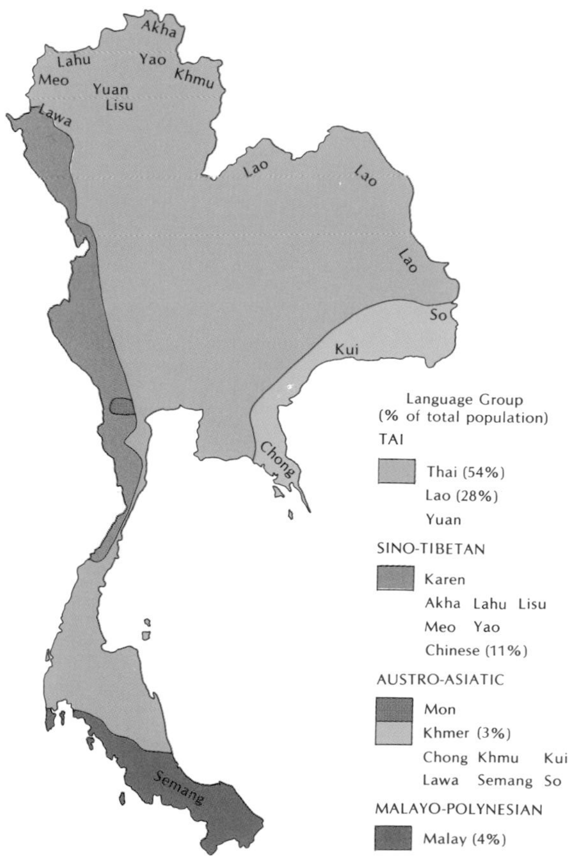

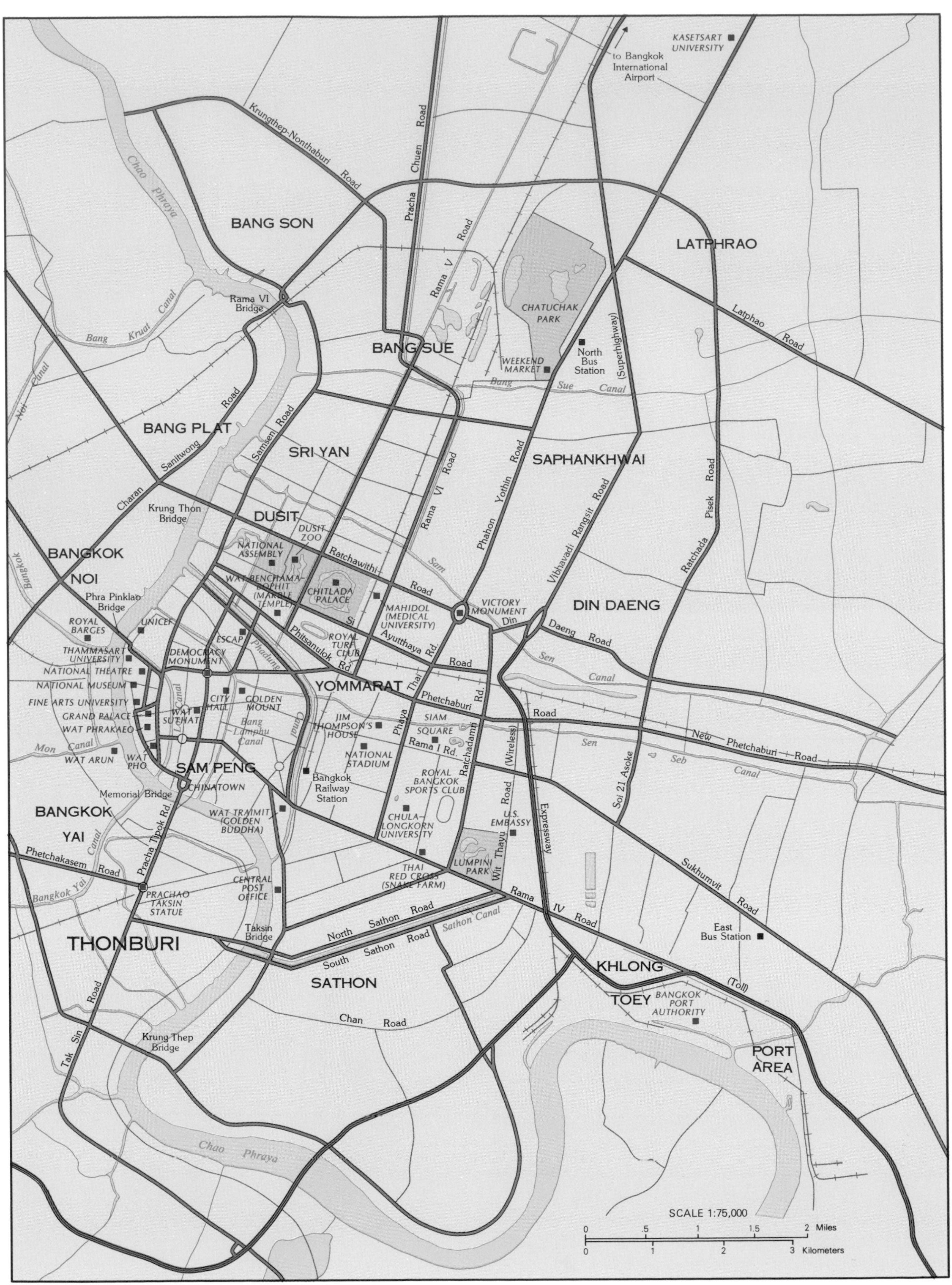


BANGKOK METROPOLITAN AREA

a required language in secondary schools and in universities, although instruction is given in Thai, the official language.

Thailand, like most nations of the region, has one predominant religion which has heavily influenced the cultural characteristics of the nation. About 95% of the population adhere to Theravada Buddhism. Like the Philippines, there is a Muslim minority in the southern part of the country that accounts for about 4% of the population. Small numbers of Christians are found in Bangkok, and in the north.

Material and nonmaterial culture in Thailand is uniquely Thai but has its basis in the Indian traditions taken from the Khmer and Mon among others; and in Buddhism, which diffused to Thailand from the Indian subcontinent. Pre-Thai indigenous culture has also helped to shape current Thai cultural patterns, especially in the rural villages. More recently, Arab, European, and American contact with Thailand has further influenced Thai cultural expression.

Wat Benchamabophit, the Marble temple, Bangkok (R. Ulack)

Democracy Monument, Bangkok (R. Ulack)

Thai art forms are evidenced in religion, in architecture, in dance and music, and in literature. Thai images of the Buddha are found throughout the country. Among the best-known Buddha images are the Reclining Buddha found in Wat (Temple) Pho and the Golden Buddha in Wat Traimit. The former is a gigantic gold-plated reclining image of the Buddha 150 feet (46 m) long and nearly 50 feet (15 m) high. The more traditional image of the Golden Buddha is unique in that it is solid gold, nearly 10 feet (3 m) high, and weighs 5½ tons. Excellent examples of Thai architecture are Bangkok's ubiquitous temples and the Grand Palace. Roofs are quite distinctive with their tiles either gilded in gold or patterned in mosaics of glazed colored glass. The Grand Palace, built in 1782, consists of several highly decorated buildings. One of these, Wat Phrakaeo, houses the Emerald Buddha, the most sacred Buddha image in Thailand. Music, literature, and other art forms also trace their origins largely to the early Hindu-Buddhist traditions.

The visitor with little time in Thailand will likely spend all or most of it in Bangkok, Southeast Asia's third most populous metropolitan area, with over five million people. Here one can enjoy major shopping areas and public markets, floating markets, famous nightlife from classical dance to the pleasure bars and massage parlors of Patpong Road, and numerous examples of Thai architectural and artistic expression. Bangkok is a relatively new city and has been the national capital only since 1782; prior to that it was a village across the river from Thon Buri, an earlier capital. Today, in addition to its national governmental and commercial functions, Bangkok plays host to international organizations including the United Nations' Economic and Social Commission for Asia and the Pacific (ESCAP), the Food and Agricultural Organization (FAO), and the World Health Organization (WHO).

# 11

# Socialist Republic of the Union of Burma

*Area:* 261,228 sq mi (676,577 sq km); almost the size of Texas

*Population:* 38,468,000 (1986)

*Population Density:* 147 persons per sq mi (57 persons per sq km)

*Urban Population:* 24%

*Annual Average Rate of Population Increase:* 2.0%

*Crude Birth Rate:* 32.9 per 1,000 population

*Crude Death Rate:* 13.4 per 1,000 population

*Infant Mortality Rate:* 104 infant deaths per 1,000 live births

*Life Expectancy:* Male—51.6 years; Female—54.6 years

*Official Language:* Burmese

*Currency:* Burmese kyat (US$1 = K6.2 in 1988)

*Capital:* Rangoon

*Form of Government:* Single-party people's republic with one legislative house, the People's Assembly.

*Chief of State:* President (Chairman of the State Council)

*Head of Government:* Prime minister

*Armed Forces (1984):* 180,500 (army—90%; navy—6%; air force—4%)

## HISTORICAL OVERVIEW

1044–1287: Pagan dynasty.

1486–1752: Toungoo dynasty.

1824–1826: First Burmese War with British; Arakan and Tenasserim ceded to British.

1852: Second Burmese War; Irrawaddy delta region (Lower Burma) ceded to Britain.

1885–1886: Third Burmese War; all remaining territories (Upper Burma) ceded to Britain.

1937: Burma detached from British India and becomes a separate British dependency with limited self-government.

1942–1945: Japanese occupation.

1948: Union of Burma achieves independence; U Nu is first prime minister.

1962: Military coup under leadership of General Ne Win; single-party (Burma Socialist Programme Party, or BSPP) dictatorial state established.

1974: New constitution promulgated aimed at transforming Burma into a democratic socialist state. Ne Win elected president by the State Council.

Burma, in part because of its self-imposed isolation since a military coup in 1962, is a nation today beset by political, social, and economic difficulties. Although well endowed with a variety of natural resources, Burma is among the poorest of the region's nations as is implied by its extremely low per capita Gross National Product (US$180 in 1983) and the fact that less than one-fifth of its population has access to safe drinking water. Like neighboring Thailand, Burma is an agricultural nation heavily dependent upon rice cultivation. Unlike Thailand, however, Burma's rice production has not increased significantly over the past quarter of a century and as a result its share of the world rice trade has decreased. Burma's foreign relations

BHUTAN
INDIA
BANGLADESH
CHINA
VIETNAM
LAOS
THAILAND
Hkakabao Razi
19,285 ft.
Highest point in Burma
Diphu Pass
16,860
Pangsau
Pass
Putao
PATKAI RANGE
HUKAWNG
VALLEY
KUMON RANGE
Mali
Nmai
Brahmaputra
NAGA HILLS
Myitkyina
Indawgyi
Lake
Chindwin
Mekong
Kunming
Ganges
Dhaka
(Dacca)
MANGIN RANGE
Bhamo
Irrawaddy
Tropic of Cancer
23 1/2° N.
Shweli
Myitnge
Namtu
Lashio
Falam
Chittagong
CHIN
HILLS
Shwebo
Salween
Monywa
Mandalay
Maymyo
Sagaing
Amarapura
SHAN
Mouths of the Ganges
Myingyan
Pagan
4,982
Mt. Popa
PLATEAU
Keng Tung
Chauk
Taunggyi
Meiktila
Inle
Lake
ARAKAN YOMA
Sittwe
(Akyab)
Boronga
Magwe
Yemethin
Pawn
Teng
Pilu
Mekong
Pyinmana
Loi-kaw
TANEN RANGE
Ramree
Allanmyo
PEGU YOMA
Cheduba
Prome
(Pye)
Toungoo
Chiang
Mai
Taungup
Pass
Pyu
Sittang
Vientiane
BAY
OF
BENGAL
Bassein
Henzada
DAWNA RANGE
Pegu
Insein
Rangoon
Pa-an
Moulmein
Pyapon
Rangoon River
Mouths of the Irrawaddy
GULF
OF
MARTABAN
Ye
Three
Pagodas
Pass
Chao Phraya
Preparis
Coco Islands
Tavoy
TENASSERIM YOMA
BILAUKTAUNG RANGE
BANGKOK
Great Tenasserim
Andaman
Islands
(India)
ANDAMAN
SEA
Mergui
Tenasserim
Mergui
Archipelago
GULF
OF
THAILAND
ISTHMUS OF KRA
SCALE 1:9,236,000
0 50 100 150 200 250 Miles
0 50 100 150 200 250 300 350 400 Kilometers
92°
96°
100°
28°
24°
20°
16°
12°

have been guided by a policy of strict neutrality, certainly in large part because of the lengthy border it shares with Asia's giants, China and India. Burma today is a party to no defense treaties or alliances although in recent years it has begun to accept foreign development assistance.

Culturally, Burma is like most other Southeast Asian nations in that it is extremely diverse ethnically but its population is quite homogeneous in terms of religion. The vast majority of Burmese (a term that refers to any citizen of Burma, regardless of ethnic group), adhere to Theravada Buddhism. Ethnically, the lowland Burman (the ethnic group that speaks Burmese, the official language) majority accounts for two-thirds of the population. A myriad of upland minority groups account for much of the rest of the population and some of these, along with the Burmese Communist Party (BCP), comprise the various insurgent groups that have been fighting government forces since independence in 1948.

## THE PHYSICAL ENVIRONMENT

In terms of landforms and drainage patterns, Burma can be divided into three distinct regions: the Western, Central, and Eastern Belts. The West extends from the Hukawng Valley in the far north to Cape Negrais and includes the north-south trending arcuate mountain ranges known as the Patkai, Naga, and Chin Hills, and the Arakan Yoma. Although these are called "hills," their elevations exceed 10,000 feet (3,050 m) in the north and decrease toward the south. Indeed, the highest peak in all of Southeast Asia, Hkakabo Razi at 19,285 feet (5,878 m), is located in the extreme north near the Tibetan border. These ranges are actually a southward extension of the Himalayas and have historically been a barrier to travel between Burma and Assam, a part of India. The Central Belt includes the vast alluvial lowlands of the Irrawaddy and the smaller Chindwin and Sittang Rivers, and comprises Burma's economic and cultural core. The Irrawaddy is navigable for over 900 miles (1,448 km) from its delta in the south to Bhamo in the north near the Chinese border. The Irrawaddy has always been Burma's major transportation route and was dubbed the "road to Mandalay" during the British colonial period. Many of the earliest capitals were located along the Irrawaddy, including Pagan, Prome (Pye), and Mandalay. The third physical region, the Eastern Belt, extends from the extreme northeast and continues southward along the border with China into the extensive Shan Plateau, and thence south to the Tenasserim coastal range. Again, elevations decrease from north to south. Burma's second great river, the Salween, begins in the Tibetan Plateau and flows south through China's Yunnan Plateau (where it runs parallel and within a few miles of the Mekong for a short distance) until it enters Burma and rushes southward through the Shan Plateau in a series of deep gorges.

With the exception of the northern mountain areas, nearly all of Burma's climate can be classified as tropical monsoon. The southwest, or summer, monsoon brings Burma's rain, which means that the vast majority of rain falls between May and October, and the remainder of the year is dry. Places along the coast receive the greatest amount of rainfall since they are the first land areas to feel the effects of the annual monsoon. Akyab and Moulmein, for example, receive more than 200 inches (500 cm) of rain a year, with over 90% falling during the short monsoon season. Inland areas surrounding Mandalay on the leeward slopes of the north-south trending western mountain ranges, receive considerably less rainfall, un-

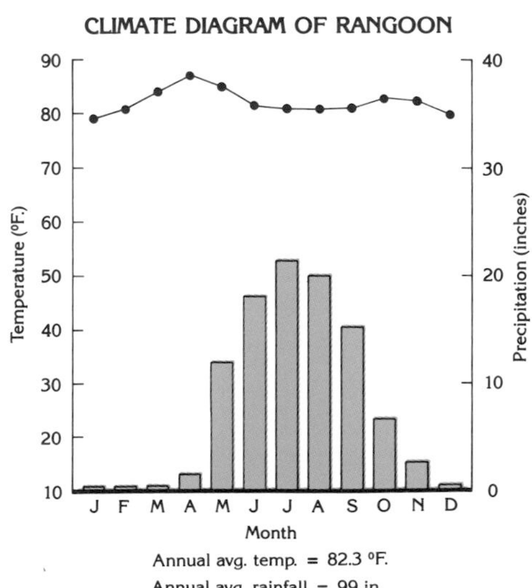

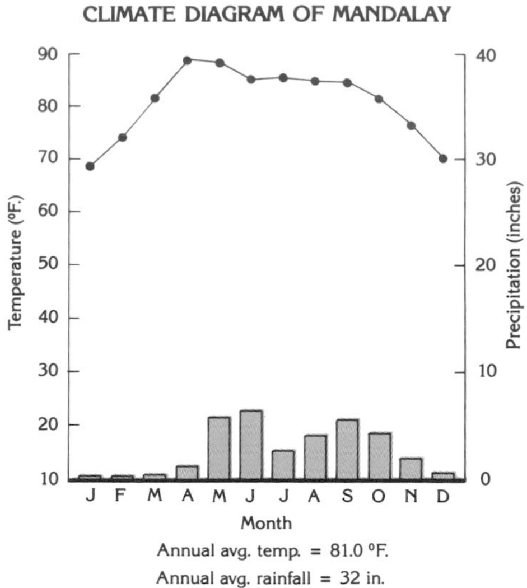

Annual avg. temp. = 81.0 °F.
Annual avg. rainfall = 32 in.

der 50 inches (125 cm) annually. Mandalay is a part of Burma's interior dry zone and rice cultivated here must be irrigated. Temperatures in Burma are typical of those found in a tropical climate region, but because much of the country is located at a more northerly latitude than the rest of the region, winters are somewhat cooler. Temperatures in the high mountain and plateau areas of the north can drop below freezing and thus snow is possible. March and April, just before the onset of the high humidity and rains of the monsoon, are the hottest and driest months in the Irrawaddy lowlands.

Flora and fauna reflect the climate characteristics of the country. It has been estimated that nearly one-half of its total area is covered by tropical rain forests, and about one-half of this area is in teak and other hardwoods such as ironwood. Teak is a major export commodity for Burma and it is estimated that some three-fourths of the world's teak reserves are located here. Bamboo is also common in the tropical forests, and in the dry zone is found grassland vegetation, thorny scrub, and even cacti. Higher elevations support oak, conifers, and other vegetation characteristic of cool climates. Burma's forests support a wide variety of fauna including elephants, tigers, wild buffalo, red deer, monkeys, bears, rhinoceros, and reptiles. Burma reportedly has among the world's highest mortality rate from snakebite; among the deadliest are the Russel's viper and king cobra. As population expands and settles in forested areas, and as the forests are destroyed, many species have become endangered.

## HISTORICAL BACKGROUND

Burma's long history has involved the interaction of the very diverse groups who today populate the lowland Irrawaddy-Sittang region and the surrounding uplands. Collectively, these peoples are today all citizens of Burma, and called Burmese, but national unity has eluded modern-day Burma, as it has historically eluded earlier Burmese empires and their rulers. Theravada Buddhism, which entered Burma over 2,000 years ago from India and Ceylon, has been the central element of the Burmese national identity. Since independence, the Western ideas of socialism and democracy have combined with Buddhist concepts to form the basis for a sometimes contradictory Burmese nationalism.

Among the earliest migrants into Burma were the Mon, who arrived over two thousand years ago. These peoples, a part of the north–south migration stream from China into mainland Southeast Asia, overthrew their Indianized predecessors and at the same time absorbed much of their culture. The Mon eventually settled in the coastal areas adjacent to the Gulf of Martaban where several Indianized Mon kingdoms, including Thaton and Pegu, emerged. It was during this time that Buddhism arrived from India, then under the rule of the emperor Asoka, a convert to Buddhism who sent missionaries outside India to carry the Buddha's teachings. According to legend it was during this time, too, that the Mon began the building of the Shwedagon pagoda, the most famous temple in Burma.

Soon the Pyu, a Sino-Tibetan speaking group from China, began migrating south into the Irrawaddy region. By the sixth century A.D. they had reached the Irrawaddy delta and had established their capital at Sri Ksetra (near Prome), where they built over 100 Buddhist monasteries. The Pyu gradually became Indianized through contact with the Mon, and soon the Pyu gained supremacy over the Mon.

Other groups, such as the Arakanese, migrated into the area and other states were established within the boundaries of present-day Burma. The next large state was that of the Burmans, a people closely related to the Pyu. The Burmans, like their predecessors, came into Burma from the north beginning about the ninth century A.D. They soon established their capital at Pagan near the confluence of the Irrawaddy and Chindwin, and it was from here that they gradually gained control of the Irrawaddy and Sittang lowland area. King Anawrahta founded the Pagan dynasty in 1044 and it was during his reign that Lower and Upper Burma were first brought under unified rule. Although the Mon were defeated during this time, their literature, art, architecture, and religion were introduced into Upper Burma and flourished there. Anawrahta was converted to Theravada Buddhism by a Mon monk and later Pagan rulers were responsible for the construction of thousands of pagodas, some of which are today considered among the greatest examples of Burmese religious architecture. The Pagan dynasty ended in 1287 with the invasion and defeat by the Chinese armies of the Mongol emperor, Kublai Khan. For the next 300 years Burma was characterized by foreign domination or disunity, with several different kingdoms controlling various parts of Upper and Lower Burma.

The reunification of much of Burma was brought about during the time of the Toungoo dynasty (1486–1752). It was originally based at Toungoo on the Sittang, and subsequently (1541) Pegu became the capital of the second Burmese empire under King Tabinshwehti. The Toungoo leaders intially defeated the Shan, the Mon, and the Siamese, and even captured Chiang Mai in 1556. In 1635 the Burman (Toungoo) capital was moved to the former Shan capital of Ava. However, by 1752 continued attacks by both the Mon and the Siamese from Ayutthaya brought about the downfall of the second Burmese empire. A third Burmese empire was established at Shwebo under Alaungpaya in 1755. Alaungpaya defeated the Mon and established a port at the small coastal town of Dagon and renamed it Yangon (Rangoon), meaning "end of strife." The city eventually became the capital of Lower Burma.

As early as the fifteenth century Europeans had begun to visit Burma. The Portuguese were among the first and signed a trade treaty with the leader of the port city of Martaban as early as 1519. Perhaps the most famous Portuguese in Burma, Philip de Brito y Nicote, actually ruled Syriam for thirteen years until he was executed after defeat by the Toungoo ruler's forces in 1613. It is said that de Brito converted perhaps 100,000 Burmese to Christianity during his reign. The Dutch and French also made contact with Burma but it was the British who left the most lasting European influence on Burma. Although British economic interest in Burma began in the early seventeenth century when ships of the British East India Company entered Burmese ports, it was not until incidents along the Burma and British India common border began to increase that friction between the two erupted. By the early 1800s fighting was frequent and the First Anglo-Burmese War (1824–26) resulted in the British takeover of Arakan and Tenasserim, primarily to deny the coast of the Bay of Bengal to the rival French. The rest of Lower Burma was ceded to the British after the Second Anglo-Burmese War in 1852. Following this, the Burmese capital was moved to Mandalay under King Mindon, and under King Thibaw British-Burmese relations deteriorated further. The Third Anglo-Burmese War resulted and in 1885 British troops entered Upper Burma and soundly defeated Burmese forces. In 1886 all of Burma was under British control and annexed as a province of British India.

British interest in Burma was almost wholly economic and it was during the colonial period that primary commodities, including rice, teak, cotton, and oil, began to be exploited for export and profit. The British opened up and greatly expanded the Irrawaddy delta to intensive rice cultivation and gave land free to prospective cultivators, many of whom migrated from central Burma's dry zone. Soon this region was the major rice-producing area in Burma. For some time prior to World War II petroleum, produced in central Burma, was after rice the second leading export of the British colony. During the British period thousands of immigrants from India also entered Burma, who, along with the

Chinese, came to monopolize the professions and commercial and financial life of the colony. Today Indians and Chinese, the vast majority of whom reside in cities, each comprise about 2% of Burma's population.

The British period in some ways facilitated the disunity of the country in that the British permitted Burma's minorities to remain autonomous and ruled the various minorities only indirectly. The majority Burmans, on the other hand, were governed much more closely and were barred from government service except for minor positions, and from the military. Nevertheless, a lasting British impact included political institutions and independence in 1948 saw the nation begin with a constitutional democracy. Burma was, however, the first former British colony to sever ties with the Commonwealth.

In 1937 Burma became a colony separate from India with a greater degree of self-government through its own Legislative Council. The indirectly ruled border states, however, remained outside the control of this council. The decade of the 1930s was also important in Burma because a new leader, Aung San, introduced Marxism as a force among university students. During World War II, even though ideologically opposed to Japan's fascism, Aung San allied his Burmese Liberation Army with Japanese forces to defeat the British-led Allied forces in the early 1940s. Bitter fighting, however, continued in Burma throughout World War II and thousands of Allied forces, Burmese, and Japanese died in the jungles of Burma. The infamous Burma Road, an all-weather route built to carry supplies to Chinese troops fighting the Japanese, General Joseph "Vinegar Joe" Stilwell, and Chennault's "Flying Tigers" are but a few of the names remembered from World War II Burma.

National elections were held in 1947 and Aung San's party won an overwhelming majority but, tragically, Aung San was assassinated that same year by right-wing extremists. In 1948 U Nu, an ally of Aung San, was asked by the British colonial government to become the first prime minister. Economically Burma's early years of independence were disastrous. Rice revenues fell drastically and military and other expenditures increased. Internal turmoil and corruption also increased and by 1958 U Nu was forced to appoint a caretaker government under General Ne Win. In 1962 Ne Win took full control after a military coup and Burma has been a dictatorship since that time following the policies set down in Ne Win's *The Burmese Way to Socialism* (1962). The current government's policies of independence, nonalignment, and friendship with all (and especially its neighbors) continues the policies of its predecessors. A more rigid, self-imposed isolation has also been in effect since 1962, although there is some evidence that this is softening. Burma's isolation has meant that it has been much less influenced by the West than other nations and as a result it is today considered among the more "exotic" Asian nations.

A new constitution in 1974 established seven states and seven divisions, all united in an administrative and political hierarchy. States and divisions are divided into townships and these are, in turn, divided into wards or village-

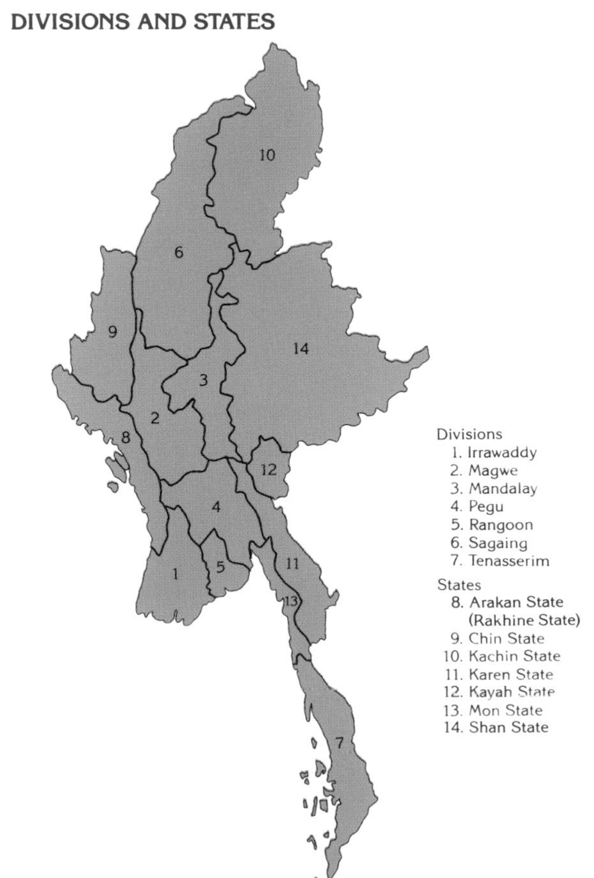

tracts. People's Councils exist at every subdivision level. At the national level, real power is vested in the Burmese Socialist Programme Party (BSPP), the only legal party. The one legislative body, the 475-member People's Assembly (Pyithu Hluttaw), is elected by the people. The Assembly elects a 29-member State Council from among its members and this council is the premier decision-making unit of government. At least one representative from each of Burma's fourteen states and divisions is on the council. The People's Assembly elects a prime minister from among its members and the State Council elects a chairman from among its members, who also is the president of the Union.

## THE ECONOMY

The economy is decidedly agricultural and dominated by rice. Nearly 57% of the total harvested area is in rice; rice and rice products account for nearly two-fifths of Burma's exports. Together with other agricultural exports including jute, rubber, maize, and beans, rice accounts for over one-half of all exports. Teak and other hardwoods account for a further one-quarter of total export earnings. The remaining principal exports are also primary commodities and include petroleum and tin. Burma was self-sufficient in petroleum until 1980, when local production began to decline. A few new oil fields have been discovered since 1980 but, more significantly, discovery of offshore natural gas fields in the Gulf of Martaban has increased energy production. In summary, Burma has rich and varied natural resources; in addition to those already noted there are significant deposits of coal, copper, zinc, tungsten, lead, gold, silver, and gemstones. Poor recovery procedures related to low capital and levels of technology, inefficient and expensive transportation, and insurgent activity have prevented higher levels of production.

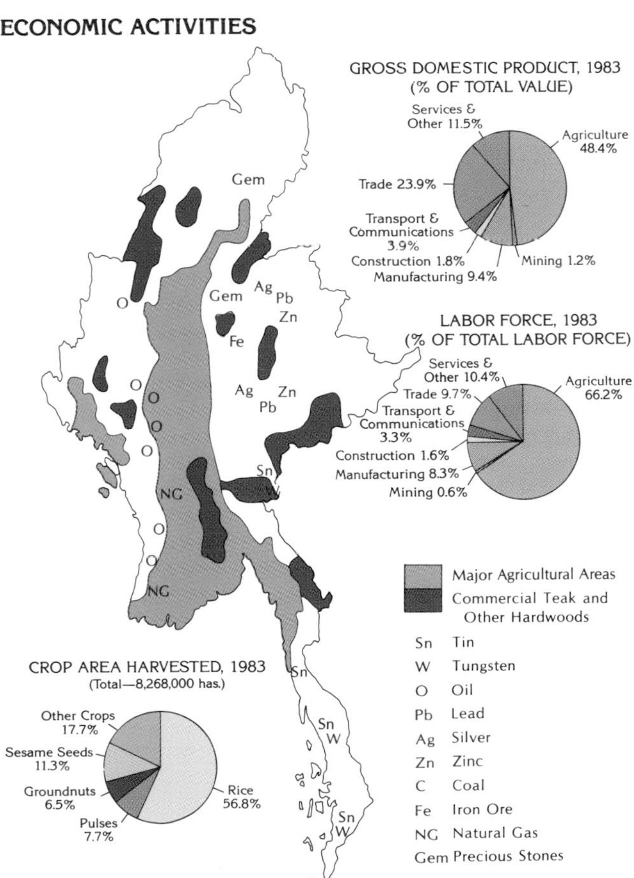


Burma comprises the major portion of the opium-producing Golden Triangle and the heart of this triangle is the Shan state. Its higher elevations offer ideal growing conditions for the poppy that produces the opium from which heroin and other drugs are derived. Whereas the new governments of Indochina have been somewhat successful in outlawing the opium trade among their upland minorities, this has not been the case in Burma. Today, many of Burma's minorities including the Palaung, Lisu, Lahu, Akha, and especially the Shan depend upon the cash crop. The Burmese government is relatively powerless in the upland areas where minority warlords are in control, and for that reason it has not destroyed the poppy fields. Today there are more poppy fields in Burma, estimated at 60,000 hectares, than in any other nation.

Manufacturing accounts for less than one-tenth of both the Gross Domestic Product and labor force. The principal industries are food processing, petroleum refining, and textiles. Because of the undeveloped industrial sector, the vast majority of imports are in machinery, transportation equipment, and other processed goods. As with most developing nations dependent upon primary commodities, a recent rise in the value of manufactured imports and a fall

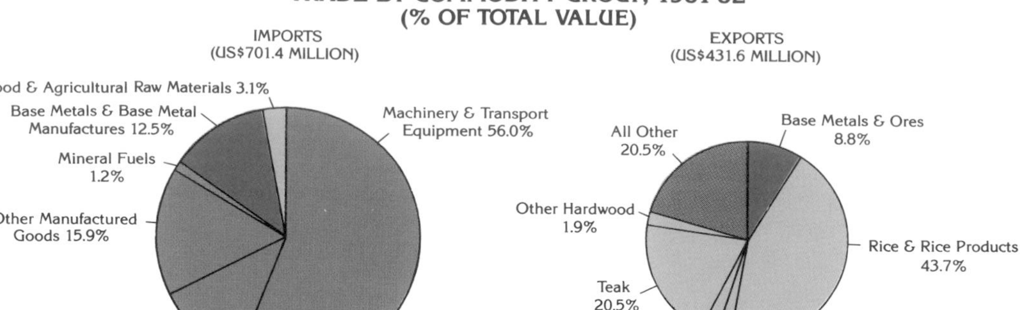


Source: *The Europa Yearbook 1986* (London: Europa Publicatons, 1986)

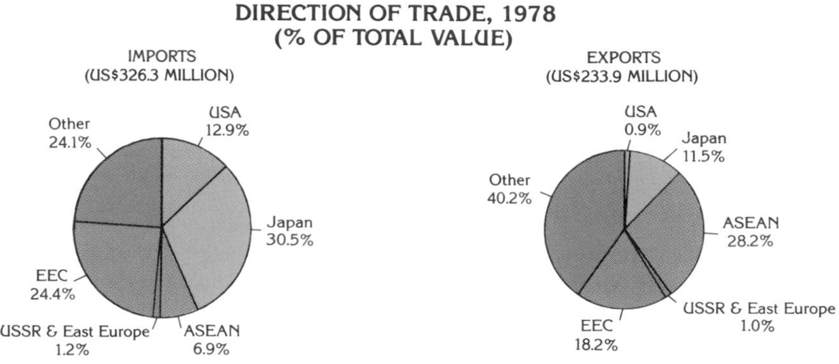


Source: *1983 International Trade Statistics Yearbook* (N.Y.: U.N., 1985)

in the value of most export commodities has caused a large trade deficit. Burma has joined the Asian Development Bank which, with the World Bank, provides most of the multilateral support. Japan is Burma's principal unilateral donor as well as its major trading partner.

## TRANSPORTATION AND TOURISM

Burma's transportation system closely parallels its drainage systems and the Irrawaddy River remains the chief artery of transportation. In addition, portions of the Salween and the Irrawaddy's major tributary, the Chindwin, are also navigable. Burma also has nearly 2,000 miles (3,200 km) of railways. The main line runs from Rangoon north through Mandalay to Myitkyina near the Chinese border. Over 14,000 miles (22,500 km) of roads, of which less than one-fifth are paved, serve the nation. Burma Airways Corporation provides both domestic and international air service. All transportation services, like most production facilities, are nationalized.

The tourist industry is undeveloped as is indicated by the fewer than 30,000 visitors who arrived in 1984, as compared to 2.3 million visitors in Thailand. Tourism certainly has potential given the nation's exotic reputation, its natural beauty, and the numerous outstanding art and architectural achievements found throughout the country, especially in Rangoon, Mandalay, and Pagan.

## PEOPLE AND CULTURE

Burma's tremendous diversity in languages was recognized at independence when the first constitution established a federal state with six autonomous units based on ethnic differences. Thus, states emerged for the Karen (9% of the population), Shan (7.5%), Kachin (2%), Chin (2%), Mon, and Arakanese, in addition to Burma

Irrawaddy river steamer, Rangoon (courtesy R. Huke)

Overcrowded bus, Rangoon (courtesy J. Baker)

## ETHNIC-LINGUISTIC GROUPS

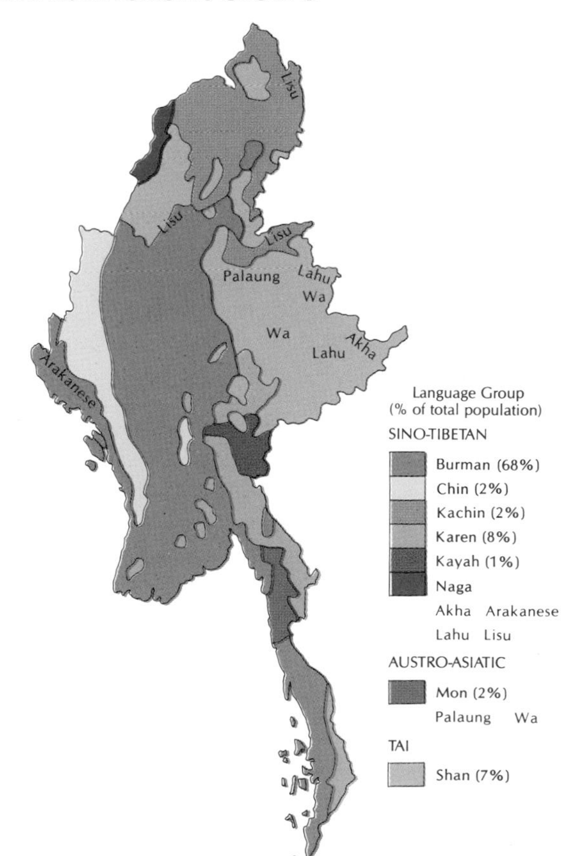

Proper, which originally contained most of the two-thirds of the majority lowlanders who spoke Burmese. Many other smaller groups are found throughout the upland areas of Burma including the Naga, Lisu, Palaung, Wa, and Lahu, and taken together, well over 100 languages and dialects are spoken by the many groups. The "long-necked" women of the 7,000-member Padaung tribe of eastern Burma maintain their individual identity and position by wearing a series of brass rings around their necks. Most of the languages spoken in Burma belong to the Sino-Tibetan language family. English is spoken as a second language among older persons and the more highly-educated. Finally, the alien Chinese and Indians comprise an important minority, especially in the coastal cities and in Rangoon.

Such ethnic diversity has been the basis for the many insurgent and dissident groups that have emerged, including the Kachin Independence Organization, the Shan State Army, the Shan United Army, and the Karen National Union, each estimated to have thousands of members. The largest insurgent group, the Burmese Communist Party, numbers as many as 15,000 members, most of whom are located near the Chinese border. This group, once supported heavily by the Beijing government, has lost strength in recent years as ties between the Chinese and Burmese governments have become closer.

**INSURGENT ACTIVITY, MID-1980s**

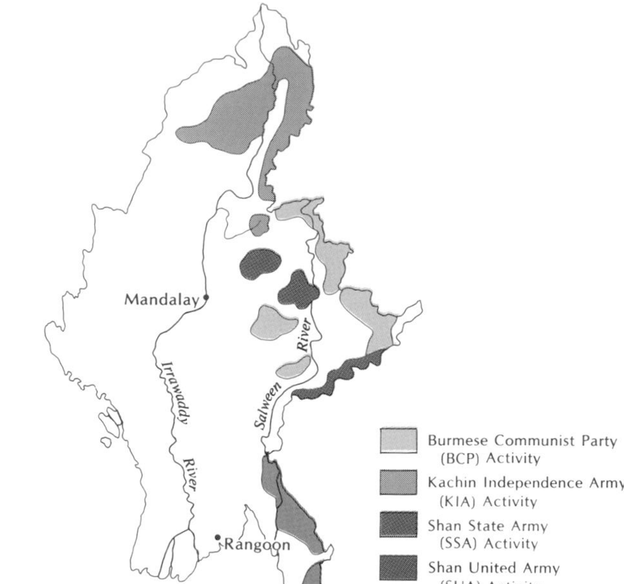


Source: *Asiaweek, August 16, 1985*

Long-necked Padaung woman (courtesy R. Huke)

Burma is fairly homogeneous in terms of religion. Over 80% are Theravada Buddhists and the remaining population includes animists in upland areas, Muslims in the south, Hindus among the Indian community, Christians, and Taoists, Confucianists, and Buddhists among the Chinese minority. Burma's art and architecture are a unique conglomeration of Indian, Buddhist, and indigenous styles. Although not necessarily the best of Burmese architecture, the Shwedagon pagoda in Rangoon is certainly the best-known representative of the Burmese style. The massive, bell-shaped main *stupa* (spire) is

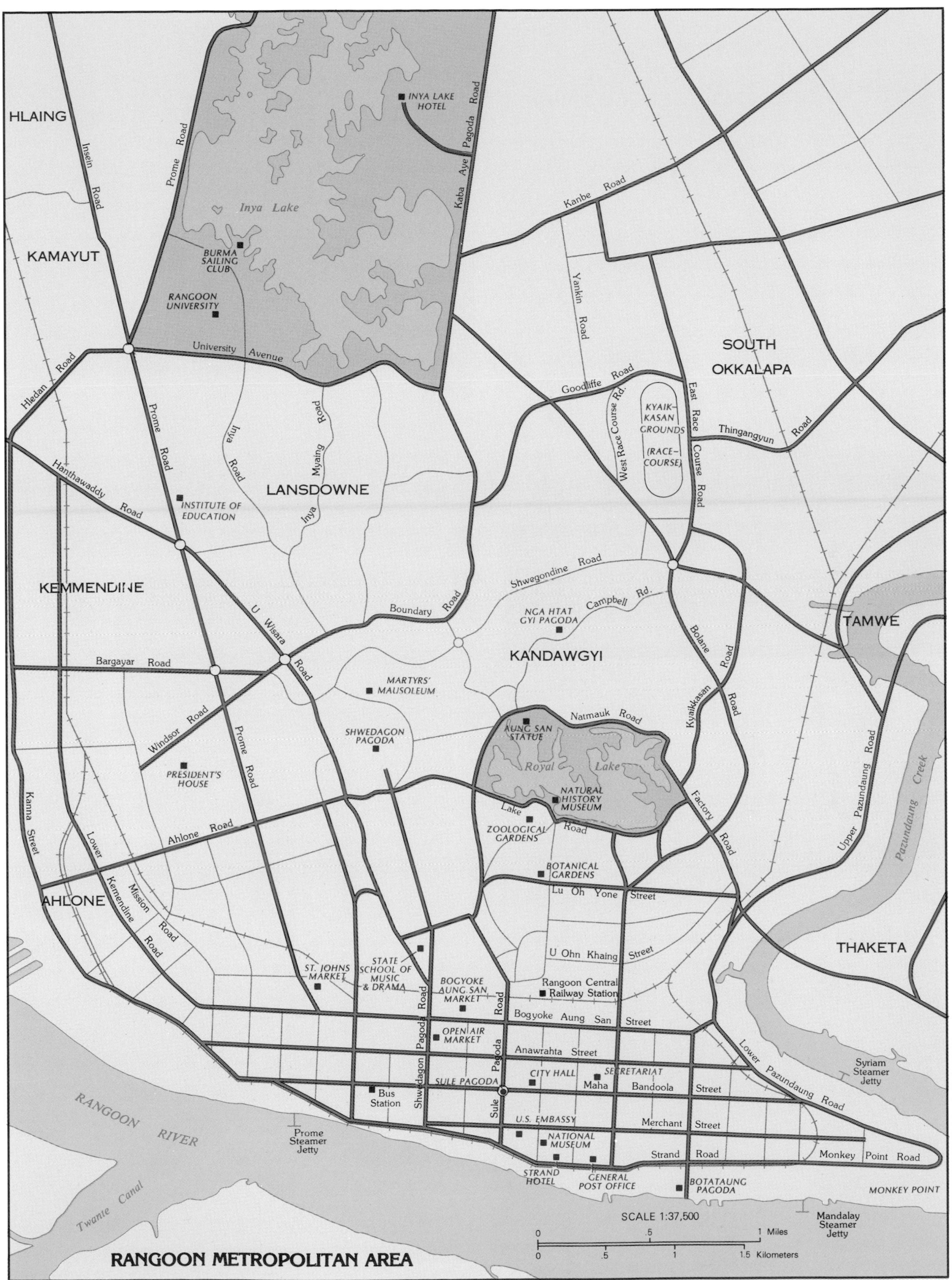

RANGOON METROPOLITAN AREA

Shwedagon pagoda, Rangoon (courtesy R. Reed)

Rangoon's tallest structure, and at 325 feet (100 m) it towers over the city. The golden, bejeweled *stupa* is surrounded by 64 smaller *stupa*s. Rangoon is unusual among Southeast Asia's largest cities in that it is devoid of tall buildings, industrial complexes, and traffic jams. Architecture representative of the British colonial period forms much of the central and riverine portions of Rangoon, which include government buildings, hotels, and shopping centers. Also unlike most other regional capitals, there is a notable absence of night life.

# 12

# *Socialist Republic of Vietnam*

*Area:* 128,052 sq mi (331,653 sq km); slightly larger than Norway or New Mexico

*Population:* 61,497,000 (1986)

*Population Density:* 480 persons per sq mi (185 persons per sq km)

*Urban Population:* 19.1%

*Annual Average Rate of Population Increase:* 2.3%

*Crude Birth Rate:* 33.6 per 1,000 population

*Crude Death Rate:* 10.3 per 1,000 population

*Infant Mortality Rate:* 69 infant deaths per 1,000 live births

*Life Expectancy:* Male—58.1 years; Female—62.5 years

*Official Language:* Vietnamese

*Currency:* Vietnamese dong (US$1 = 368 dong in 1988)

*Capital:* Hanoi

*Form of Government:* Single-party socialist republic with one legislative house.

*Chief of State:* President

*Head of Government:* Premier

*Armed Forces (1985):* 1,027,000 (army—97%; air force—2%; navy—1%)

## HISTORICAL OVERVIEW

111 B.C.–939 A.D.: Tonkin and northern Annam ruled by China.

1009–1225: Ly dynasty.

1225–1400: Tran dynasty.

1428–1788: Le dynasty.

1471: Final conquest of Champa; push southward begins in earnest.

1672: Vietnam divided at the 17th Parallel; Trinhs rule northern Vietnam; Nguyens rule southern part.

1802: Northern and southern kingdoms united and renamed Vietnam under Gia Long who founded the Nguyen dynasty.

1859: French occupy Saigon.

1862: Cochin China becomes a French colony.

1884: Annam and Tonkin proclaimed French protectorates.

1887: Annam, Tonkin, Cochin China, and Cambodia brought together as "Union Indochinoise."

1930: Emergence of the Communist Party of Indochina under Ho Chi Minh.

1940–1945: Japanese occupation.

1945: Viet Minh proclaim the Democratic Republic of Vietnam with Ho Chi Minh as president.

1949: French establish State of Vietnam.

1954: French forces defeated by Viet Minh at Dien Bien Phu; Vietnam partitioned at 17°N latitude; French forces withdrawn from Vietnam; Ngo Dinh Diem becomes president in the South.

1961: United States joins war on side of the South.

1969: Ho Chi Minh dies.

1973: United States forces withdrawn after Paris Agreement.

1975: Remaining United States citizens withdrawn.

1976: Country's reunification proclaimed; Saigon renamed Ho Chi Minh City.

1978: Vietnam invades Kampuchea.

CHINA
Nanning
Ha Giang
Cao Bang
Lao Cai
Highest Point in Vietnam 10,310
Fan Si Pan
NUI CON VOI
FAN SI PAN
Lai Chau
Lang Son
Dien Bien Phu final battle with France
Dien Bien Phu
SIP SONG CHAU THAI
Son La
Thai Nguyen
Bac Ninh
Bac Giang
Viet Tri
Hanoi
Hai Duong
Haiphong
Hon Gai
Hoa Binh
Thai Binh
Nam Dinh
Ninh Binh
Zhanjiang
GULF OF TONKIN
Hainan Strait
Haikou
HAINAN
Thanh Hoa
LAOS
Vinh
Ha Tinh
Vientiane
Porte d'Annam
ANNAMITE CHAIN
Dong Hoi
Mekong
SOUTH CHINA SEA
Quang Tri
Hue
THAILAND
Da Nang
Cham
Hoi An (Faifo)
Re
Quang Ngai
8,366
Ngoc Linh
Kontum
KONTUM PLATEAU
Pleiku
Bin Dinh
Qui Nhon
BANGKOK
Tonle Sap
Srepok
CAO NGUYEN DAC LAC
Tuy Hoa
KAMPUCHEA
Ban Me Thuot
Ninh Hoa
MNONG PLATEAU
Nha Trang
Gia Nghia
Da Lat
Cam Ranh
Cam Ranh Bay Naval Base (USSR)
CAO NGUYEN DI LINH
Phan Rang
GULF OF THAILAND
Phnom Penh
Tay Ninh
Dong Nai
Bien Hoa
Ho Chi Minh City
Phan Thiet
Cholon
Cao Lanh
Tan An
My Tho
Long Xuyen
Ben Tre
Vung Tau
Hon
Quan Phu Quoc
Rach Gia
Vinh Long
Can Tho
Hau Giang
Mouths of the Mekong
CA MAU PENINSULA
SCALE 1:7,000,000
0 50 100 150 200 250 Miles
0 50 100 150 200 250 300 350 400 Kilometers
Ca Mau
Bac Lieu
Pte. de Ca Mau (Mui Bai Bung)
Con Son

Over thirty years of war, beginning with that against French colonial forces in the 1940s and ending with the withdrawal of American forces in 1975, has meant great turmoil for Vietnam and its economy. The war and its aftermath caused many thousands of Vietnamese to flee the nation and become a part of the huge refugee movement. Internally, there has also been tremendous population redistribution since 1975 as many Vietnamese from the North have migrated southward. The economy of Vietnam was seriously disrupted as a result of the war but some progress toward reconstruction has been made since 1975. Vietnam also is gradually opening up to Western development aid and tourism. Development plans and foreign diplomatic relations, however, have been seriously disrupted by Vietnam's 1978 invasion and subsequent occupation of Kampuchea. Heavy budgetary spending on military equipment and the army, the world's fourth largest, numbering over one million, has greatly hampered economic progress.

## THE PHYSICAL ENVIRONMENT

As is so of most of Southeast Asia, Vietnam can be described as rugged. The range known as the Annamite Cordillera, where the highest elevations are over 10,000 feet (3,000 m), stretches for most of the 1,000-mile north-south extent of Vietnam. The southern part of Vietnam is dominated by the Mekong delta and lowlands, which account for much of the nation's lowland area, about 25% of the total area. Alluvial soils of the Mekong region are very fertile and this area has historically been one of the world's great rice surplus-producing regions. As one travels north of the Mekong lowlands and Ho Chi Minh City into central Vietnam, the topography is much more varied and includes coastal lowlands and the rugged mountain terrain of the Annamite Chain. Most of northern Vietnam is mountainous or hilly and here is located the country's highest elevation, Fan Si Pan (10,310 ft or 3,142 m). The limited lowlands consist of the narrow floodplain and delta of the Red River (or Song

Perfume River (courtesy W. Duiker)

Koi) and the coastal plain. The lowlands of the north are intensively cultivated and rural population densities here are among the highest in the world.

Most of Vietnam is affected by a tropical monsoon climate. Ho Chi Minh City, for example, receives 77 inches (196 cm) of rainfall annually and nearly three-quarters of the total falls between June and September as a result of the summer, or southwest, monsoon. Da Nang, on the coast in central Vietnam, also experiences the monsoon but in this case it is the winter, or northeast, monsoon and therefore nearly four-fifths of Da Nang's 77 inches (196 cm) of annual precipitation falls between September and December. In the lowland areas of southern and central Vietnam the average annual temperature of about 80°F (27°C) varies little from month to month. Northern Vietnam, on the other hand, experiences a more humid subtropical climate. Temperatures are cooler here with the annual average lowland temperature in the North about 75°F (24°C) and monthly variations ranging between 60° and 85°F (16° and 29°C). Highland areas throughout the country experience cooler and often wetter conditions. As was so in other Southeast Asian hill areas, colonial administrators and the local elite journeyed to the upland resorts during the summers to get relief from the hot, humid, and malarial conditions of the lowland capitals. Such mountain resorts in Vietnam include Da Lat, Tam Dao, and Sapa. Vietnam, along with the Philippines, experiences the majority of typhoons that affect the region, and they are regular occurrences here during the late summer.

The drainage basins of Vietnam's two major rivers contain one of the nation's principal natural resources: extremely fertile alluvial soils. Little natural vegetation remains in these lowland areas, now densely settled, where nearly all of the nation's rice is produced. Historically, the Mekong delta region has been one of the world's major rice-exporting regions but this has not been the case since the 1960s as a result of the war. Upland areas, which constitute about three-quarters of the land area, are covered by forests and it is estimated that up to one-half of the nation is forested. Bamboo, and hardwoods including mahogany, teak, rosewood, and ebony, are found. The forests, and the fauna, suffered as a result of the bombing that occurred until 1975. And over time, increasing numbers of Montagnards (upland minority groups) and shifting cultivation have further affected the flora and fauna of the uplands, which include honey bears, deer, monkeys, elephants, and wild cats such as tigers, leopards, and civets. Rhinoceros have been extinct in Vietnam since the 1940s. As is so all over the sparsely populated upland areas of Southeast Asia, there is a great variety of birds, insects, and reptiles.

CLIMATE DIAGRAM OF HO CHI MINH CITY

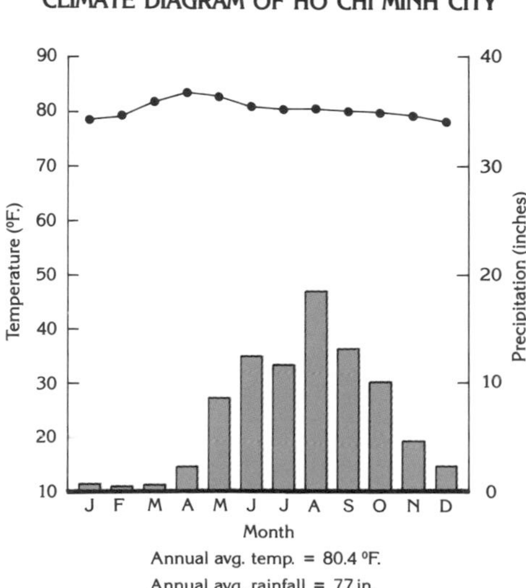


Annual avg. temp. = 80.4 °F.
Annual avg. rainfall = 77 in.

CLIMATE DIAGRAM OF HANOI

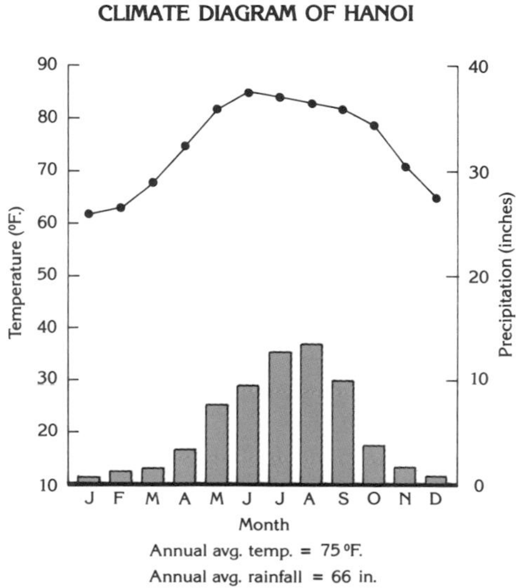


Annual avg. temp. = 75 °F.
Annual avg. rainfall = 66 in.

## HISTORICAL BACKGROUND

Evidence of an advanced culture in Indochina can be dated to the Mesolithic age (more than 10,000 years ago). Named the Bacson-Hoabinhian culture, after the provinces in Tonkin where the most numerous artifacts have been found, their economy was characterized by some form of rudimentary cultivation. In fact, the geographer Carl Sauer proposed in 1952 that sedentary cultivation was first practiced in mainland Southeast Asia, rather than in the Near East (Sauer, 1952). Racially, these were probably early Melanesoid and Australoid peoples, the ancestors of some of the contemporary Southeast Asian hill tribes, and of those who eventually migrated south and east into island Southeast Asia, New Guinea, Australia, and the Pacific.

The early ancestors of the present Vietnamese majority migrated from southern China to the Red River delta area where they gradually mixed with local peoples of Indonesian stock. A distinct Vietnamese ethnic group and local culture began to emerge, probably during the first millennium B.C. During the time of China's Han dynasty the northern half of Vietnam was annexed, and the area was a Chinese colony for a thousand years (between 111 B.C. and 939 A.D.). During this time northern Vietnam was influenced by Chinese culture and, "the(se) northern Annamite lands gradually acquired the character of a demographic extension of southern China rather than a typical part of Southeast Asia" (Fisher, p. 531). The Chinese introduced their systems of law, religion, and art, and techniques of rice cultivation, such as irrigation, double cropping, and diking. The northern Vietnamese learned much from the Chinese but assimilation was by no means complete, and the Vietnamese did preserve much of their own traditional lifeways.

HISTORIC BOUNDARIES

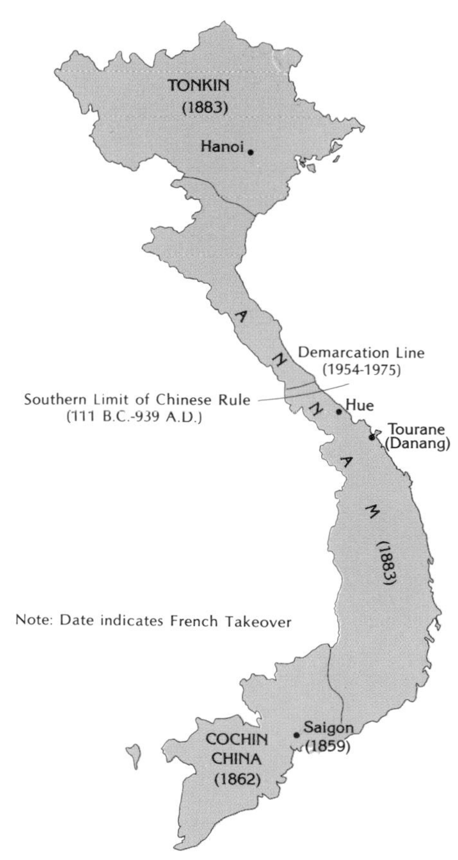


In the southern part of Vietnam two great Indianized coastal states emerged, Funan from the first to the sixth centuries A.D. and Champa between the second and fifteenth centuries. Funan, with its capital at Vyadhapura and centered on the plains of the Mekong delta, was for a time the most powerful among the peninsular states. By the sixth century Funan had weakened and was defeated by Chenla, the precursor of the great Angkor empire of Cambodia. Champa was gradually defeated by the Annamites from the north and the Khmers from the west, and by the latter part of the fifteenth century, during the time of the Le dynasty, most of what had been Champa and Funan had been annexed by Nam Viet in northern Vietnam. What is most important to remember is that the states of southern Vietnam, and for that matter most of the rest of pre-European Southeast Asia, were culturally influenced by India moreso than by other external entities. The major exception was northern Vietnam, more influenced by China, and this is a major reason for the existing cultural differences between the northern and southern parts of the nation.

During the fifteenth and sixteenth centuries it became increasingly difficult for the rulers of the Le dynasty to maintain control over Vietnam. Several local territorial families began to gain power, most notably the Nguyen family in

One-pillar pagoda, Hanoi (courtesy W. Duiker)

the South and the Trinh family in the North. In the seventeenth century the Nguyen family constructed a wall across the country at about the 17th Parallel and thus divided the country between North and South, thereafter known to the Europeans as Tonkin and Cochin China, respectively. The power of the Nguyens in Cochin China increased and by 1802 the clan had captured Hue and Hanoi in the North, thus reuniting Vietnam and establishing the Nguyen dynasty with Gia Long as emperor. A new, central, capital was established at Hue, the ancestral home of the Nguyen family.

European contact with Vietnam began in the fifteenth century. Portuguese Jesuit priests were among the first Europeans and missions were established in Tonkin, as they had been in China and Japan. After the decline of Portuguese power and the withdrawal of brief Dutch and English interests in the mid-seventeenth century, the French took the lead in missionary work and trading interests in Indochina, at least until the French Revolution, when France became more concerned with problems at home. The French met resistance from Vietnamese rulers who gradually became more hostile to Western intervention generally. Through the efforts of a French missionary, Pigneau de Behaine, Nguyen rulers (including Gia Long) in Cochin China began to accept French advice and military help. However, there ensued a period in which French advisers and missionaries were dismissed or persecuted in large part because of anti-Christian and anti-Western feelings. Missionary propaganda and French capitalists who saw a need for an overseas market persuaded Napoleon III to intercede. In 1858 a French naval force attacked the city of Tourane (Da Nang) and made it a French base. After much resistance from the Vietnamese, Saigon was taken in 1859 and by 1867 all of Cochin China had become a colony. By 1883 Annam and Tonkin were declared French protectorates and thus the European colonization of Vietnam had been completed. By 1893 these three areas were merged with Cambodia and Laos to form French Indochina.

Throughout the colonial period, Vietnamese resistance to French rule persisted. During the 1920s a young revolutionary named Ho Chi Minh formed the Vietnamese Revolutionary Youth League and in 1930 this was succeeded by the Communist Party of Indochina, also under Ho Chi Minh. In 1940 Japanese forces, with the cooperation of the French, occupied Vietnam. Ho Chi Minh's forces, called the Viet Minh, occupied Hanoi after Japan's surrender to allied forces. Ho proclaimed the Democratic Republic of Vietnam with himself as president. French forces returned to Vietnam in 1946 and, following unsuccessful negotiations between the French and Ho Chi Minh's government, war broke out. In 1949 the French established the State of Vietnam in the south. War continued and in 1954, at Dien Bien Phu, French forces were defeated. The Geneva Agreement of 1954 provided for a provisional partition of Vietnam at the 17th Parallel. Later in 1954 French forces withdrew from the south and Ngo Dinh Diem proclaimed himself president of the Republic of Vietnam. Diem refused to participate in the national elections that had been agreed upon at Geneva. Diem was opposed in the South by the insurgent Viet Cong, former members of the Viet Minh. Beginning in 1959 the North Vietnamese government actively assisted the Viet Cong, and in 1961 the United States joined the war on the side of the Saigon government. The next fourteen years were characterized by a series of American-supported military regimes in the South, periods of intense bombing of the North by the United States, failed peace agreements, and offensives by North Vietnamese and Viet Cong forces. In 1973 a withdrawl of American forces began, and in 1975, following a major Communist offensive, Saigon fell. The country's reunification was proclaimed one year later. The nation was renamed the Socialist Republic of Vietnam, and Saigon was renamed Ho Chi Minh City, in honor of the leader who died in 1969.

The war and its aftermath brought about the exodus of hundreds of thousands of refugees from Vietnam, as well as from Cambodia and Laos. Many Vietnamese fled by sea and those "boat people" who were not killed by pirates or ill health were given first asylum in one of a number of refugee camps found throughout the region (see map in Chapter 4). Hundreds of thousands of such refugees have since been resettled in the United States and Canada, among other nations. Other refugees from Vietnam, most notably ethnic Chinese, fled by land to China.

The exodus of ethnic Chinese became especially significant in 1979 when fighting broke out between Chinese and Vietnamese troops along the border between those two nations. The fighting was a result of a punitive attack by China into Vietnam in retaliation for Vietnam's invasion and subsequent installation of a pro-Vietnamese government in Kampuchea. It was in 1978 that Vietnamese forces entered Kampuchea and since then relations with many nations, especially China and the ASEAN nations, have been strained. Although Vietnam has said it would withdraw its troops from Kampuchea by 1990, there remained over 150,000 Vietnamese forces in Kampuchea in the mid-1980s and 40,000 in Laos, also a Vietnamese client state.

Relations with the Soviet Union remain strong and the Russians maintain military bases in Vietnam, one a large naval facility at Cam Ranh Bay, the former American naval base. Vietnam has indicated that it would like to establish normal relations with the United States, but the American government has rejected this possibility in large part because of the unresolved question of American soldiers who are still missing in action (MIA). A return to more normal relations with Western nations is likely, however, after this question and the issue of Kampuchea are settled.

The most important political institution is the Vietnamese Communist Party, headed by a Secretary General and governed by an all-powerful politburo. Legislative power is vested in the 496-member National Assembly, elected by universal suffrage every five years. Theoretically the Assembly has wide law-making authority but in practice it simply gives formal approval to proposals from higher authority. The country is divided into provinces and municipalities which are directly under central authority, and further subdivided into districts, towns, and vil-

**PROVINCES & CITIES**

lages, which in turn are under the authority of locally elected People's Councils.

## THE ECONOMY

As is so elsewhere in the region, the economy is dominated by agriculture with nearly 70% of the labor force involved in farming and fishing activities. Mining and manufacturing, on the other hand, account for only 3% of the labor force, but almost one-quarter of the material product by value.

Vietnam's shape has been likened to "two bags of rice hanging from a pole" and it is certainly rice that is at the forefront of the nation's agricultural economy. Over two-thirds of Vietnam's total cultivated area (8.3 million hectares, or one-quarter of its total area) is in rice, with the majority of this in the South. Historically, the fertile alluvial Mekong delta region has produced a great surplus and as a result the nation had once been a rice exporter. The war ended the surplus production and as of the mid-1980s Vietnam still had to import some rice, but production has increased in recent years. Although considerable private enterprise was permitted to thrive in the South until 1978, collectivization has been gradually extended into the South through the establishment of "New Economic Zones." Area under rice cultivation has increased in such zones, as has the population. This has occurred through major transfers of population from the North to South, and from the major urban centers to the countryside, especially in the period from 1976 to 1980. Since 1976 it is estimated that over 2.5 million persons have moved to the New Economic Zones. Out-migration from the southern urban areas to these zones has been offset by the movement of northerners into southern cities, and recently it has been reported that there has been considerable return migration from the Zones. Nonetheless, this government policy of intervention has significantly altered the population distribution of the nation in a short period of time.

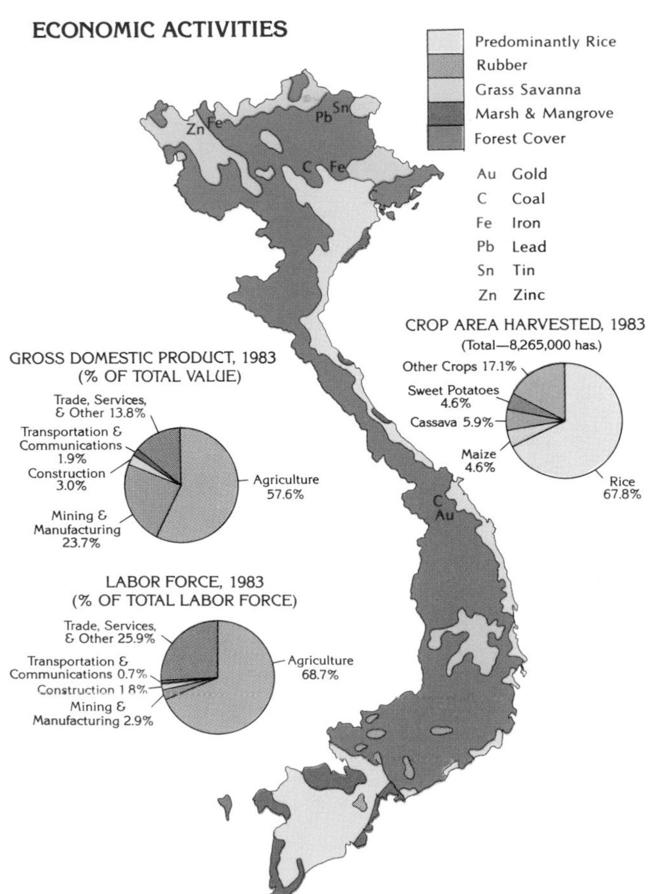


Other important agricultural commodities produced in Vietnam are maize, cassava, sweet potatoes, fruits and vegetables, and several export-oriented crops, most important of which are sugarcane, coconuts, and rubber.

Vietnam, especially the North, has an abundance of several minerals. Coal has been the most important of these resources and has been a major export commodity. In 1982 Vietnam exported about 800,000 metric tons of coal, mostly to non-Communist nations. Other important minerals, all produced in the North, are tin, copper, chromite, phosphate rock, and iron. Beginning in 1979, Vietnam began production of extensive offshore petroleum deposits and this production, in addition to significant thermal and hydroelectric power, has helped to make Vietnam less dependent upon energy imports. The limited heavy industry that exists is located principally in the North, in the Hanoi-Haiphong area. Some machinery, steel, cement, and phosphate fertilizer is produced in the North based in part on locally produced raw material and hydroelectric energy. Textile products and processed food are manufactured in the North and South. Manufactured items are

**TRADE BY COMMODITY GROUP, 1980**
**(% OF TOTAL VALUE)**

IMPORTS
(VALUE UNKNOWN)

All Other Imports
14.9%
Machinery
23.2%
Food & Food
Products 17.2%
Fuel & Raw
Materials 44.7%

EXPORTS
(VALUE UNKNOWN)

Food & Agricultural
Raw Materials 8.6%
Handicrafts
18.6%
Manufactured Goods
72.8%

*Source: Encyclopedia Britannica (Chicago: Encyclopedia Britannica, 1984)*

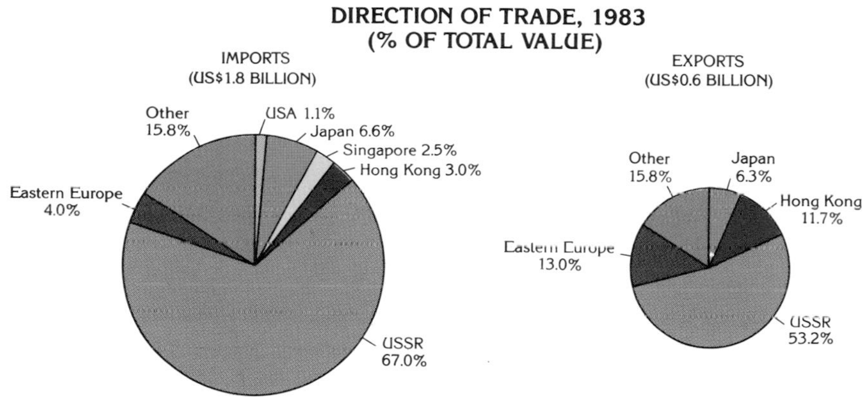


*Source: The Europa Yearbook 1986 (London: Europa Publications, 1986)*

the major imports with agricultural machinery, transportation equipment, and chemical fertilizers accounting for most of the value.

In summary, the northern and southern parts of Vietnam complement each other; the South has the agricultural surplus and the North contains the industrial and mineral core of the nation.

## TRANSPORTATION

There are over 1,500 miles (2,400 km) of railways in Vietnam and 37,000 miles (59,000 km) of roads, 16% of which are paved. Both systems connect Hanoi and Ho Chi Minh City with each other and with the other important urban centers in the country. Long-distance bus service also connects the nation's two major cities, as does Air Vietnam, which offers four flights daily between them. Foreign visitors can arrive on weekly international flights to Hanoi or Ho Chi Minh City from Moscow, Vientiane, Rangoon, Bangkok, East Berlin, or Paris. By far the most important port is Haiphong, an urban area with a population of over one million.

## PEOPLE AND CULTURE

Although dialect and other differences exist, ethnically the Vietnamese constitute the vast majority of the population and comprise between 85 and 90% of the total. A variety of other ethnic groups make up the remainder, the two most important of which are the Chinese and the mountain tribal groups, collectively called Montagnards. The approximately one million Chinese account for nearly 2% of the total, their proportion and absolute num-

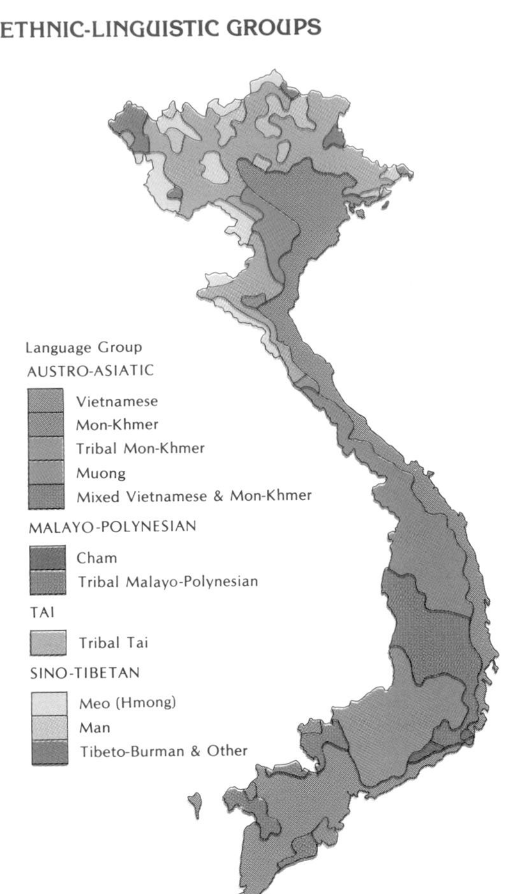

Cathedral, Ho Chi Minh City (courtesy W. Duiker)

Cholon (Chinatown), Ho Chi Minh City (courtesy W. Duiker)

HO CHI MINH CITY METROPOLITAN AREA

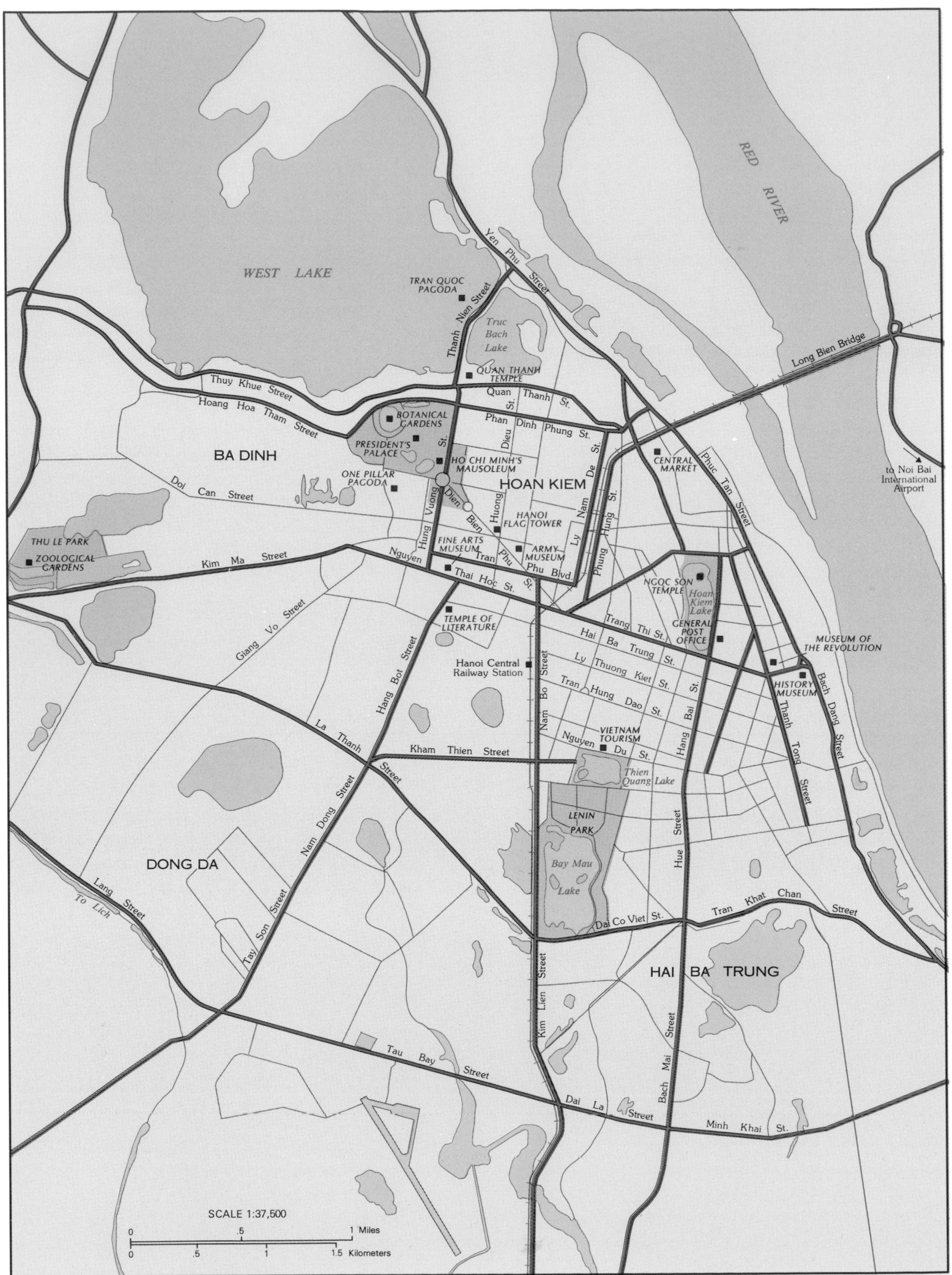


HANOI METROPOLITAN AREA

bers somewhat less in recent years because of the flight of many Chinese as a result of fighting between China and Vietnam over Kampuchea. Most Chinese reside in the South, and many of these reside in Cholon, historically the Chinese area of what is now metropolitan Ho Chi Minh City. As is so in other Southeast Asian nations, the Chinese in Vietnam have in the past controlled a disproportionate share of rice trading, rice and corn milling, real estate, shipping, and banking. The 1978 government ban on private trade in Vietnam seriously affected the Chinese business community and this also was a reason for the flight of Chinese from the country.

Montagnards consist of about thirty upland tribal groups of differing cultural backgrounds who speak a variety of languages from one of two major families, Malayo-Polynesian or Austro-Asiatic (Mon-Khmer). Other minorities include over one-half million Cambodians near the southern border of Kampuchea and several thousand Cham in coastal central Vietnam, descendents of those who lived in the once powerful state of Champa.

Like other Asian groups, there are large numbers of Vietnamese emigrants who reside outside Vietnam, most notably the refugees of the 1970s and 1980s. In Kampuchea, there are thousands of Vietnamese who have settled, especially in Phnom Penh. There are fears among many Kampucheans that this is a part of a deliberate policy that ultimately will lead to the total Vietnamization of Kampuchea.

Traditional Vietnamese religion includes elements of Chinese religious beliefs including Mahayana Buddhism, Confucianism, and Taoism. Buddhism is the largest religion, and Roman Catholicism, brought to Vietnam by the Portuguese and French, is an important minority religion, especially in the South. Approximately 6% of the population are Roman Catholic. A number of Buddhist sects exist, the best known of which are both from the South, the Cao Dai, an amalgam of Eastern and Western traditions, and the Hoa Hao, a radical form of Buddhism. Some upland tribal groups follow animistic beliefs.

Traditional Vietnamese art and architecture have been heavily influenced by China, especially in the North, and by India (via Cambodia), most notably in the South. More recently, there is evidence of French style. Vietnamese forms of opera and the country's favorite literary genre, poetry, flourish in the cities.

Ho Chi Minh City and Hanoi are, respectively, Southeast Asia's fourth and fifth largest metropolitan areas and despite the war and bombing, much evidence of the nation's long and varied history can still be seen. Hanoi under French rule became one of Asia's most attractive cities and the broad, tree-lined boulevards and parks can still be visited. Numerous pagodas and the mausoleum in honor of Ho Chi Minh are other important sites in Hanoi. Pagodas, the Notre Dame Basilica, the Central Market, and an excellent National Museum are among the important attractions in Ho Chi Minh City, located on the banks of the Saigon River. The city of Cholon, Vietnam's "Chinatown," is a part of the Ho Chi Minh City metropolitan area, and here can be found the narrow streets, shop-houses, and temples typical of Chinatowns throughout the region. The infamous pre-1975 Saigon nightlife no longer exists in the city; there are very few bars and prostitutes in Ho Chi Minh City and practically none in Hanoi.

# 13

# *People's Republic of Kampuchea**

*Area:* 69,900 square miles (181,040 sq km); about the size of Missouri or Uruguay

*Population:* 7,477,000 (1986)

*Population Density:* 107 persons per sq mi (41 persons per sq km)

*Urban Population:* 13.9%

*Annual Average Rate of Population Increase:* 2.5%

*Crude Birth Rate:* 42.3 per 1,000 population

*Crude Death Rate:* 17.6 per 1,000 population

*Infant Mortality Rate:* 140 infant deaths per 1,000 live births

*Life Expectancy:* Male—45.3 years; Female—48.2 years

*Official Language:* Khmer

*Currency:* 1 new riel = 100 sen (US$ = 4 riels in 1985)

*Capital:* Phnom Penh

*Form of Government:* Single-party people's republic

*Chief of State:* President

*Head of Government:* Prime minister

*Armed Forces (1984):* 30,000 (army—100%); in addition, approximately 180,000 Vietnamese troops were stationed in Kampuchea

## HISTORICAL OVERVIEW

802: Jayavarman II founds the Angkorian Empire.

12th Century: Angkor Wat built under Suryavarman II; Angkor Thom built under Jayavarman VII.

1431: Angkor abandoned.

1863: French protectorate of Cambodge (Cambodia) established.

1941: Norodom Sihanouk, aged 18, is crowned king.

1949: French granted limited independence within the French Union.

1953: Full independence granted by France.

1970: Sihanouk deposed by right-wing General Lon Nol; Khmer Republic proclaimed.

1975: Phnom Penh falls to Communist Khmer Rouge.

1976: Country renamed Democratic Kampuchea; Khieu Samphan becomes president and Pol Pot is named prime minister.

1978: Vietnamese forces invade Kampuchea.

1979: Phnom Penh falls to Vietnamese forces; People's Republic of Kampuchea proclaimed; Heng Samrin becomes president.

At its zenith in the twelfth century, the Khmer (or Angkorian) empire was the center of power in mainland Southeast Asia. Its capital, the great temple cities of Angkor Wat and Angkor Thom, were among the world's largest cities of the time. Today, the area that was the heart of this great empire, called Cambodia by some and Kampuchea by others, is among the poorest and least developed of the world's nations, in part because of the wartime atrocities carried out, especially since 1975. This relatively small nation is perhaps the single key to peace in Southeast Asia today. Invaded by Vietnam in

*The United Nations recognizes a coalition government-in-exile headed by Prince Norodom Sihanouk. The official name is the Coalition Government of Democratic Kampuchea.

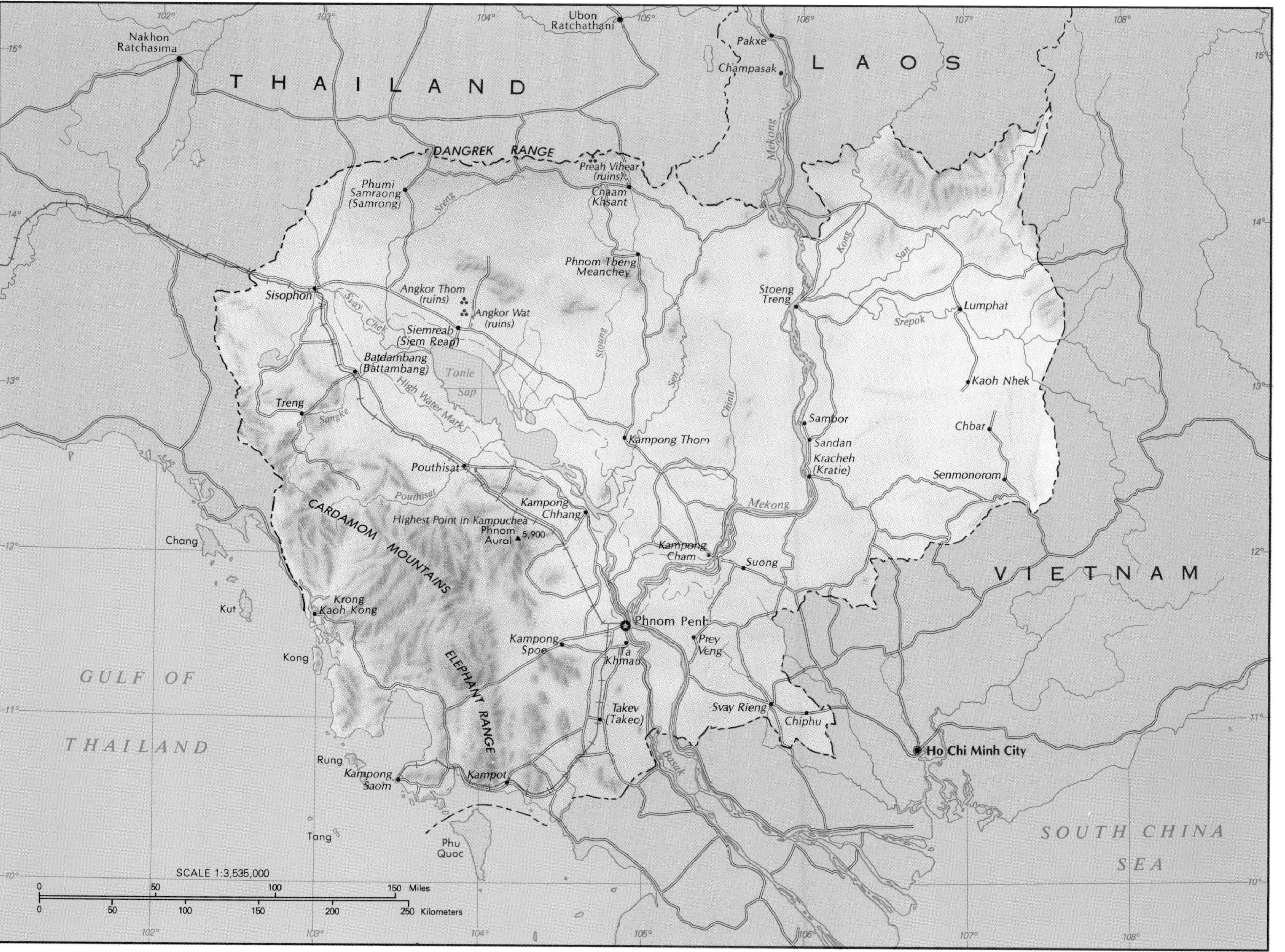
THAILAND
LAOS
VIETNAM
SOUTH CHINA SEA
GULF OF THAILAND
Nakhon Ratchasima
Ubon Ratchathani
Pakxe
Champasak
Mekong
DANGREK RANGE
Preah Vihear (ruins)
Chaam Ksant
Phumi Samraong (Samrong)
Sreng
Phnom Tbeng Meanchey
Sisophon
Angkor Thom (ruins)
Angkor Wat (ruins)
Sway Chek
Siemreab (Siem Reap)
Stoung
Sen
Chinit
Batdambang (Battambang)
Tonle Sap
High Water Mark
Treng
Sangke
Kampong Thom
Pouthisat
CARDAMOM MOUNTAINS
Kampong Chhang
Highest Point in Kampuchea
Phnom Aural 5,900
Kampong Cham
Suong
Chang
Kut
Krong Kaoh Kong
Kong
Phnom Penh
Kampong Spoe
Ta Khmau
Prey Veng
ELEPHANT RANGE
Takev (Takeo)
Svay Rieng
Chiphu
Basak
Rung
Kampong Saom
Kampot
Tang
Phu Quoc
Ho Chi Minh City
Stoeng Treng
Kong
San
Srepok
Lumphat
Kaoh Nhek
Sambor
Sandan
Kracheh (Kratie)
Chbar
Senmonorom
SCALE 1:3,535,000
0 50 100 150 Miles
0 50 100 150 200 250 Kilometers
102° 103° 104° 105° 106° 107° 108°
15° 14° 13° 12° 11° 10°

1978, the country has been a Vietnamese colony since 1979. The once great Khmer peoples, some maintain, are undergoing a purposeful policy of "Vietnamization" whereby the country will one day become a part of Vietnam.

## THE PHYSICAL ENVIRONMENT

Except for the microstates of Singapore and Brunei, Kampuchea is the smallest nation in area in the region. Much of this compactly shaped nation is a relatively flat, fertile alluvial area drained by the Mekong and its tributaries. The Mekong averages about 1.25 miles (2 km) in width throughout most of its course in Kampuchea and is interrupted by rapids and falls between the Laotian border and the city of Kracheh (Kratie) further south. The volume of water carried by the river varies greatly throughout the year, and during the wet season, from June to October, the river is especially flood prone. When the flow is heavy, water is diverted via the Tonle River (which reverses its direction of flow) to the Tonle Sap (or "Great Lake"). During such times the lake swells to an area that is more than twice the size it occupies in the dry season. The frequent floodwaters carry rich sediments, and thus the high fertility of the alluvial soils is constantly renewed. Historically the area has been one of the world's major rice surplus regions and the lake is among the world's richest sources for freshwater fish.

The major upland areas and the highest elevations of the country are in the southwest between the Tonle Sap and the Gulf of Thailand. Here are the Cardamom and Elephant ranges and the nation's highest peak, Phnom (Mount) Aural, nearly 6,000 feet (1,800 m) in elevation. This southwestern upland area has been the base of the anti-Vietnam insurgent movement that emerged after the 1979 takeover. The Dangrek Range forms the northern border with Thailand, and east of the Mekong the lowland area gradually ascends to a region of densely forested mountains and plateaus in the northeast along the border with Vietnam and Laos.

The climate is controlled by the monsoons; the wet season occurs from May to November,

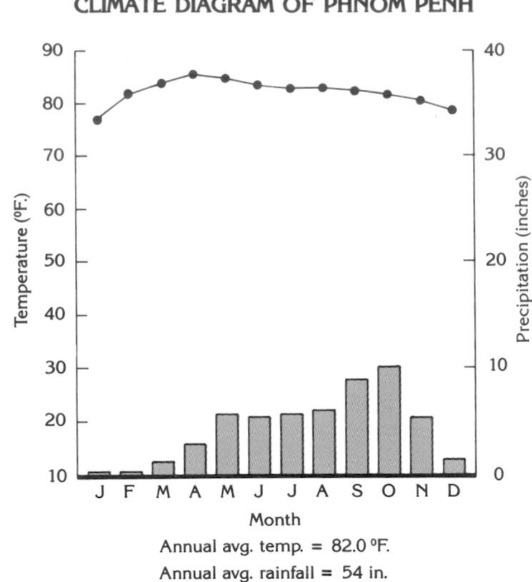


when the summer (high-sun) monsoon brings strong prevailing winds from the southwest. During the rest of the year, the light winds of the winter (low-sun) monsoon come from the northeast and bring much less rain. In all, about three-quarters of the rain falls during the southwest monsoon season.

About three-quarters of Kampuchea's land area is in forest and woodland and there is a smaller area of savanna or grassland. Important forest species include bamboo, rattan, and various palms. Virgin rain forests exist on the lower windward slopes of the Cardamom and Elephant ranges in the southwest. Mangrove forests fringe the coastal areas. Animal life is typical of that of much of mainland Southeast Asia and includes elephants, tigers, and smaller cats such as the leopard. There are several varieties of venomous snakes including the cobra and Russell's viper.

## HISTORICAL BACKGROUND

Although debated, the origins of Kampuchea can probably be traced to the Indianized kingdom of Funan, which was established in the vicinity of the Mekong delta region sometime between the first and third centuries A.D. Later Khmer traditions derived directly from the Indianized heritage of Funan. The successor state to Funan was Chenla, a Khmer-based empire that incorporated Funan and lasted from the fifth to the seventh century before it came under the suzerainty of the Javanese.

In the first few years of the ninth century, Jayavarman II threw off Javanese domination and founded the Angkorian empire. Following the lead of Indianized states elsewhere in the region, he became the first "god-king" of the empire. Although a hydraulic system was developed during the time of the Chenla empire, one legacy of this early Angkorian period may have been the development of a more advanced hydraulic system that, among other things, supplied irrigation water to produce enough rice for the population of nearly one million that inhabited the immediate vicinity of the Angkorian capital. In the ninth century Theravada Buddhism was introduced and the first Angkorian capital, Yasodharapura, was built during the reign of Yasovarman I (Coedes, 1963). Later capitals built in the same general locale were Angkor Wat and Angkor Thom. The Khmer empire attained its zenith in the twelfth century and the magnificent capital of Angkor Wat was among the largest and finest of the temple complexes that existed at the time (see photo in Chapter 2). Like the many other temples, Angkor Wat closely reflected aspects of Hinduism; in this case it was the physical representation of the Hindu cosmology. In 1178 the neighboring kingdom of Champa invaded Angkor but Jayavarman VII soon expelled the Cham and by the close of the twelfth century had extended the boundaries of the empire to their greatest, from the Annamite Chain in the north to the Malay Peninsula in the south.

The death of Jayavarman VII in 1218 marked the beginning of the end for the Khmer empire. The Siamese began a series of invasions and in 1394 they captured the capital; in 1431 the capital was abandoned and a new capital was established at Lovek. Although the Khmer attempted to reinstate their power at various times, continued invasions from Siam and, later, from Vietnam, curtailed such attempts. By the seventeenth century the former Khmer empire was a vassal state of Siam and Vietnam, which it remained until the arrival of the Europeans.

In 1863 the French declared Cambodia a protectorate and in 1887 it became a part of the larger French Indochinese Union. During World War II Cambodia, like virtually all of Southeast Asia, was a part of the Japanese empire. Following the war Cambodia resumed its colonial relationship with France and by 1949, under the leadership of King Norodom Sihanouk, Cambodia received limited independence within the French Union. In 1953 full independence was achieved.

Prince Sihanouk (who abdicated his throne in favor of his father) was an extremely popular leader among the Khmer people and remained the head of state in Cambodia until 1970, when he was deposed by a right-wing coup headed by General Lon Nol. Sihanouk established good relations with both China and Vietnam, and was critical of the American role in Southeast Asia. Faced with a Communist insurgency movement, the Khmer Rouge, Sihanouk found it increasingly difficult to keep Cambodia out of the Vietnam War. After he was deposed in 1970 Sihanouk formed a government-in-exile, which included the Communist Khmer Rouge. Lon Nol was supported by the United States but as the American war effort wound down, the Khmer Rouge gained power and brought about the fall of Phnom Penh in April, 1975. For a brief time after the Khmer Rouge victory Sihanouk was restored as head of state but never effectively returned to power and only stayed in the country briefly.

Under Khmer Rouge leadership, soon dominated by Pol Pot, a program of radical social change was carried out whereby the cities and towns were largely evacuated and hundreds of thousands of people, many of them well educated, were put to death by the new regime. Pol Pot established close links with China beginning in 1975 while relations with Vietnam, on the other hand, deteriorated.

In 1978 the Vietnamese began their invasion of Kampuchea and in January, 1979 Phnom Penh fell. The People's Republic of Kampuchea was proclaimed and Heng Samrin became the new leader. The Khmer Rouge fled to the uplands of the southwest and to areas near the Thai border to fight a guerrilla war against the Vietnamese. It is estimated that about 30,000 Khmer Rouge forces are engaged in the war against the Vietnamese in Kampuchea. The Vietnamese takeover of Kampuchea was soundly condemned by the majority of the world's nations, and today the ASEAN nations, as well as the United Nations, recognize a coalition government-in-exile, headed by Prince Sihanouk, as the legitimate government.

After the 1979 takeover by Vietnam, difficulties continued for the Khmer people and many died of starvation, disease, or as casualties of war. Thousands fled the country to end up in refugee camps, mostly in Thailand near the Kampuchean border. The ASEAN nations, and especially Thailand, are strongly opposed to the Vietnamese colonization of Kampuchea and have even given support to the armed forces of the Khmer Rouge. The United States and China find themselves allies in the opposition to the Soviet-supported Vietnamese takeover of Kampuchea. In short, until the Vietnamese forces leave Kampuchea (which Vietnam has stated it will do by 1990) there is little hope for peace or cooperation as it relates to Southeast Asia either between Vietnam and ASEAN, or among the superpowers.

A major potential tragedy in Kampuchea is related to what has been called the policy of "Vietnamization" whereby Vietnamese are settling in Kampuchea until gradually, it is feared, the Khmer population will be assimilated. In addition to some 180,000 Vietnamese troops stationed in Kampuchea, it is estimated that there may be several hundred thousand Vietnamese settlers. Many have settled in the cities and towns but others are also settling in rural villages, especially on the banks of the major rivers and around the Tonle Sap, where they have become fishermen.

Kampuchea is a single-party people's republic with one legislative house, the 117-member National Assembly. A Council of State is elected from among the members of the Assembly. Local administration is carried out by People's Committees. Kampuchea is divided into twenty provinces which are in turn subdivided into municipalities, districts, communes, and wards.

## THE ECONOMY

The economy is predominantly an agricultural one but since 1975 there have been severe food

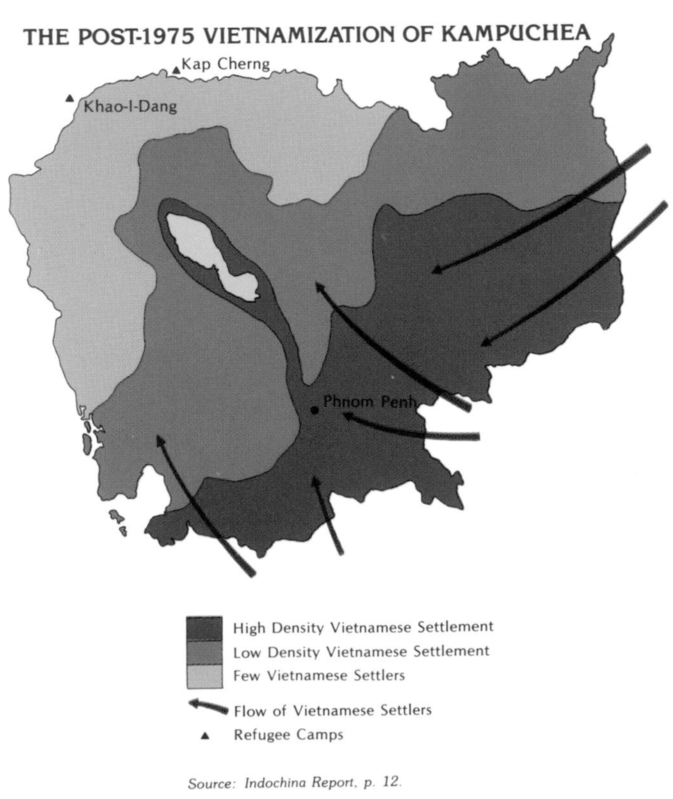


Source: *Indochina Report*, p. 12.

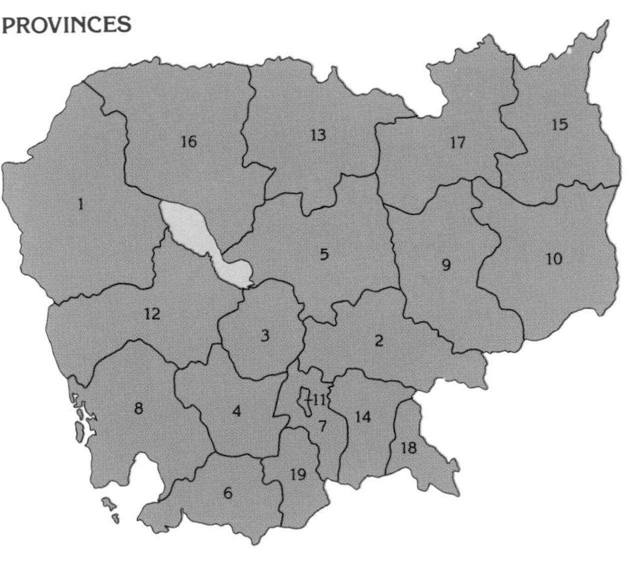


1. Batdambang
2. Kampong Cham
3. Kampong Chhnang
4. Kampong Spoe
5. Kampong Thum
6. Kampot
7. Kandal
8. Kaoh Kong
9. Kracheh
10. Mondol Kiri
11. Phnom Penh
12. Pouthisat
13. Preah Vihear
14. Prey Veng
15. Rotanokiri
16. Siemreab-Otdar Meanchey
17. Stoeng Treng
18. Svay Rieng
19. Takev

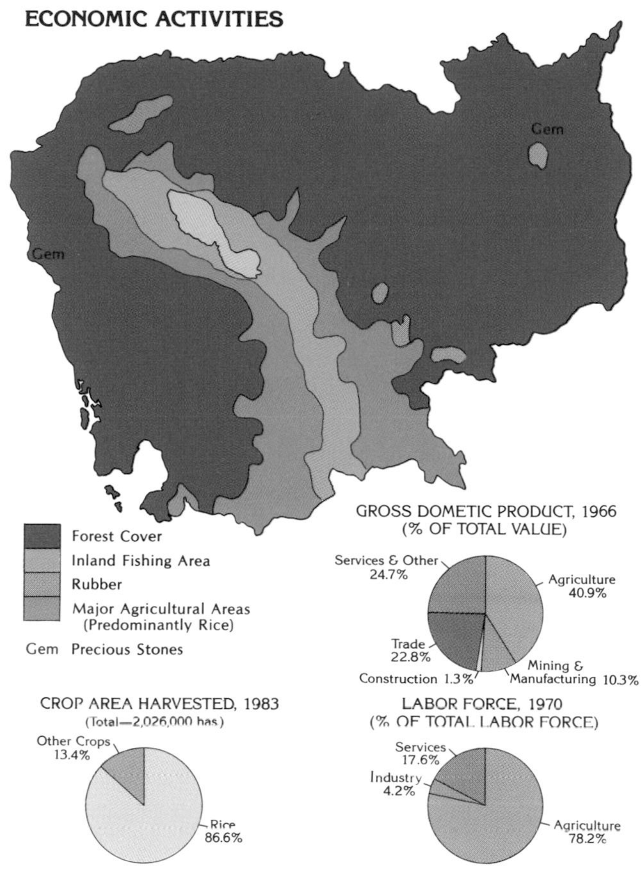


shortages. Historically, Kampuchea has been an exporter of rice but the country has had to import rice nearly every year since 1975. In 1975 Pol Pot nationalized all sectors of the economy and agriculture was collectivized. Most of the urban population was driven into rural areas where they were forced to work on the land. While the aim was to produce a surplus of rice and other crops the food shortages continued, due partly to flooding or droughts.

Other crops that Kampuchea has produced under normal conditions include rubber, pepper, sesame, maize, sweet potatoes, dry beans, and cassava. Since 1982, according to FAO, production in most crops has improved. Increase in livestock production, notably pigs, water buffalo, and cattle, has also reportedly increased. Fish production, especially in the rich waters of the Tonle Sap, has had the most success; it is estimated that production tripled between 1980 and 1985. Considerable potential also exists in timber production, but this is little developed.

Kampuchea has very limited mineral resources and these include iron ore, phosphate, and precious stones. Currently, phosphates are the only mineral commercially produced. Manufacturing was devastated during the war years and is still little developed but some recovery is evident, mostly in the area of rice and food processing.

The few exports are agricultural commodities such as fish, rubber, and logs. Currently, trade is almost wholly with Vietnam and the Soviet Union (diagram illustrates direction of trade in 1973).

## TRANSPORTATION

The war years destroyed much of the transportation system in Kampuchea. Gradually the roads and railroads have been restored; for example, the railway that links Phnom Penh and Kampong Som (formerly Sihanoukville, completed in 1960), the country's major seaport, was reopened in 1979. Total railway mileage is currently about 400 miles (645 km) and roads ac-

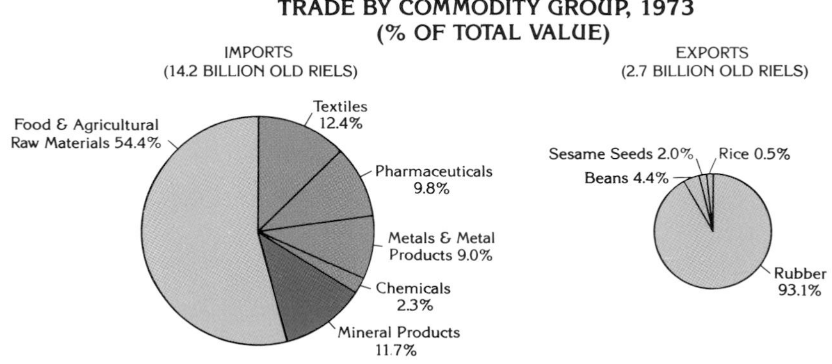


*Source: Encyclopedia Britannica (Chicago: Encyclopedia Britannica, 1985)*

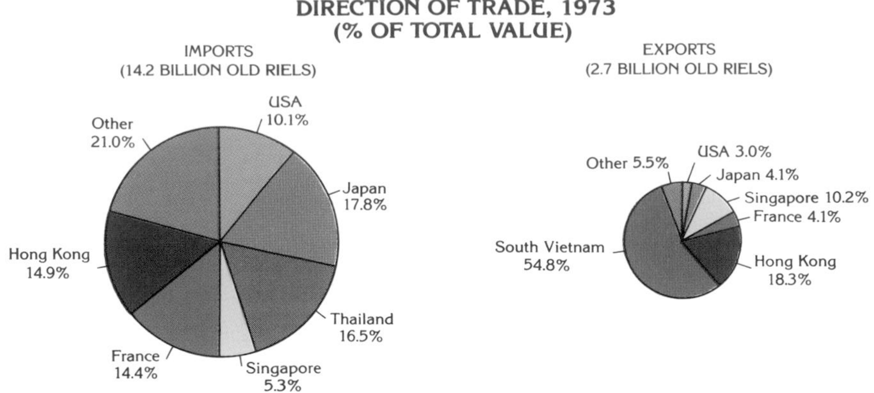


*Source: Encyclopedia Britannica (Chicago: Encyclopedia Britannica, 1985)*

count for over 8,000 miles (12,870 km); about 20% of the roads are paved. Inland waterways constitute another major transportation route, although these are annually affected by heavy rains and floods. Phnom Penh has an international airport and scheduled flights run to Ho Chi Minh City, Hanoi, and Vientiane via Air Kampuchea, Air Vietnam, and Lao Aviation.

## PEOPLE AND CULTURE

Over 90% of the population belong to the Khmer ethnic group. Before 1975 the largest minority ethnolinguistic groups included the Chinese, Vietnamese, Cham, and various upland tribal groups. In 1970 when the right-wing Lon Nol regime came to power many Vietnamese fled Cambodia and with the ascendency of the Khmer Rouge in 1975 other ethnic minority peoples were expelled from the country, or fled. Thousands of Chinese, for example, sought refuge in nearby Vietnam. After 1978 there was a new immigration of Vietnamese and today the Vietnamese again comprise perhaps 5% of the Kampuchean population. The distribution of ethnic groups, and of the population more generally, has been altered greatly as a result of the turmoil that began about 1970. Given such instability and the dearth of information available, it is not possible to depict the distribution of ethnic groups in the nation today (the map included shows the situation about 1970).

The Khmer are followers of Theravada Buddhism, introduced in the tenth century. Until 1975 Buddhism was the state religion and it is estimated that in the 1980s perhaps 85% of the population still adhered to the faith. Minority populations generally followed other religions; for example, the Cham are Muslims (3% of the population), and the Chinese and Vietnamese follow one or another of the Chinese religions.

Expressions of material and nonmaterial cul-

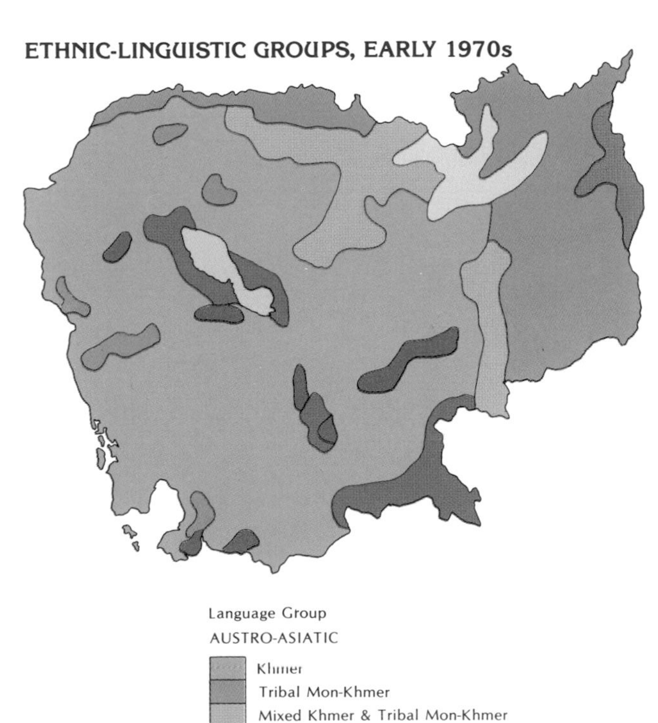

Phnom Penh, 1985 (courtesy W. Duiker)

**PHNOM PENH, EARLY 1970s**

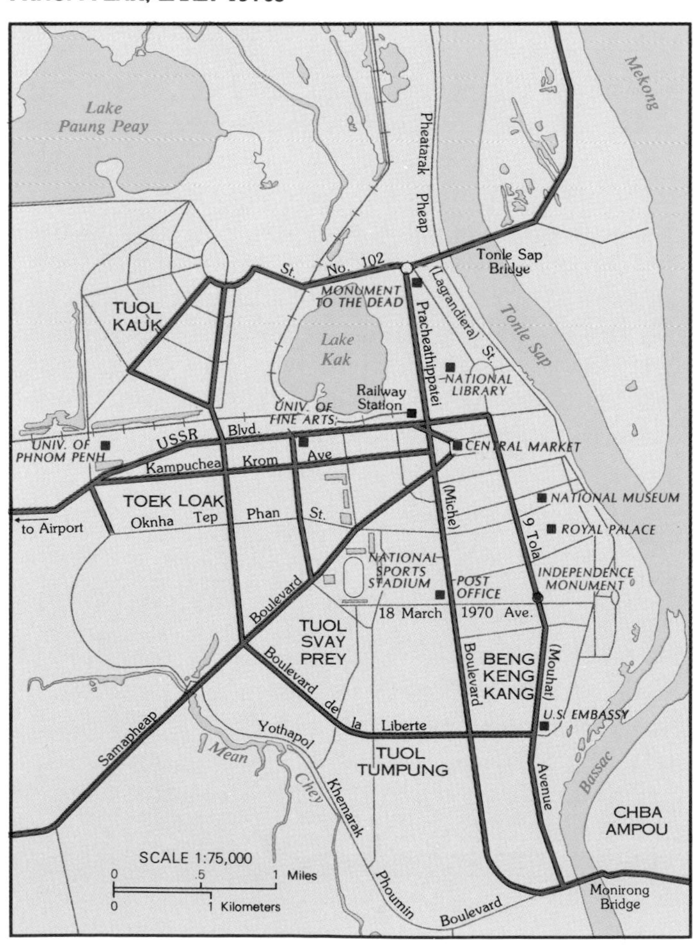


ture of the Khmer have their origins in the Indian traditions, which can be traced to Funan, Chenla, and of course, the Angkorian empire. This is epitomized in the magnificent architecture of Angkor Wat but it is also evidenced in the music, dance, and drama for which the Khmer are famous. Highly stylized Khmer classical ballet adapted from the Indian tradition can be witnessed in Phnom Penh's School of Fine Arts.

After 1975 and the expulsion of most city dwellers to rural areas, Kampuchea has been the least urbanized nation in the region. Before 1975 Phnom Penh, the nation's capital and largest city, had a population of about 1,000,000 (map of Phnom Penh shows situation in early-1970s). Following the Khmer Rouge expulsion of city dwellers to rural areas after 1975, Phnom Penh and other cities became veritable ghost towns. As late as the early 1980s the population of the capital was perhaps 200,000 and it is estimated that today its population may have returned to as many as 700,000. Migrants from rural areas are moving to the city, commercial activity is increasing, and even a few tourists are showing up in the city and staying in one of the three hotels that were in full operation in the mid-1980s. The five main city markets, the National Museum, and the Royal Palace are among the few attractions for visitors to the city.

# 14

# *Lao People's Democratic Republic*

*Area:* 91,430 sq mi (236,804 sq km); slightly smaller than the United Kingdom or Michigan

*Population:* 3,704,000 (1986)

*Population Density:* 41 persons per sq mi (16 persons per sq km)

*Urban Population:* 15.9%

*Annual Average Rate of Population Increase:* 2.4%

*Crude Birth Rate:* 41.9 per 1,000 population

*Crude Death Rate:* 17.9 per 1,000 population

*Infant Mortality Rate:* 137 infant deaths per 1,000 live births

*Life Expectancy:* Male—45.4 years; Female—49.3 years

*Official Language:* Lao

*Currency:* Laotian new kip (US$ = 350 new kips in 1988)

*Capital:* Vientiane

*Form of Government:* Unitary single-party people's republic

*Chief of State:* President

*Head of Government:* Prime minister

*Armed Forces (1984):* 53,700 (army—93%; navy—3%; air force—4%)

## HISTORICAL OVERVIEW

1353: Kingdom of Lan Xang unifies scattered principalities under King Fa Ngum; lasts 350 years.

1893: Laos becomes a protectorate of France.

1949: Laos becomes independent within the French Union.

1953: Full independence recognized by France.

1965: De facto partitioning of Laos established.

1975: Monarchy abolished; People's government established.

1977: Twenty-five-year treaty of friendship between Laos and Vietnam signed.

Formerly a part of French Indochina, Laos is today one of the Southeast Asia's poorest and least developed nations. It is unique in the region in that it is a landlocked nation but is similar to the other nations in terms of its cultural diversity. Located between much more powerful neighbors including Burma, China, Vietnam, and Thailand, Laos has been of great strategic importance and as a result it has a long history of foreign encroachment. A Communist nation, Laos' foreign policy is today closely related to that of Vietnam and the Soviet Union. Since the 1960s, and especially since 1975, many ethnic Lao have fled the country for Thailand, and today Thailand has a larger Lao-speaking population than does Laos itself.

## THE PHYSICAL ENVIRONMENT

Laos, like much of the regional landscape, can be characterized as very rugged. The principal mountain range, the Annamite Cordillera, trends northeast-southwest. The highest peak, Phou Bia, is over 9,000 feet (2,740 m) high. Mountain ranges are incised by narrow river valleys, most of which are southwest-flowing tributaries of the Mekong River, which accounts for most of the nation's western boundary. One vital

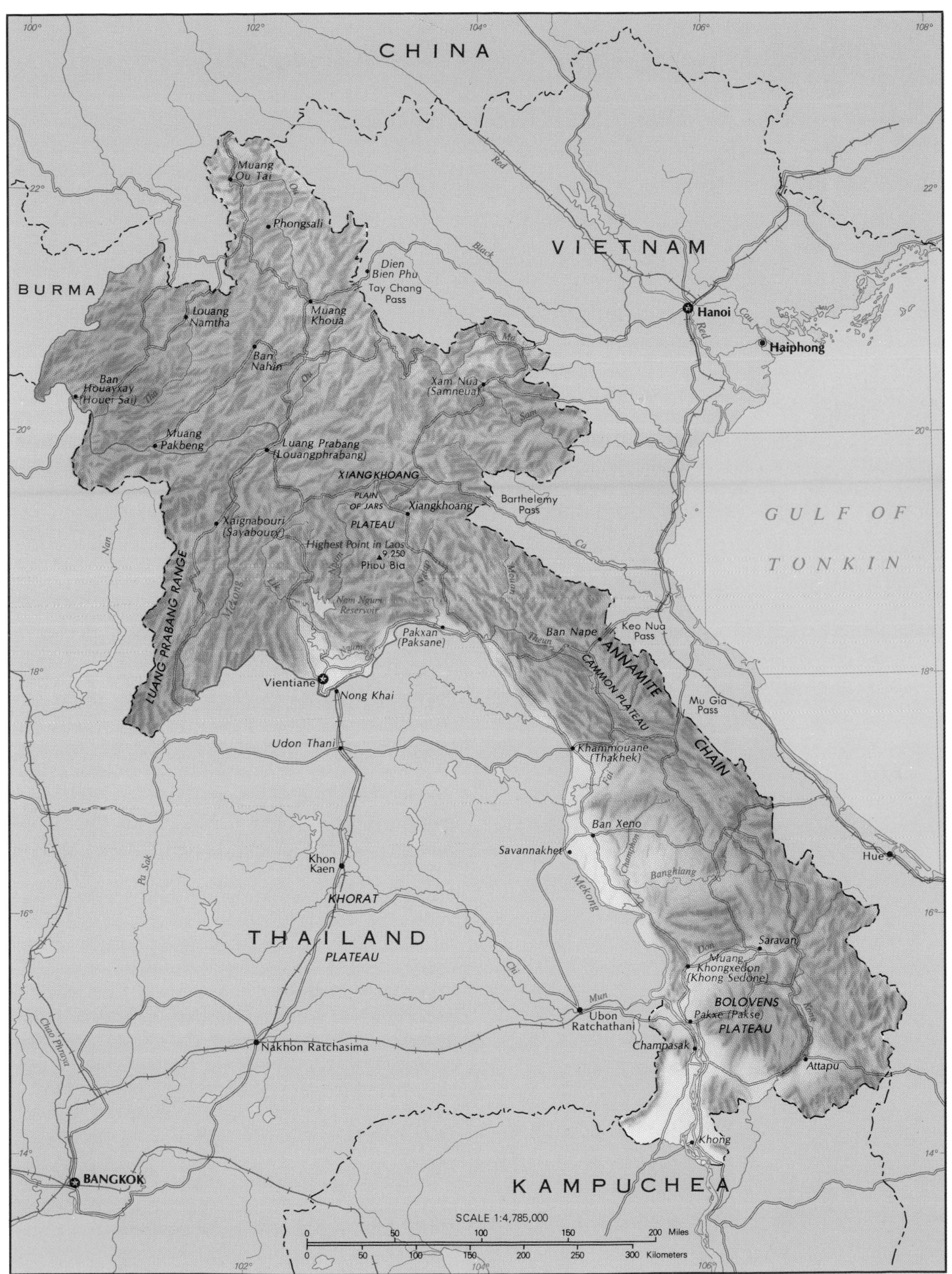
CHINA
VIETNAM
BURMA
THAILAND
KAMPUCHEA
GULF OF TONKIN
Muang Ou Tai
Phongsali
Dien Bien Phu
Tay Chang Pass
Louang Namtha
Muang Khoua
Ban Nahin
Ban Houayxay (Houei Sai)
Xam Nua (Samneua)
Muang Pakbeng
Luang Prabang (Louangphrabang)
XIANGKHOANG
PLAIN OF JARS
PLATEAU
Xiangkhoang
Barthelemy Pass
Xaignabouri (Sayaboury)
Highest Point in Laos 9,250
Phou Bia
LUANG PRABANG RANGE
Nam Ngum Reservoir
Pakxan (Paksane)
Ban Nape
Keo Nua Pass
ANNAMITE CHAIN
CAMMON PLATEAU
Vientiane
Nong Khai
Mu Gia Pass
Udon Thani
Khammouane (Thakhek)
Ban Xeno
Savannakhet
Khon Kaen
KHORAT
PLATEAU
Saravan
Muang Khongxedon (Khong Sedone)
BOLOVENS PLATEAU
Pakxe (Pakse)
Ubon Ratchathani
Champasak
Attapu
Nakhon Ratchasima
Khong
BANGKOK
Hanoi
Haiphong
Hue
Red
Black
Ma
Ca
Sam
Mekong
Chi
Mun
Nan
Pa Sak
Chao Phraya
Banghiang
Kong
Don
Theun
SCALE 1:4,785,000
0 50 100 150 200 Miles
0 50 100 150 200 250 300 Kilometers
100° 102° 104° 106° 108°
22° 20° 18° 16° 14°

low-lying area is the centrally located Plain of Jars, on which were fought many battles during the recent war years. This landform feature derived its name from large prehistoric stone jars unearthed there.

The climate is controlled largely by the monsoon. The rainy season is from May to October when the southwest winds bring heavy rains to much of the country; dry winds from the northeast dominate much of the rest of the year. Total annual precipitation amounts vary somewhat throughout the country from the fertile Bolovens Plateau in the far south, which receives an annual average of over 100 inches (250 cm), to Luang Prabang in the north, which receives about 50 inches (125 cm) annually.

Rugged topography, a monsoonal climate, and low population densities suggest that much of the land is still in natural vegetation and this is indeed the case. It is estimated that over 60% of the country is still covered by forest, of which there are three major types: dense, humid forests characteristic of tropical rainforest and monsoon climate regions; dry and more open monsoon forests; and a smaller area of coniferous forests, mostly in the north. Commercially, teak and rosewood are the most important species and bamboo is found widely throughout the country. In addition, there are areas of grassland and savanna vegetation including the Plain of Jars and the Bolovens Plateau. There is an abundance of wildlife including elephants, tigers, wild buffalo, deer, monkeys, and pythons. As in Thailand and Burma, elephants are captured and used as beasts of burden.

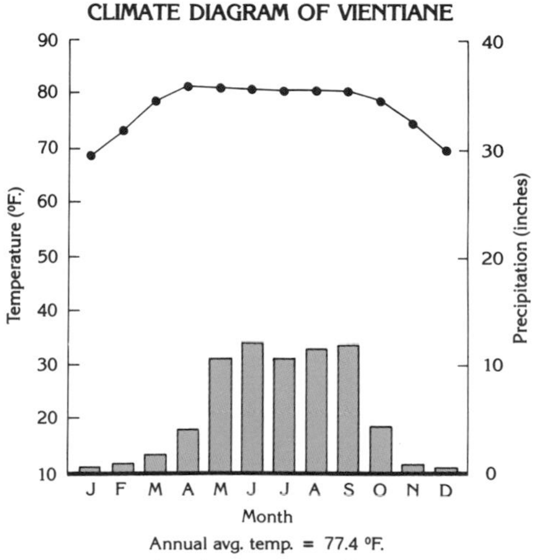


## HISTORICAL BACKGROUND

Present-day Laos derived its name from the Lao, a branch of the Tai ethnolinguistic groups that migrated south from the Chinese areas of Sichuan and Yunnan. Before the fourteenth century A.D. much of present-day Laos was under the suzerainty of, first, the kingdom of Nan Chao centered in southwest China and, second, the later Khmer empire. Given this background, it is evident that Laos was influenced culturally by both China and India. From the Chinese, for example, the Tai-speaking peoples may have adopted terracing of hill slopes and lowland wet rice cultivation and from the Khmer they adopted writing, mythology, and the notion of the god-king.

The recorded history of Laos begins in 1353 when King Fa Ngum, who was brought up in the Angkorian capital, united scattered principalities in present-day Laos and northeast Thailand to form the Lao kingdom of Lan Xang (literally, "Million Elephants"). It was during the reign of Fa Ngum that Theravada Buddhism was established as the state religion; it was also during this time that the Prabang, a gold statue of Buddha, was brought to Laos. This statue, located in the ancient Lan Xang capital of Muong Swa (present-day Luang Prabang), remains the principal religious symbol in Laos today. Initially, the majority of the people maintained their animistic beliefs although gradually, especially after the establishment of numerous Buddhist *wat*s (temples) and schools, the religion became more widely accepted, although it has never completely replaced the ancient worship of spirits. In the sixteenth century the capital was moved to Vientiane where the king built a new temple compound, Wat Keo, and a *stupa,* That Luang (Royal Spire), the most revered in Laos.

In the seventeenth century a period of disunity began which led to the disintegration of the empire, and by the early eighteenth century three separate Lao states had emerged, centered

Buddhist monks exiting from the Royal Palace in Luang Prabang (courtesy J. Halpern)

on Vientiane, Luang Prabang, and Champasak in the south. During the nearly two centuries before French rule these states acted as a buffer zone between Siam and Vietnam and were under the suzerainty of one of these more powerful neighbors.

Of the several European colonizers in Southeast Asia, the French were the first to make contact with Laos. Following the establishment of protectorates in Cambodia, Cochin China, Annam, and Tonkin by the 1880s, the French began to show an interest in Laos, ostensibly because of the important Mekong route to China coupled with Vietnamese claims to Laos. In 1893 France laid claim to Laos and by 1907, through a series of treaties with the Siamese, all of what became known as French Indochina was under French rule. That portion of the former Lan Xang empire that today comprises northeast Thailand remained a part of Siam. Thus, as occurred elsewhere in Southeast Asia and throughout the former colonial world, the imposition of European-drawn boundaries divided a major ethnic group (the Lao) into two separate political units. Otherwise, French rule in Laos was less noticeable than European colonization elsewhere in the region, in part because of its relatively late arrival in Laos, and in part because of the remoteness of the country. The French ruled largely through local elites, particularly tribal chiefs, who sometimes were educated in the ways of the French.

World War II and Japanese occupation had little effect on Laos. The Lao, characterized as easy-going with a penchant for enjoying themselves (*muan*), showed little resentment toward the new occupiers. Indeed, after over two centuries of occupation by either Chinese, Burmese, Siamese, Vietnamese, or French, this was viewed by most Laotians as simply another, temporary chapter in the history of the kingdom.

After the defeat of the Japanese and a period of internal conflict, the French returned to occupy most of Laos in 1946. Under French guidance, Laos became semi-independent within the

French Union in 1949 and in 1953 full independence was granted to the kingdom of Laos. Beginning in 1950 the Royal Government was opposed by insurgents known as the Pathet Lao, who were Communists supported by the Viet Minh of North Vietnam. Led by Prince Souphanouvong, a half brother of the Royal Government leader Prince Souvanna Phouma, and Kaysone Phomvihane (today the general secretary of the Lao People's Revolutionary Party), the Pathet Lao gradually gained control of the eastern half of the country. By 1965 the de facto partitioning of Laos had been completed. The Pathet Lao fought with the Viet Minh against French and, later, American forces until 1975. The Ho Chi Minh Trail, the Communist supply lifeline to South Vietnam, passed through Pathet Lao territory in southern Laos. This area, and the Plain of Jars to the north, were the two regions in Laos that were the most heavily bombed by American planes during the Vietnam War. In 1975, following the end of the war, the Pathet Lao gained control of the entire country, ended the monarchy, and declared the Lao People's Democratic Republic. Armed opposition to the present government exists among some hill tribes but it has been effectively contained.

Since the end of the war Laos has been heavily dependent upon military and economic aid from Vietnam and, more recently, the Soviet Union. In 1977 Laos and Vietnam signed a twenty-five-year friendship treaty, and Laos supported the Vietnamese invasion of Kampuchea in 1978. Similarly, Laos supported the Vietnamese in their recent border conflict with China. It is estimated that today (1988) some 50,000 Vietnamese troops are stationed in Laos. Since 1975 relations with Thailand have been mixed as a result of boundary disputes, refugee movements, and other political disagreements. In the latter case, it is estimated that 400,000 refugees, or over 10% of Laos' total population, has fled the country since 1975. Trade relations have been maintained between the two countries during most of the 1980s; Laos exports considerable amounts of electricity to Thailand, especially from Nam Ngum Dam. It is estimated that one-half of Laos' hard currency income is derived from electricity sold in Thailand.

Interestingly, the United States has main-

GEOPOLITICAL SITUATION, EARLY 1970s

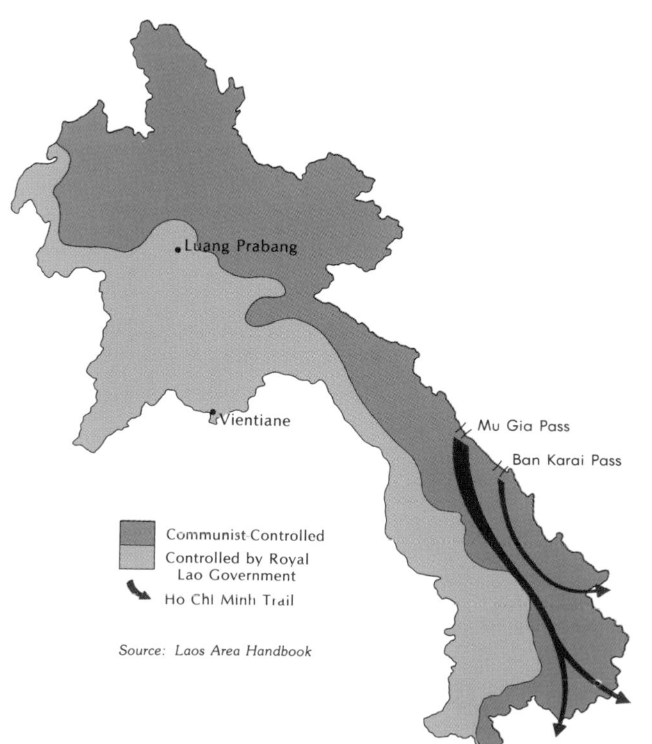


PROVINCES

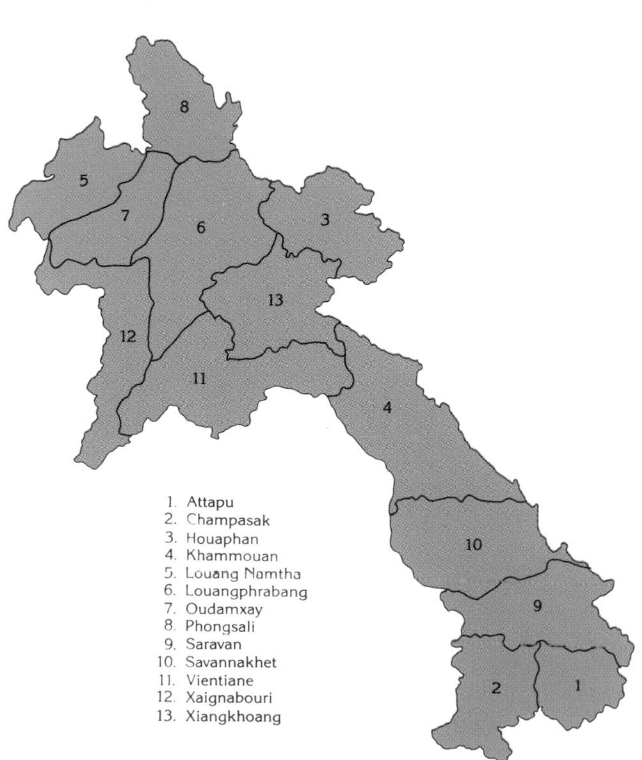

tained its embassy in Vientiane ever since 1975 and today it is the only American embassy in any of the three former Indochinese states. Since 1985 there have been further indications that links with the United States, and with China, may be strengthened.

Laos is today a unitary single-party people's republic with one legislative house, the National Congress of People's Representatives, which consists of 264 delegates elected by local authorities. Political power is vested in the Lao People's Revolutionary Party (LPRP). The chief of state is the president and the head of government is the prime minister, who is also secretary general of the LPRP.

The country is divided into thirteen provinces which are subdivided into districts; these are further subdivided into towns and villages. At each level there is a People's Revolutionary Committee which is controlled by the Central Committee of the LPRP.

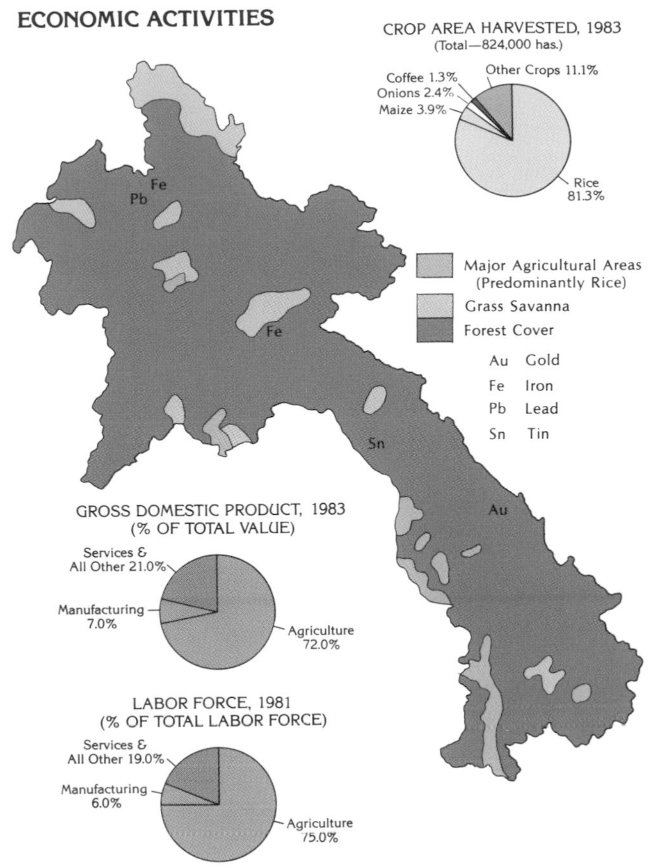


## THE ECONOMY

Fully three-quarters of the national labor force is engaged in agricultural activities. The major crops produced on the 5% of land in agriculture include rice, coffee, sweet potatoes, cassava, maize, and tobacco. The northern part of the country is a part of the Golden Triangle and thus the opium poppy is also widely grown in the upland areas. In recent years Laos has occasionally been self-sufficient in rice, but due to periods of flooding or drought, it has been imported in other years.

Other resources that have been commercially important to the export economy are timber and forest products, tin, precious stones, and hydroelectric power. Laos has other mineral resources that could become commercially important and these include iron ore, coal, lead, zinc, and small deposits of gold and silver. Also, petroleum deposits are said to exist in the Vientiane valley area.

There is very little manufacturing activity in Laos and this is reflected in the fact that only 7% of the Gross Domestic Product is derived from, and 6% of the national labor force is dependent upon, manufacturing. The only manufacturing that exists is food and beverage processing, furniture, cigarette-making, and local handicrafts, such as the traditional costumes of the Hmong hill tribe. Laos suffers from a

Fishermen with nets, Laos (courtesy J. Halpern)

**TRADE BY COMMODITY GROUP, IMPORTS—1974 & EXPORTS—1980 (% OF TOTAL VALUE)**

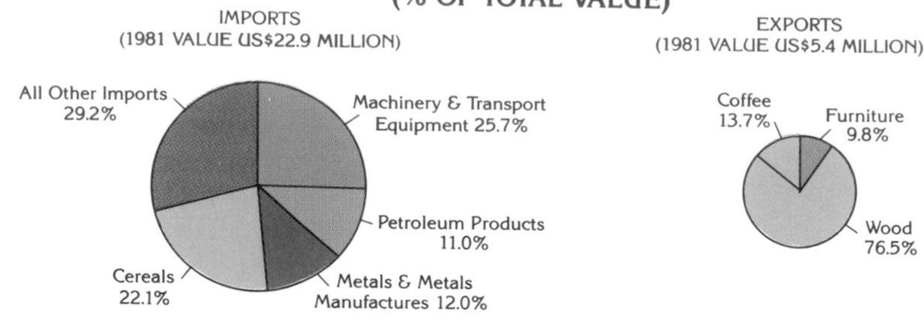


*Source: Encyclopedia Britannica (Chicago: Encyclopedia Britannica, 1984)*

**DIRECTION OF TRADE, 1984 (% OF TOTAL VALUE)**

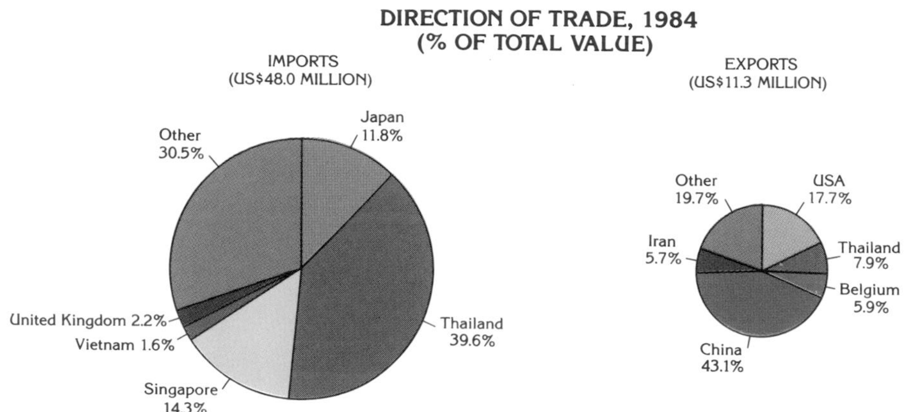


*Source: Encyclopedia Britannica (Chicago: Encyclopedia Britannica, 1985)*

chronic balance-of-trade deficit since it must import food and agricultural products and most manufactured items.

Laos remains one of the world's poorest and least developed nations in terms of most of the indices normally used to measure level of economic development. Thus, in the early 1980s it was estimated that the per capita Gross National Product was but US$80.

## TRANSPORTATION

Laos is landlocked and thus is unique in the region in that it does not have a seaport. A major transportation artery is the Mekong and it is on this great river that the country's principal city and capital, Vientiane, is located. Also located on the Mekong are the other major cities of Luang Prabang, Savannakhet, and Pakxe (Pakse). Over 7,500 miles (12,000 km) of road exist, of which only 15% are paved. The major road, Route 13, extends from Luang Prabang to Vientiane and then south through Pakxe to the Kampuchean border. There are no railroads in Laos. The national airline, Lao Aviation, serves the nation's seven airports with scheduled flights.

## PEOPLE AND CULTURE

The people of Laos are officially divided into four ethno-political categories: the Lao Lum, or valley Lao, which comprise about one-half of the population; the Lao Tai, or tribal Tai; Lao Theung ("Lao of the mountainsides"), or Mon-Khmer; and Lao Soung ("Lao of the mountaintops"), which include the Yao (Man) and Hmong (Meo or Miao). The mountain peoples are sometimes called *Kha,* a pejorative term meaning slave. The vast majority of persons who belong to the Lao Tai and Lao Soung live in upland area tribal groups, known as *muong.* In all, there are about 70 separate ethnic groups in Laos.

While animistic beliefs and traditions are still dominant among large numbers of hill tribes, the religion of the majority of the population is

**ETHNIC-LINGUISTIC GROUPS**

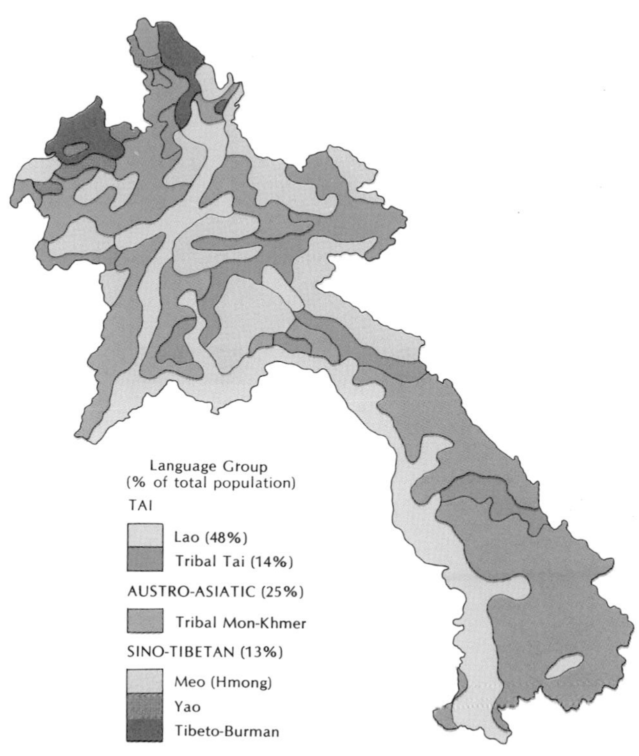


Theravada Buddhism, which entered the area in the fourteenth century. This Indian form of Buddhism, along with Hindu influences, has been the major influence on art, literature, music, and dance. Except for Vientiane, there is little of the imprint of the West that is found elsewhere in the region. Religious sculpture, stories, art, and myths all have their origin in the Indianized expressions that came by way of Siam, the Angkorian empire, or Burma. The symbolic use of the snake on religious and royal buildings, for example, represents the spirit of water and protects the king, and has its basis in Indian influences.

Laos has the smallest proportion of urban dwellers of any Southeast Asian nation with the possible exception of Kampuchea since 1975. Vientiane is by far the largest city with a population of over 200,000, but it is still much smaller than any other Southeast Asian capital. It has been described as a "dusty and torpid provincial town masquerading as a capital city and sleeping on the banks of the Mekong" (Wheeler, p. 569). Places to visit in the city are the open

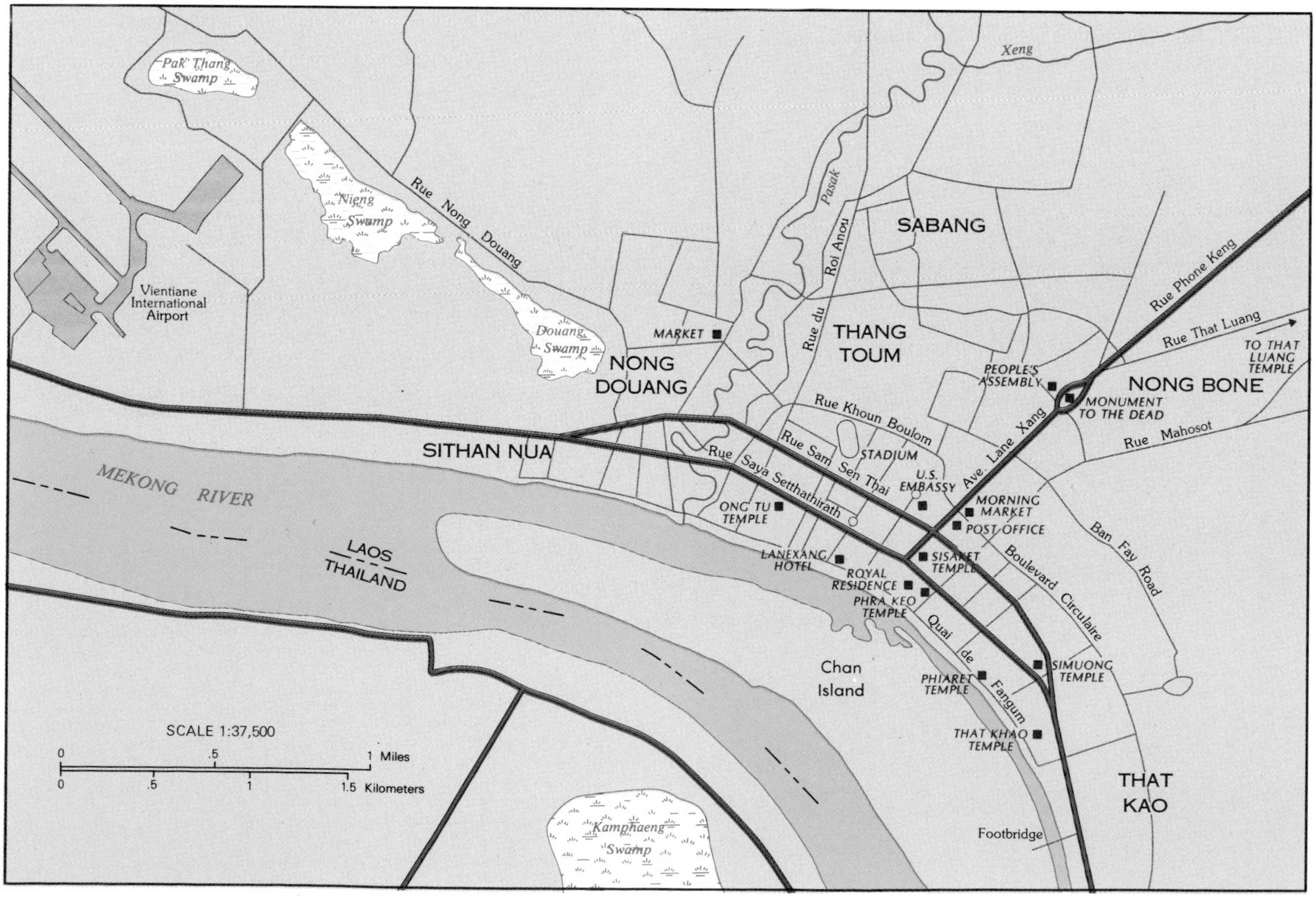

Ferry crossing on Nam Ngum River (courtesy A. Lind)

markets, especially the Morning Market, and the numerous Buddhist temples. Especially well known among the latter are the Wat Keo, built originally to house the Emerald Buddha which is now in Bangkok, and the Wat Khao. Several war monuments and the People's Assembly are also attractions to the tourists who find their way to this out-of-the-way country. A suburb known as Kilometer 6, located on the outskirts of the city, once housed the American diplomatic and military community. Only one reasonably good tourist hotel, the Lanexang (named after the earlier Lao empire), exists in all of Vientiane.

# Selected Bibliography

## ATLASES AND MAPS


Apa Maps (Apa Productions; published by Nelles Verlag GmbH, Munich). Fold-out road maps (scale = 1:1,500,000) for tourists, including city maps and places of interest. Complements the Apa "Insight Guides" (see Travel Guides section in this bibliography. Includes the following: "Bali," "Malaysia," "Philippines," "Thailand," "Western Indonesia."

*Atlas Ganaco* (Bandung: Penerbit Ganaco N.V., 1976).

*Atlas Penggunaan Tanah Republik Indonesia (Land Use Atlas of the Republic of Indonesia)* (Jakarta: Departemen Dalam Negeri, 1984).

Bartholomew World Travel Map. "Asia: South-East" (Edinburgh: John Bartholomew & Sons Ltd., 1985). Scale = 1:5,800,000.

Barton, Thomas F., Robert C. Kingsbury, and Gerald R. Showalter. *Southeast Asia in Maps* (Chicago: Denoyer-Geppert Company, 1970).

Clyde Surveys Limited. Maps published by Clyde Surveys, Maidenhead, Berkshire, England include: "Singapore: A Clyde Leisure Map for the Tourist."

Dewan Bahasa dan Pustaka, *Atlas Kabangsaan Malaysia* (Kuala Lumpur: Dewan Bahasa dan Pustaka, Kementerian Pelajaran Malaysia, 1977).

Hall, D. G. E. *Atlas of South-East Asia* (London: MacMillan and Company Limited, 1964).

Hildebrand's Travel Maps (published in Germany by Karto & Grafik). Detailed fold-out maps for tourists with textual tourist information and city map insets. The following maps are included (with varying scales): "Map #26: Western Indonesia, Sumatra, Java, Bali, and Celebes"; "Map #27: Thailand, Burma, Malaysia, and Singapore"; "Map #30: Philippines."

Huke, Robert E. *Agroclimatic and Dry-Season Maps of South, Southeast, and East Asia* (Los Baños, Philippines: International Rice Research Institute, 1982). Scale of maps included = 1:6,336,000.

Jin-Bee, Ooi (ed.). *Atlas for Singapore* (Singapore: Longman Singapore Publishers Ltd., 2nd ed., 1985).

Leong, Goh Cheng and Soo Fong Beng. *Modern Certificate Guides: South-East Asia* (Kuala Lumpur: Oxford University Press, 1976).

Morgan, Joseph R. and Mark J. Valencia (eds.). *Atlas for Marine Policy in Southeast Asian Seas* (Berkeley, California: University of California Press, 1983).

National Geographic Society (Washington, D.C.). "The Peoples of Mainland Southeast Asia" (March, 1971), Scale = 1:3,168,000; "The Philippines" (July, 1986), Scale = 1:2,844,000; "Southeast Asia" (December, 1968), Scale = 1:6,000,000; "Viet Nam, Cambodia, Laos, and Thailand" (February, 1967), Scale = 1:1,900,800.

Onorato, Michael P. *Historical Atlas of the Far East in Modern Times* (Chicago: Denoyer-Geppert, 1967).

Prescott, J. R. V., H. J. Collier, and D. F. Prescott. *Frontiers of Asia and Southeast Asia* (Melbourne: Melbourne University Press, 1977).

Sandy, I Made. *Atlas Indonesia* (Jakarta, 1986).

United Nations, Economic Commission for Asia and the Pacific. "A Practical Guide to Motorists: Asian Highway Route Map. Indonesia, Route A-2/A-25, Banda Aceh-Jakarta-Denpasar" (March, 1978). Scale = 1:1,250,000. Includes inset maps of cities along route (Medan, Semarang, Surabaya, Bandung, Jakarta, Yogyakarta, and other, smaller cities); "A Practical Guide to Motorists: Asian Highway Route Map. Singapore to Vientiane, Route A-2/A-12, Via Bangkok & Kuala Lumpur" (March, 1976). Scale = 1:1,250,000. Includes inset maps of Vientiane, Bangkok, Singapore, Kuala Lumpur.

United States, Army Map Service, Corps of Engineers. "Indonesia" (1968); Stock No. 1106X9WT. Scale = 1:5,000,000. Miller Oblated Sterographic Projection. Includes nearly the entire region; "Krung Thep" (1955); Sheet #ND 47-12. Scale =

1:250,000. Reverse side includes map of "Krung Thep (Bangkok), Thailand and Vicinity" at scale of 1:35,000; "Rangoon" (1954); Sheet #NE47-13. Scale = 1:250,000. Reverse side includes map of "Rangoon and Vicinity" at scale of 1:50,000.

United States, Central Intelligence Agency. *Indochina Atlas* (Washington, D.C.: CIA, October, 1970).

United States, Central Intelligence Agency and Defense Mapping Agency. Individual nation maps include the following: "Brunei" (1984). Scale (approx.) = 1:950,000; "Cambodia" (undated). Scale = 1:1,740,000. Also includes three thematic maps; "Cambodia" (1986). Scale = 1:1,400,000; "Indonesia" (1972). Scale = 1:7,740,000. Includes four thematic maps (Population; Economic Activity; Ethnolinguistic; Vegetation); "Kampuchea: Internal Administrative Divisions" (1980). Scale = 1:1,740,000; "Laos" (1970). Scale = 1:1,750,000. Includes three thematic maps (Economic Activity; Population; Ethnic Groups); "Malaysia and Brunei" (1978). Scale = 1:3,600,000. Includes four thematic maps (Agriculture and Land Use; Industry and Mining; Ethnic Groups; Population); "North Vietnam" (1971). Scale = 1:1,750,000; "Singapore" (1973). Scale = 1:345,000. Also one thematic map (Economic Activity); "Southeast Asia" (1982). Scale = 1:2,000,000. Lambert Conformal Conic Projection of mainland only; "Thailand" (1974). Scale = 1:3,500,000. Includes five thematic maps (Vegetation; Administrative Divisions; Economic Activity; Ethnic Groups; Population); "Vietnam" (1985). Scale (approx.) 1:6,970,000.

United States, Defense Mapping Agency Aerospace Center. "Operational Navigation Charts." Scale = 1:1,000,000. Detailed topographic maps of the entire region. There are 19 charts that cover the Southeast Asian region.

United States, Department of the Army. *Insular Southeast Asia: A Bibliographic Survey* (DA Pamphlet 550-12). (Washington, D.C.: U.S. Government Printing Office, 1971). Includes the following full-color maps: "Indonesia." Scale = 1:7,740,000. Also four thematic maps (Population; Ethnolinguistic; Economic Activity; Vegetation); "Malaysia and Brunei." Scale = 1:3,525,000. Also four thematic maps (Agriculture and Land Use; Mining and Industry; Selected Ethnic Groups; Population); "Singapore." Scale = 1:338,000. Also one thematic map (Economic Activity).

United States, Department of the Army. *Peninsular Southeast Asia: A Bibliographic Survey of the Literature* (DA Pamphlet 550-14). (Washington, D.C.: U.S. Government Printing Office, 1972). Includes the following full-color maps: "Burma." Scale = 1:3,990,000. Also three thematic maps (Ethnic Groups; Land Use and Economic Activity; Population); "Cambodia." Scale = 1:1,740,000. Also three thematic maps (Ethnic Groups; Population; Land Use and Economic Activity); "Laos." Scale = 1:1,750,000. Also three thematic maps (Economic Activity; Population; Ethnic Groups); "Thailand." Scale = 1:3,000,000. Also five thematic maps (Vegetation; Administrative Divisions; Economic Activity; Ethnic Groups; Population).

United States, Department of State, Department of the Geographer and Global Issues. "South China Sea: Conflict Potential" (1983).

United States, Department of State, Office of the Geographer. "Composite Theoretical Division of the Seabed" (1978).

## SELECTED WORKS

*Asiaweek.* "Rangoon in Front," Vol. 11, No. 33 (August 16, 1985); 18–31.

Buchanan, Keith. *The Southeast Asian World: An Introductory Essay* (New York: Taplinger Publishing Co., 1967).

Burling, Robbins. *Hill Farms and Paddy Fields* (Englewood Cliffs, N.J.: Prentice-Hall, 1965).

Buttinger, Joseph. *The Smaller Dragon: A Political History of Vietnam* (New York: Frederick A. Praeger, 1958).

Cady, John F. *Southeast Asia: Its Historical Development* (New York: McGraw-Hill Book Company, 1964).

Coedes, George. *Angkor: An Introduction* (New York: Oxford University Press, 1963).

Dobby, E. H. G. *Southeast Asia* (London: University of London Press, 1973, 11th edition).

Dommen, Arthur J. *Laos: Keystone of Indochina* (Boulder, Colorado: Westview Press, 1985).

Duiker, William J. *Vietnam Since the Fall of Saigon* (Athens, Ohio: Ohio University Center for Southeast Asian Studies, 1985).

Dutt, Ashok K. (ed.). *Southeast Asia: Realm of Contrasts* (Boulder, Colorado: Westview Press, 1985).

Esterline, John H. and Mae H. Esterline. *How the Dominoes Fell: Southeast Asia in Perspective* (Lanham, Maryland: Hamilton Press, 1986).

Etcheson, Craig. *The Rise and Demise of Democratic Kampuchea* (Boulder, Colorado: Westview Press, 1984).

Fisher, Charles A. *South-East Asia: A Social, Economic and Political Geography* (London: Methuen & Co. Ltd., 2d ed, 1966).

Fryer, Donald W. *Emerging Southeast Asia: A Study in Growth and Stagnation* (New York: John Wiley & Sons, 2d ed, 1979).

Geertz, Clifford. *Agricultural Involution: The Process of Ecological Change in Indonesia* (Berkeley, California: University of California Press, 1963).

Guoxing, Ji. "Current Security Issues in Southeast Asia," *Asian Survey* 26, No. 9 (September, 1986): 973–90.

Hall, D. G. E. *A History of Southeast Asia* (London: Macmillan, 4th ed, 1981).

Harrison, Brian. *South-East Asia: A Short History* (New York: St. Martin's Press, 1967).

*Indochina Report.* "The Vietnamisation of Kampuchea: A New Model of Colonialism," October, 1984.

Karnow, Stanley. *Vietnam: A History* (New York: The Viking Press, 1983).

Kent, George and Mark J. Valencia (eds.). *Marine Policy in Southeast Asia* (Berkeley, California: University of California Press, 1985).

Keyes, Charles F. *The Golden Peninsula: Culture and Adaptation in Mainland Southeast Asia* (New York: Macmillan, 1977).

Kunstadter, Peter (ed.). *Southeast Asian Tribes, Minorities, and Nations,* 2 vols. (Princeton, N.J.: 1967).

LeBar, Frank M. (ed.). *Ethnic Groups of Insular Southeast Asia* (New Haven: Human Relations Area Files, 1972).

______, Gerald C. Hickey, and John K. Musgrave. *Ethnic Groups of Mainland Southeast Asia* (New Haven: Human Relations Area Files, 1964).

Leifer, Michael. *Conflict and Regional Order in South-East Asia* (London: The International Institute for Strategic Studies, Adelphi Papers No. 162, 1981).

Leinbach, Thomas R. and Richard Ulack. "Cities of Southeast Asia." In Stanley D. Brunn and Jack F. Williams (eds.), *Cities of the World: World Regional Urban Development* (New York: Harper & Row, 1983).

McCloud, Donald G. *System and Process in Southeast Asia: The Evolution of a Region* (Boulder, Colorado: Westview Press, 1986).

McGee, T. G. *The Southeast Asian City: A Social Geography of the Primate Cities of Southeast Asia* (New York: Frederick A. Praeger, 1967).

Peacock, James L. *Indonesia: An Anthropological Perspective* (Pacific Palisade: Goodyear Publishing Co., 1973).

Sauer, Carl O. *Agricultural Origins and Dispersals* (New York: American Geographical Society, 1952).

Solheim, Wilhelm G., II. "An Earlier Agricultural Revolution," *Scientific American* 226, No. 4 (April, 1972); 34–41.

Spencer, Joseph E. and William L. Thomas. *Asia, East by South: A Cultural Geography* (New York: John Wiley & Sons, 1971).

Steinberg, David Joel (ed.). *In Search of Southeast Asia: A Modern History* (Honolulu: University of Hawaii Press, 1985).

Sternstein, Larry. *Thailand: The Environment of Modernisation* (Sydney, Australia: McGraw-Hill, 1976).

Tate, D. J. M. *The Making of Modern South-East Asia.* Vol. 1, *The European Conquest;* Vol. 2, *The Western Impact* (Kuala Lumpur: Oxford University Press, 1971, 1979).

Taylor, Alice (ed.). *Focus on Southeast Asia* (New York: Praeger Publishers, 1972).

United States, Dept. of the Army. Area Handbook Series. (Washington, D.C.: U.S. Government Printing Office). Published country studies include: *Burma* (DA Pamphlet #550-61, 1983); *Khmer Republic (Cambodia)* (#550-50, 1973); *Indonesia* (#550-39, 1983); *Laos* (#550-58, 1985); *Malaysia* (#550-45, 1984); *Philippines* (#550-72, 1984); *Singapore* (#550-184, 1977); *Thailand* (#550-53, 1981); *North Vietnam* (#550-57, 1967); *South Vietnam* (#550-55, 1967).

Vesilind, Priit J. "Monsoons: Life and Breath of Half the World," *National Geographic* 166, No. 6 (December, 1984); 712–47.

Wernstedt, Frederick L. and Joseph E. Spencer. *The Philippine Island World: A Physical, Cultural, and Regional Geography* (Berkeley, California: University of California Press, 1967).

Wheatley, Paul. *Nagara and Commandery: Origins of the Southeast Asian Urban Traditions* (Chicago: University of Chicago, Dept. of Geography Research Papers, 1983).

Williams, Lea E. *Southeast Asia: A History* (New York: Oxford University Press, 1976).

White, Peter T. "The Temples of Angkor: Ancient Glory in Stone," *National Geographic* 161, No. 5 (May, 1982): 552–89.

______ . "The Poppy," *National Geographic* 167, No. 2 (February, 1985): 142–89.

Yeung, Yue-man and C. P. Lo (eds.). *Changing South-East Asian Cities: Readings on Urbanization* (New York: Oxford University Press, 1976).


## STATISTICAL AND GOVERNMENT SOURCES


Domschke, Eliane. *Handbook of National Population Censuses: Africa and Asia* (New York: Greenwood Press, 1986).

*Encyclopedia Britannica* (Chicago: Encyclopedia Britannica, Inc., 15th edition, 1985).

*The Europa Yearbook 1986: A World Survey* (London: Europa Publications Limited, 1986).

*The Far East and Australasia 1987* (London: Europa Publications Limited, 1986).

Indonesia, Biro Pusat Statistik (Bureau of Statistics). *Statistical Yearbook of Indonesia 1982* (Jakarta: Biro Pusat Statistik, 1983).

Malaysia, External Information Division, Ministry of Foreign Affairs. *Malaysia in Brief 1985* (Kuala Lumpur: 1985).

Mayerchak, Patrick M. *Scholar's Guide to Washington, D. C. for Southeast Asian Studies* (Washington, D. C.: Smithsonian Institution Press, 1983).

Philippines, National Economic and Development Authority. *Philippine Yearbook, 1985* (Manila: National Census and Statistics Office, 1985).

Population Reference Bureau, Inc. "1987 World Population Data Sheet" (Washington, D. C.: Population Reference Bureau, Inc., 1987).

Singapore, Ministry of National Development, Planning Department. *Report of Survey, Revised Master Plan, 1985* (Singapore: Planning Department, 1985).

Thailand, National Statistics Office. *Statistical Yearbook Thailand* Number 33, 1981–1984 (Bangkok: National Statistics Office, 1985).

United Nations. *The Law of the Sea: Official Text of the United Nations Convention on the Law of the Sea* (New York: U. N., 1983).

United Nations, Conference on Trade and Development (UNCTAD). *Yearbook of International Commodity Statistics, 1985* (New York: U. N., 1985).

United Nations, Dept. of International Economic and Social Affairs. *1983 International Trade Statistics Yearbook* (New York: U. N., 1985).

______ . *Statistical Yearbook, 1982* (New York: U. N., 1985).

United Nations, Economic and Social Commission for Asia and the Pacific (ESCAP). "1986 ESCAP Population Data Sheet" (Bangkok: ESCAP Population Division, 1986).

United Nations, Food and Agriculture Organization. *1984 FAO Production Yearbook* (Rome: FAO, 1985).

United States, Central Intelligence Agency, National Foreign Assessment Center. "Kampuchea: A Demographic Catastrophe" (Washington, D. C.: C. I. A., May, 1980).

United States, Bureau of the Census. *The Population of Vietnam* (Washington, D. C.: Bureau of the Census, October, 1985). International Population Report (Series P-95, No. 77) by Judith Banister.

United States, Department of State. *World Refugee Report, September 1986* (Washington, D. C.: Bureau for Refugee Programs, Dept. of State, 1986).

United States Committee for Refugees. *World Refugee Survey, 1985 in Review* (New York: American Council for Nationalities Service, 1986).

Wernstedt, Frederick L. *World Climatic Data,* Vol. V, Southern Asia, Australasia, and Ocean Islands (Lemont, Pennsylvania: Climatic Data Press, 1972).

World Bank. *World Development Report 1987,* and prior years (New York: Oxford University Press, 1987).

World Resources Institute. *World Resources 1986* (New York: Basic Books, Inc., 1986).

## TRAVEL GUIDES

*All-Asia Guide* (Far Eastern Economic Review, Limited, 1986, 14th ed). Distributed by Charles E. Tuttle Co., Inc. of Rutland, Vermont and Tokyo, Japan.

*Baedecker's Bangkok* (Norwich, England: Jarrold and Sons Ltd., 1987). Includes detailed fold-out city map.

*Baedecker's Singapore* (Norwich, England: Jarrold and Sons Ltd., 1987). Includes detailed fold-out city map.

DeLand, Antoinette. *Fielding's Far East* (New York: Fielding Travel Books, c/o William Morrow & Co., Inc., 1987).

Divine, Elizabeth and Nancy L. Braganti. *The Traveler's Guide to Asian Customs and Manners* (New York: St. Martin's Press, 1986).

*Fodor's Southeast Asia 1987* (New York: Fodor's Travel Guides, 1986). Excludes Kampuchea, Laos, and Vietnam. Fodor also publishes a *City Guide to Singapore.*

*Insight Guides* (Apa Productions Ltd., 5 Lengkong Satu, 1441 Singapore). Excellent text and color photography with maps; perhaps the best current guides to individual countries. They include the following: *Bali; Burma; Indonesia; Java; Malaysia; Philippines; Singapore; Thailand.*

Wheeler, Tony. *South-East Asia on a Shoestring* (Berkeley, California: Lonely Planet Publications, 1985). Lonely Planet also publishes the following: *Bali and Lombok: A Travel Survival Kit; Burma: A Travel Survival Kit* (1985); *Malaysia, Singapore, and Brunei: A Travel Survival Kit; The Philippines: A Travel Survival Kit; Thailand: A Travel Survival Kit.*

## SELECTED PERIODICALS

*ASEAN Economic Bulletin.* Published three times a year since 1984 by the Institute of Southeast Asian Studies, Singapore.

*Asian Survey*. Published monthly by the University of California Press.

*Asiaweek*. Published weekly since 1975 by Asiaweek, Ltd., Hong Kong. Similar in format to *Time* Magazine.

*Far Eastern Economic Review*. Published weekly since 1946 by Far Eastern Economic Review Limited, Hong Kong; a wholly owned subsidiary of Dow Jones and Company, Inc. Excellent magazine for financial and other news. Indispensable for the businessman and diplomat working in Asia.

*Journal of Asian Studies*. Quarterly since 1956 (previously the *Far Eastern Quarterly*). Academic journal of the Association for Asian Studies, the principal Asian interdisciplinary professional organization in the United States. Located at 1 Lane Hall, University of Michigan, Ann Arbor, Michigan 48109.

*Southeast Asian Affairs*. Published annually since 1974 by the Institute of Southeast Asian Studies, Singapore. Reviews the significant developments and trends in the region, with particular emphasis on the ASEAN countries.

*Southeast Asian Business*. Quarterly journal published by the Southeast Asian Business Education and Resources Program (SEABERP), Center for South and Southeast Asian Studies, University of Michigan (130 Lane Hall, Ann Arbor, Michigan). Covers the region's economic, political, and business news on a country-by-country basis. Valuable resource for academics, businessmen, and government workers.

# *Index*

The main page references to the ten individual nations are given in **boldface** type. Each will usually contain the following basic information: key geographical, demographic, and political data; an historical overview; a country reference map; several thematic maps; maps of the major metropolitan areas; several photographs; pie graphs of economic and trade data; climate diagrams; and textual information included under the subheadings "The Physical Environment," "Historical Background," "The Economy," "Transportation," and "People and Culture." Additionally, topical information on individual countries can be found under a number of topical headings including "Agriculture," "American influence," "Climate," "Independence," "Religion," "Rice," and so forth.

## A


Abaca, 67
Accessibility, 1,26
Aceh, 55
Aetas, 65
Agrarian Law (Indonesia), 53
Agricultural involution, 55
Agriculture, 3,5,11–14
  Brunei, 96
  Burma, 117,120
  Indonesia, 55–56
  Kampuchea, 140–41
  Laos, 149
  Malaysia, 79–80
  Philippines, 67,68
  Singapore, 89–90
  Thailand, 101,104–105
  Vietnam, 130
Aguinaldo, Emilio, 66
Agus River, 5
Akha, 117
Akyab, 113
Alaungpaya, 115
Alluvial soils. *See* Soils
American influence, 1,18–21,28
  Kampuchea, 139,140
  Laos, 148,149
  Philippines, 62–64,66–67,71
  Thailand, 109
  Vietnam, 129
Anawrahta, King, 115
Angeles City, 67
Angkor Thom, 16,18,136,139
Angkor Wat, 136,139,143
Angkorian Empire. *See* Khmer
Anglo-Burmese Wars, 115
Anglo-Dutch Treaty of London, 77–78
Animism, 30,59,82,96,102,120,135, 146,150
Annam, 127,128
Annamite Cordillera, 125,144
Apo, Mount, 64
Aquino, Benigno, 69
Aquino, Corazon, 68, 70
Arabic influence, 1,15,18,66,109
Arakan, 115
Arakan Yoma, 113
Arakanese, 114–15,118
Architecture
  Brunei, 98
  Burma, 115,120–22
  Indonesia, 59
  Kampuchea, 143
  Laos, 151
  Malaysia, 84
  Philippines, 73
  Singapore, 92
  Thailand, 110
  Vietnam, 135
Art
  Burma, 120–22
  Indonesia, 59
  Kampuchea, 143
  Laos, 151
  Malaysia, 82–84
  Philippines, 73
  Singapore, 92
  Thailand, 103,110
  Vietnam, 135
Asahan River, 5
Asoka, 114
Association of Southeast Asian Nations (ASEAN), 21,22,23,54,76,79,87,95,140
Association of Sons of the People. *See* Katipunan
Aung San, 116
Australian Realm, 7,52
Australoids, 15,127
Austro-Asiatic languages, 26,106,107,135
Austronesian languages. *See* Malayo-Polynesian languages
Ava, 115
Ayutthaya empire, 16,87,103


## B


Bacson-Hoabinhian culture, 127
Baguio, 64–65
Bahasa Indonesia, 50,59
Bahasa Malaysia, 82
Bali, 28,32,52,58,59
Bamboo, 3,8,114,126,138,146
Bandar Seri Begawan, 96
Bandicoots, 52
Bandung, 38,50
Bangkok, xi,38,101,106,109,110
Banteng, 102
*Barangays*, 66,67
Barisan Range, 51
Batak, 30,52,59
Batavia, 61

Batdambang (Battambang), xi
Batik, 1,57,59,61,82
Batu Caves, 84
Bauxite, 10,57,80
Beaches, 81,106
Beans, 11,117,141
Bears, 102,114,126
*Becak*, 58
Behaine, Pigneau de, 128
Belait River, 93
*Bemo*, 58
Bencoolen, 78
Bengal, Bay of, 115
Bengali, 92
Betel nut, 73
Bhamo, 113
Bicol Peninsula, 64
Birds' nests (for soup), 93
Birds-of-paradise, 52
Boat people, 41,129
Bolovens Plateau, 146
Bonifacio, Andres, 66
Bontoc, 65
Border disputes, 23,24,66,79,148
Borneo, 16,34,51,76,78,93,94
Borobudur, 18,58,59,61
Brahmanism, 28
British. *See* European influence
British Commonwealth members, 79,87
British North Borneo Company, 78
Brooke, James, 78,94
Brunei, **93–98**
Brunei Bay, 94
Brunei River, 96
Buddhism, 15-18,28-29,52,82,92,135
  Mahayana, 29,135
  Theravada, 2,29,99,102,109,113,114, 115,120,139,146,142,150-51
Buffalo. *See* Water buffalo
Buffer state, 99
Buffer zone, 103
Bukit Timah, 85
Burling, Robbins, 15
Burma, **111–22**
Burma Road, 116
Burmans, 115
Burmese, 27,103,114
Burmese Communist Party (BCP), 113,120
Burmese Liberation Army, 116
Burmese Socialist Programme Party (BSPP), 117

C

Cam Ranh Bay, 23,129
Cameron Highlands, 76
Canals (Bangkok), 106
Cantonese, 92
Cao Dai (Buddhism), 135
Cardamom Mountains, 138
Cassava, 3,13,55,96,105,130,141,149
Catholicism, 29-30,62,66,135
Cebu, 19,66,70,71
Cebuano, 71
Cengkareng, 58
Central Belt (Burma), 113
Central Cordillera (Philippines), 65
Central Plain (Philippines), 7,68
Central Plain (Thailand), 101,102
Chakkri dynasty, 103
Cham, 135,139,142
Champa, 16,127,135,139
Champasak, 147
Changi, 90
*Changwat*, 104
Chao Phraya, 4,32,101,105,106
Chao Praya Chakkri, 103
Chemicals, 96
Chenla, 127,138-39,143
Chiang Mai, 101,102,106,115
Chin, 27,118
Chin Hills, 113
Chindwin, 113,118
Chinese influence, 1,15,26,27,29
  Brunei, 94,96
  Burma, 114,115-16,120
  Indonesia, 54,59
  Kampuchea, 139,140,142
  Laos, 146,148-49
  Malaysia, 77,81-82
  Philippines, 65,66
  Singapore, 87,92
  Thailand, 102,103
  Vietnam, 127,129,131-35
Chinese language, 26,27,82,92,107
Cholon, 135
Christianity, 19,28,29-30,59,66,82,92, 96,109,115,120. *See also* Catholicism; Protestantism
Chromite, 10,130
Chulalongkorn, King (Rama V), 103
Churchill, Sir Winston, 98
Cigarette-making, 149
Cinchona, 13
Clark Air Base, 67

Climate, 2-5
  Brunei, 93
  Burma, 113-14
  Indonesia, 51
  Kampuchea, 138
  Laos, 146
  Malaysia, 76-77
  Philippines, 64-65
  Singapore, 86
  Thailand, 101-102
  Vietnam, 126
Coal, 10,117,130,149
Coastal Plain (Thailand), 101
Cobras, 77,102,114,138
Cochin China, 128
Cocoa, 80
Coconut oil, 67
Coconuts, 3,13,55,67,96,130
Coen, Jan Pieterszoon, 61
Coffee, 13,55,96,149
*Cogon* (grass), 11
Colombo Plan, 79
Colonialism, 19-21,45. *See also* American influence; European influence
  Brunei, 94,95
  Burma, 115-16
  Indonesia, 53-55
  Kampuchea, 139
  Laos, 147-48
  Malaysia, 74-76,77-79
  Philippines, 62-64,66-67
  Singapore, 87
  Vietnam, 128-29
Communism, 21,23-24,25,54,67,79, 87,103,129
  expansionism, 23,25
  insurgencies, 23-24,69,79,139,148
Communist Party of Indonesia (PKI), 23-24,54,87,128
Conflicts, 1,23-25,102,115,138-40
  border disputes, 23,24,66,79,148
  insurgencies, 23-24,38,41-43,54,69, 79,120,138,148
  maritime claims, 25,57
  revolutionary social change, 23,66
  Vietnam expansionism, 23,25
  Vietnam War, 128-29,139,148
Confucianism, 82,92,120,135
Continental shelf, 8,15
Copper, 3,10,57,67,80,117,130
Copra, 13,67
Cordillera Central, 64
Core-periphery areas, 19
Corn. *See* Maize
Corregidor Island, 67
Cotton, 115
Crocodiles, 77,102
Crown Colony, 87,89
Cultural change, 30-31
Culture System, 53

## D

Da Lat, 126
Da Nang, 23,126,128
Dagon, 115
Dams, 101,148
Dangrek Range, 138
*Datu*, 66
De Brito y Nicote, Philip, 115
Death March, 67
Deforestation, 6,8,65,77,102
Democratic Republic of Vietnam, 128
Denpasar, 58
Dien Bien Phu, 128
Doi Inthanon, 101
Domino theory, 23
Dusun, 96
Dutch. *See* European influence
Dvaravati empire, 16

## E

Earthquakes, 4
East India Company, 78,87,115
East Indies, 53
East Timor, 54
Eastern Belt (Burma), 113
Ebony, 8,126
Electricity, 148
Electronics, 81,89
Elephant Mountains, 138
Elephants, 77,102,114,126,138,146
Emergency, 79
Employment, 40-41
  formal sector, 41
  informal sector, 40-41
*Encomienda* system, 66
English language, 21,28,64,71,82,92, 107-109,120
Eurasian plate, 50

European influence, 1,12–13,18–21, 28,29–30,103,109. *See also* Colonialism
British, 13,19–21,53,76,78,79,81,87, 94–95,115–16,128
Dutch, 13,19–21,53–55,61,76,77–78,115,128
French, 19,115,128,135,139,147–48
Portuguese, 19,53,54,74–76,77,78,115,128,135
Spanish, 19,28,53,62,66
Export-Processing Zones (EPZ), 69
Exports. *See* Trade, foreign

F

Family planning, 34
Fa Ngum, King, 146
Fan Si Pan, 125
Fauna, 7–8,51
Brunei, 93
Burma, 114
Indonesia, 52
Kampuchea, 138
Laos, 146
Malaysia, 77
Philippines, 65
Singapore, 92
Thailand, 102
Vietnam, 126
Federated Malay States, 78
Federation of Malaya, 79
Federation of Malaysia, 54,76,87
Fish, 14,96,130,138,141
Fisher, Charles, 7
Flora. *See* Vegetation
Flying Tigers, 116
Food processing, 57,117,130,149
Forest products, 96,149
Forests, 3,8–10,51–52,65,77,86,93,102, 114,126,138,146
Foreign investments, 22,57
Foreign relations, 21–23. *See also* Trade, foreign
Formal sector. *See* Employment
Fraser's Hill, 76
Free Papua Movement, 54
French. *See* European influence
French Indochina, 147
Fruit, 96,130
Funan, 16,127,138–39,143
Furniture, 149

G

Galleon Trade, 66
Gaur, 77,102
Geertz, Clifford, 55
Gemstones, 10,105,117,141,149
Geneva Agreement of 1954, 128
Genting Highlands, 76
George Town (Penang), 78,81,87
Gia Long, 128
Gibbons, 102
Gold, 67,117,149
Golden Crescent, 105
Golden Triangle, 13–14,105,117,149
Government. *See* Political systems
Greater Sunda Islands, 50
Green Revolution, 12,55,68,80
Gurkhas, 95

H

Hainanese, 92
Haiphong, 130,131
Hakka, 92
Handicrafts, 57,149
Hanoi, x,23,38,128,130,135
Heng Samrin, 139
Heroin, 13–14
Hill stations. *See* Upland resorts
Hill tribes, 15,27,30,117,126,127,150
Hindi language, 27,92
Hinduism, 15–16,28,52,59,82,92,120, 139,151
Hkakabo Razi, 113
Hmong, 149,150
Ho Chi Minh, 128
Ho Chi Minh City,x,38,126,128–29,135
Ho Chi Minh Trail, 148
Hoa Hao (Buddhism), 135
Hokkien, 92
Hornbills, 77,93
Hue, 128
Hukawng Valley, 113
Hukbalahap movement, 24
Hydroelectric power, 5,149

I

Iban, 82,96
Ice Age. *See* Pleistocene epoch
Ifugao, 65
Iligan City, 5

Import substitution, 57,81
Imports. *See* Trade, foreign
Independence
  Brunei, 94,95
  Burma, 116
  Indonesia, 54
  Kampuchea, 139
  Laos, 147-48
  Malaysia, 78-79
  Philippines, 67
  Singapore, 79,87
  Vietnam, 128-29
Indian influence, 1,2,15-18,27-28,29
  Burma, 114,115-16,120
  Indonesia, 52,59,61
  Kampuchea, 138-39,142-43
  Laos, 146,151
  Malaysia, 77
  Philippines, 66
  Singapore, 87,92
  Thailand, 102,109
  Vietnam, 127
Indo-Australian plate, 50
Indochina, xi,66
Indonesia, **47-61**
Industrialization. *See* Manufacturing
Informal sector. *See* Employment
Insurgencies, 23-24,38,41-43,54,69, 79,120,138,148
Intensive subsistence cultivation, 11,102,127
International Rice Research Institute, x,68
Irian Jaya, 26,30,43,50,51,52,54,59
Iron ore, 10,80,130,141,149
Ironwood, 52,114
Irrawaddy, 4,32,113,114,115,118
Irrigation, 5,101,114,139
Islam, 18,28,29
  Brunei, 94,96,98
  Burma, 120
  Indonesia, 50,53,59
  Kampuchea, 142
  Malaysia, 77,82
  Philippines, 66
  Singapore, 92
  Thailand, 109

J

Jakarta, 37,38,50,51,55,58,59-61
Japanese influence, 22,23,28
  Brunei, 94
  Burma, 116
  Indonesia, 53
  Kampuchea, 139
  Laos, 147
  Philippines, 67
  Singapore, 87
  Thailand, 103
  Vietnam, 128
Java, 4,6,15,16,18,30,32,37,50,51,52,53, 55,58,59,61
Java man, 51
Java Trench, 50
Javanese, 59,139
Jayavarman II, 139
Jayavarman VII, 139
Jeepney, 40,70
Johore, 77,78
Johore Strait, 86
Jurong Industrial Estate, 86,89
Jute, 13,117

K

*Kabupaten,* 55
Kachin, 27,118
Kachin Independence Organization, 120
Kalimantan, 30,37,50,51,52
Kampong Ayer, 96
Kampong Som (Sihanoukville), 141
Kampuchea, **136-43**
Kapuas River, 51
Karen, 27,107,118
Karen Baptists, 30
Karen National Union, 120
Katipunan, 66
Kaysone Phomvihane, 148
*Kecamatan,* 55
Kedah, 77,78
Kediri empire, 18
Kelantan, 78
*Kha,* 150
Khlong Toei, 106
Khmer, 16,25,77,102,103,107,109,127, 136,138-40,142-43,146
Khmer Rouge, 38,139-40,142-43
Khorat Plateau, 101
Kinabalu, Mount, 51,76
Komodo dragon, 52
Kota Kinabalu, 81
Kracheh (Kratie), xi,138
Krakatoa, 3,50
*Kris,* 73

Kuala Lumpur, 76,78,79,81,83–84
Kuala Trengganu, xi
Kublai Khan, 115
Kuching, 81

L

Labuan, 81,94
Lahu, 117,120
*Lalang* (grass), 11
Lan Xang, 146,147
Land reclamation (Singapore), 86
Land reform (Philippines), 68
Langkasuka, 77
Languages, 19,21,26–28. *See also individual languages, language families*
  Brunei, 96
  Burma, 26–27,118–20
  Indonesia, 50,59
  Kampuchea, 142
  Laos, 150
  Malaysia, 82
  Philippines, 71
  Singapore, 92
  Thailand, 106–109
  Vietnam, 135
Lao, 107,146
Lao Lum, 150
Lao People's Revolutionary Party (LPRP), 149
Lao Soung, 150
Lao Tai, 150
Lao Theung, 150
Laos, **144–52**
Lapu-Lapu, 66
Laterization. *See* Soils
*Lauan,* 65
Law of the Sea, 25
Le dynasty, 127
Lead, 10,117,149
Lee Kuan Yew, 87
Legaspi, Miguel Lopez de, 66
Leopard, 8,52,126,138
Lesser Sunda Islands, 50,51,52
Leyte, 66
Light, Francis, 78
Light Rail Transit (LRT), 70
Lisu, 117,120
Lolo, 107
Lon Nol, 139,142
Los Banos, 68
Lovek, 139
Luang Prabang, 146–47,150
Lumber, 57,67,77,93
Lutong, 95
Luzon, 12,64,65,66,68,70

M

MacArthur, General Douglas, 67
McGee, T.G., 16
Mactan Island, 66,70
Madura, 32,50
Madurese, 59
Magellan, Ferdinand, 19,66
Mahayana Buddhism. *See* Buddhism
Mahogany, 65,126
Main Range (Malaysia), 76
Maize, 3,13,55,68,101,105,117,130, 141,149
Majapahit, 16,18,52–53,77,87,94
Makati, 73
Malacca (Melaka), 16,18,19,53,74,77–78,87
Malacca, Strait of, 74,76,77,78
Malay, 59,66,77,82,87,92,96,107
Malay Peninsula, 5,18,34,52,53,65,76
Malayan Communist Party, 79
Malayan Democratic Union (MDU), 87
Malayan Union, 79,87
Malayo-Polynesian languages, 26,50,59,71,106,107,135
Malaysia, **74–84**
Mandalay, 113,114,115,118
Manila, 38,64–65,66,67,69,70,71–73
Manioc. *See* Cassava
Manufacturing
  Brunei, 96
  Burma, 117
  Indonesia, 57
  Kampuchea, 141
  Laos, 149–50
  Malaysia, 80–81
  Philippines, 69
  Singapore, 87–89
  Thailand, 105–106
  Vietnam 130–31
Marcos, Ferdinand, 67,68,69,70
Maria Christina Falls, 5
Maritime boundaries, 25,57
Martaban, 115
Martaban, Gulf of, 114,117
Marxism, 54,116
Master Plan (Singapore), 87
Mataram, 18,52
Maxwell Hill, 76

Mayon Volcano, 64
Medan, 38,50,58
Mekong, 4,32,101,125,126,127,130,138, 144,147,150
Melaka. *See* Malacca
Melanau, 82
Mellanesoids, 15,127
Merdeka Square, 59
*Mestizo*, 66
Metropolitan Rapid Transit system (MRT), 90
Migration, 4,92. *See also* Settlement, pre-colonial
  internal, 37,130
  labor, 23,40,78,81,89
  refugees, 30,36-38,41-43,54,66,99, 103-104,129,135,140,148
  rural-to-urban, 31,37,41,143
  Transmigration, 30,37,54-55
  Vietnam, 37,130
Military alliances, 22-23
Minangkabau, 30,52
Mindanao, 5,34,37,64,65,66
Mindon, King, 115
Mindoro Island, 65
Missing-in-Action (MIA) soldiers, 129
Mohammed, Sultan, 94
Moken, 107
Moluccas, 19,50,52,53
Mon, 77,102,107,109,114,115,118
Mon-Khmer languages, 150
Mongoloids, 15,52,62,65,77
Monitor lizard. *See* Komodo dragon
Monkey-eating eagle, 8,65
Monkeys, 93,102,114,126,146
Monsoons. *See* Climate
Montagnards, 126,131,135
Moulmein, 113
*Muan*, 147
Muara, 96
Muda River, 80
Multinational corporations, 22,69
*Muong*, 150
Muong Swa, 146
Murut, 96
Muslim, *See* Islam
Myitkyina, 118

N

Naga, 27,120
Naga Hills, 113
Nam Ngum Dam, 148
Nam Viet, 127
Nan Chao, 146
Napoleon III, 128
Natural gas, 3,10,50,56-57,95,117
Natural resources, 3,10
  Brunei, 95-96
  Burma, 117
  Indonesia, 56-57
  Kampuchea, 141
  Laos, 149
  Malaysia, 76,77,80
  Philippines, 67
  Singapore, 86
  Thailand, 102,105
  Vietnam, 126,130
Ne Win, 116
Negeri Sembilan, 78
Negrais, Cape, 113
Negritos, 15,65,77
New Economic Zones, 29,31,37,130
New Order (Indonesia), 54
New People's Army (NPA), 24,69
Ngo Dinh Diem, 128
Nguyen family, 127-28
Nickel, 10,57
Norodom Sihanouk, 139-40

O

Oil palm, 13,79-80,81
Olongapo City, 67
Opium, opium poppy, 13-14,105, 117,149
Orangutan, 8,52,77
Orchids, 52
Organization of Petroleum Exporting Countries (OPEC), 10
Oriental Realm, 7,52
Outer Islands, 34,37,53,55

P

Padaung, 120
Padi. *See* Rice
Pagan, 16,113,115,118
Pahang, 78
Pakxe (Pakse), 150
Palaung, 117,120
Palaung-Wa, 27
Palawan Island, 65
Palembang, 18,52
Palm oil. *See* Oil palm

Panay, 65,70
Papua New-Guinea, 24,26,43,50,54
Papuan languages, 26,59
Pathet Lao, 148
Patkai Hills, 113
Pattaya, 106
Pedicab, 40
Pegu, 114,115
Penang. *See* George Town
Penang Island, 78
People's Action Party (PAP), 87
Pepper, 80,96,141
Perak, 78
Perlis, 78
Pertamina, 56,57
Petroleum, 3,10,50,56–57,76,80,89,95, 115,117,130,149
Petroleum refining, 89,95,117
Pewter, 84
Philippine plate, 50
Phillippines, **62–73**
Phnom Aural, 138
Phnom Penh, x,37,135,139,142,143
Phosphate, 10,130,141
Phou Bia, 144
Phuket, 106
Plain of Jars, 146,148
Plantation agriculture, 12–13,19,53
Plate tectonics. *See* Tectonic activity
Pleistocene epoch, 7–8,15,51,52,65
Pol Pot, 38,139,141
Political boundaries, 18–19
Political systems, 18–23
  Brunei, 95
  Burma, 116–17
  Indonesia, 55
  Kampuchea, 140
  Laos, 149
  Malaysia, 79
  Philippines, 67
  Singapore, 87
  Thailand, 104
  Vietnam, 129–30
Pontianak, 51
Population characteristics, 4,32–38,43
  Brunei, 93
  Burma, 111
  Indonesia, 47,50
  Kampuchea, 136
  Laos, 144
  Malaysia, 74,76
  Philippines, 62
  Singapore, 85
  Thailand, 99
  Vietnam, 123
Port Kelang, 81
Portuguese. *See* European influence
Prambanan, 18,59,61
Precious stones. *See* Gemstones
Primate cities, 19,38–41
Prome (Pye), 113
*Propinsi*, 55
Protestantism, 30
Puntiak Jaya, 51
Pythons, 146
Pyu, 114

## Q

Quezon City, 73

## R

Raffles, Thomas Stamford, 53,78,87
Rama Thibodi I, 103
Rama V. *See* Chulalongkorn, King
Rangoon, 5,40,115,118,122
Rattan, 8,52,138
Red River, 4,32,125,127
Refugees. *See* Migration
Religion, 28–30. *See also individual religions*
  Brunei, 96
  Burma, 120
  Indonesia, 50,59
  Kampuchea, 142
  Laos, 146,150–51
  Malaysia, 82
  Philippines, 66
  Singapore, 92
  Thailand, 99,109
  Vietnam, 135
Remittances, 23
Resorts, 3,76,81,106,126
Rhinoceros, 8,52,77,102,114,126
Rice, 3,4,11–13
  Brunei, 96
  Burma, 111,115,117
  Indonesia, 55
  Kampuchea, 138,139,141
  Laos, 149
  Malaysia, 80
  padi, 11–12
  Philippines, 68
  terraces, 12,65,146
  Thailand, 101,102,104–105
  Vietnam, 125,126,130
Rizal, Jose, 66

Rosewood, 8,126,146
Roxas, Manuel, 67
Rubber, 3,13
  Brunei, 96
  Burma, 117
  Indonesia, 55,57
  Kampuchea, 141
  Malaysia, 76,78,79–80,81
  processing, 57
  Singapore, 87,89
  Thailand, 101,105
  Vietnam, 130
Russell's viper, 114,138
Russia. *See* Soviet influence

## S

Sabah, 34,43,76,78,79,81,94
Saigon. *See* Ho Chi Minh City
Sailendra, 18
Salween, 4–5,113,118
*Samlors,* 106
Sandalwood, 8
Sanskrit, 15
Sapa, 126
Sarawak, 34,76,77,78,79,80,81,82,94
Sauer, Carl, 11,127
Savanna, 138,146
Savannakhet, 150
Sawmilling, 89
*Sawah* (wet-field), 11
Sedentary cultivation. *See* Intensive subsistence cultivation
Selangor, 78
Semang, 77
Semarang, 38,50
Senoi, 77
Sesame, 141
Settlement, pre-colonial, 15–18. *See also specific groups of peoples*
  Brunei, 94
  Burma, 114–15
  Indonesia, 52–53
  Kampuchea, 138–39
  Laos, 146–47
  Malaysia, 77
  Philippines, 65–66
  Singapore, 87
  Thailand, 102–103
  Vietnam, 127–28
Shadow plays, 59
Shan, 27,115,117,118
Shan Plateau, 113
Shan State Army, 120
Shan United Army, 120
Shatter belt, 1,3,26
Shifting cultivation, 6,11,77,126
Ship building, 89
Shwebo, 115
Siam, 139,147
Sichuan, 146
Sihanouk. *See* Norodom Sihanouk
Silver, 67,117,149
Singapore, 76,78,79,**85–92**
Singapore River, 87
Singhasari, 52
Sino-Tibetan languages, 26,106,107,120
Sittang River, 113
Slash-and-burn agriculture. *See* Shifting cultivation
Slum areas, 40,61,73,87
Snakes, 77,102,114,138,146
Soils, 5–7,12
  alluvial, 6–7,11,102,125,126,130,138
  fertility, 5–6,12,55,102
  laterization, 5,102
  volcanic, 4,6–7,50–51
Soliman, Rajah, 66
Souphanouvong, 148
Southeast Asia Treaty Organization (SEATO), 22–23
Souvanna Phouma, 148
Soviet influence, 23,28,129,144,148
Soviet-Chinese split, 23
Spanish. *See* European influence
Spanish-American War, 19,66
Spanish language, 28
Spice Islands, 19,53
Spice trade, 19,77
Spices, 13,53
Squatter areas, 40,61,73,87
Sri Ksetra, 114
Srivijaya, 16–18,52,53,77,87
Stilwell, General Joseph, 116
Strait of Malacca, 74,76,77,78,81
Straits Settlements, 76,94,78,87
*Stupa,* 120,122,146
Subic Bay Naval Base, 67
Sugar cane, 3,13,55,67,96,105,130
Suharto, 54–55
Sukarno, 53–54
Sukhothai, 102–103
Sulawesi, 50,52
Sulu Archipelago, 66,94
Sumatra, 5,16,29,30,37,50,51,52,59
Sunda Shelf, 8,51,65,76
Sunda Strait, 3
Sundanese, 59

Surabaya, 38,50
Sweet potatoes, 130,141,149
Syriam, 115

T

Taal, Lake, 64
Tabinshwehti, King, 115
Tabon Caves, 65
Tagalog, 71
Tahan, Gunung (Mount), 77
Tai languages, 26,106,107,146
Tak Sin, 103
Tam Dao, 126
Taman Negara (national park), 77
Tamaraw, 65
Tamil, 27,82,92
Tanjung Perak, 58
Tanjung Priok, 58
Taoism, 82,92,120,135
Tapir, 52,77,102
Tea, 13
Teak, 3,8
  Burma, 114,115,117
  Indonesia, 52
  Laos, 146
  Thailand, 101,102
  Vietnam, 126
Tectonic activity, 3-4,50,64,76,101
Telugu, 92
Temasek, 87
Tenasserim, 115
Tenasserim Yoma, 113
Teochew, 92
Terengganu, 78
Ternate, 19
Terraces, rice. *See* Rice
Textiles, 57,81,89,105,117,130
Thai, 25,77,107,109
Thailand, **99–110**
Thailand, Gulf of, 138
Thaton, 114
Theravada Buddhism. *See* Buddhism
Thibaw, King, 115
Thon Buri, 103,110
Tidore, 19
Tiger, 8,52,77,102,114,126,138,146
Timber, 80,81,141,149
Tin, 3,10
  Burma, 117
  Indonesia, 57
  Laos, 149
  Malaysia, 76,78,80
  Singapore, 87,89
  Thailand, 101,105
  Vietnam, 130
Toba, Lake, 5,51
Tobacco, 13,149
Tonkin, 128
Tonle River, 138
Tonle Sap, 138,140,141
Toungoo dynasty, 115
Tourane. *See* Da Nang
Tourism, 3,23
  Brunei, 98
  Burma, 118
  Indonesia, 58
  Kampuchea, 143
  Laos, 151–52
  Malaysia, 76,81,84
  Philippines, 71–73
  Singapore, 90–92
  Thailand, 106,110
  Vietnam, 135
Trade, foreign, 21–22
  Brunei, 95–96
  Burma, 117–18
  Indonesia, 55–58
  Kampuchea, 141
  Laos, 149–50
  Malaysia, 79–81
  Philippines, 67–70
  Singapore, 87–90
  Thailand, 105–106
  Vietnam, 130–31
Transmigration, 30,37,54–55
Transportation, 19
  Brunei, 96
  Burma, 118
  Indonesia, 58
  Kampuchea, 141–42
  Laos, 150
  Malaysia, 81
  Philippines, 70
  Singapore, 90
  Thailand, 106
  Vietnam, 131
Treaty of Saragossa, 53
Trinh family, 128
Tungsten, 117
Typhoons, 65,126

U

U Nu, 116
Unfederated Malay States, 78

United East Indies Company, 53
United Nations, xi,21,25,87,95
United States. *See* American influence
Upland minorities. *See* Hill tribes
Upland resorts, 3,64,76,81,126
Urban characteristics, xi,38-41
Urdu, 92

V

Vegetables, 90,130
Vegetation, 7-10
  Brunei, 93
  Burma, 114
  Indonesia, 51-52
  Kampuchea, 138
  Laos, 146
  Malaysia, 77
  Philippines, 65
  Singapore, 86,92
  Thailand, 102
  Vietnam, 126
Vientiane, x,106,146,147,149,150,151
Viet Cong, 128-29
Viet Minh, 128,148
Vietnam, **123-35**
Vietnam War, 128-29,139,148
Vietnamese Communist Party, 129
Vietnamese language, 26,131
Vietnamese occupation of Kampuchea, 23,25,103,129,135, 136-38,139-40,142,148
Vietnamese Revolutionary Youth League, 128
Volcanic soils, 4,6-7,50-51
Volcano Island, 64
Volcanoes, 3,50,64
Vyadhapura, 127

W

Wa, 120
Wallace's Line, 7-8,52
Water buffalo, 11,114,141,146
Wat Keo, 146,152
*Wats,* 146
*Wayang kulit,* 59
Weber's Line, 7
West Irian. *See* Irian Jaya
Western Belt (Burma), 113
Western influence, 18-21,31,103. *See also* American influence; European influence
Wheat, 56

Y

Yang di-Pertuan Agong, 79
Yao (Man), 150
Yasodharapura, 139
Yasovarman I, 139
Yogyakarta, 55,61
Yuan, 107
Yunnan, 146

Z

Zinc, 10,117,149